Religion, Spirituality & Secularity in Multi-Religious India

Religion, Spirituality & Secularity in Multi-Religious India

Visions & Experiments

Editor
Israel Selvanayagam

The Association of Theological Teachers in India (ATTI)

&

Christian World Imprints™

First Published in 2017 by

Association of Theological Teachers in India (ATTI)
thru **Rev. Dr. H. G. Mithra, Secretary, ATTI**
Union Biblical Seminary
PUNE 411037 / MAHARASHTRA
hid3_mithra@rediffmail.com
Phone: 09421200718

&

Christian World Imprints™
Christian Publishing & Books from India
H-12 Bali Nagar, New Delhi-110015
info@christianworldimprints.com
www.ChristianWorldImprints.com
Phone: +91 11 25465925

ISBN: 978-93-5148-213-0 (HB) ISBN: 978-93-5148-214-7 (PB)

Cataloging in Publication Data--DK
Courtesy: D.K. Agencies (P) Ltd. <docinfo@dkagencies.com>

Conference on Implicit Religion and Secular Spirituality in India (2016 : Hyderabad, India; Gauhati, India)
Religion, spirituality & secularity in multi-religious India : visions & experiments / editor, Israel Selvanayagam.
pages cm
"Two Conferences on Implicit Religion and Secular Spirituality in India (held in Hyderabad and Gauhati in August and November 2016 respectively)"--Foreword.
ISBN 9789351482130 (HB) ISBN 9789351482147 (PB)

1. Implicit religion--India--Congresses. 2. Spirituality--India--Congresses. 3. Religious pluralism--India--Congresses. 4. Secularism--India--Congresses. I. Celvanāyakam, Israyēl, editor. II. Association of Theological Teachers in India, publisher. III. Title. IV. Title: Religion, spirituality and secularity in multi-religious India.

BL1055.C66 2016 DDC 200.954 23

Printed in India

IN RESPECTFUL MEMORY OF

EDWARD IAN BAILEY (1935-2015)

Contents

Foreword

I am so glad that the papers presented at the two Conferences on Implicit Religion and Secular Spirituality in India (held in Hyderabad and Gauhati in August and November 2016 respectively) are being published by the Association of Theological Teachers in India (ATTI). It is very good that the Revd. Dr. Israel Selvanayagam used his tenure as the President of ATTI to organize these conferences and to encourage the writing of these papers on a topic that has thus far not been, as far as I am aware, much researched in India. These papers are an important addition to the body of literature on the whole question of the forms of 'religion' and 'spirituality' that at first glance are not within the ambit of what one would normally study as religion and spirituality.

The concept of Implicit Religion and Secular Spirituality brings to the fore the fact that a very large number of people in India have 'ultimate commitments' and 'integrating foci' that are not the usual ones associated with Indic religions and spirituality but may be things like, cricket, the nation-state or even naturopathy. Their whole life revolves around these foci and their commitment to them orders their lives in a way that for conventionally religious people, God, Scripture and Ritual may do. Further, research into what the religious themes may be in seemingly secular things like films or plays is a very valid exercise and I pray that this volume may just be the first in a series of studies of implicit religion and secular spirituality in India and perhaps later in South Asia as well.

December 2016

Revd. Dr. Sunil M. Caleb
Principal, Bishop's College, Kolkata

Preface

The history and background of the production of this book may be very interesting. It was in September 1996, I started to teach at the Wesley College, Bristol, England. Being new to the situation, I was exploring particularly avenues of theological discussions. I was pleased to discover that there was the Bristol Theological Society. For that academic term, their first session was in the Baptist College on a Monday evening of the same month. According to the agreement of my appointment, every Monday I was scheduled to teach at Queens College, Birmingham. This particular Monday, I rushed by train to be in time for the theological seminar. From the Temple Meads station, I took a taxi to the Baptist College. But only on arrival I realized that taxi wallas would not accept credit cards and I felt embarrassed. After a while a person with clerical collar appeared who was walking towards the building. I approached him and told him of my plight. He gave the necessary amount and I noted his address. Next morning, I sent a cheque with a thank-you note which impressed him!

The clergyman was Edward Bailey, the longstanding Rector of St. Michael parish church in Winterbourne, a suburb of Bristol. Visits between our two families were exchanged. Edward was most passionate when he shared the story of establishing what was then known as the Centre for the Study of Implicit Religion and Contemporary Spirituality. I do not want to repeat the story here as he has detailed it in the first chapter of this book. Also, he had special interest in India where he spent more than a year (1959-60) in preparation for his priestly training, based at the United Theological College, Bangalore where Russel Chandran was the Principal. He visited the adjacent institution, Christian Institute for the Study of Religion and Society, Bangalore and regularly consulted P. D. Devanandan and M. M. Thomas who developed ideas about the theological significance of Asian revolution and Indian renaissance with the western impact of secularism. Obviously, Edward was influenced by those theologians who found in genuine secularism, a medium of God's continuing revelation.

Professor Baily was not only interested in the academic study of society and spirituality, but also had a pastoral heart and social concern. When I introduced the Rural Development Movement of my village, he raised contributions through his church as well as St. Michael's School over which he had pastoral charge. He organized events at his home and invited me to preach few times at his services. Because of long years of remaining in the same place he came to be regarded as a friend of his parishioners and leader of the local community.

I moved to Birmingham to be the Principal of the United College of the Ascension from January 2001. Subsequently, Edward invited me to the annual Denton Conference and I was inclined not to reject his offer of becoming a trustee of his Centre. Probably, he thought that having a non-white who had long experience of teaching Religions and Interfaith Dialogue would bring a new perspective. He encouraged me to review books for *The Journal of Implicit Religion* and to present papers at the Conference. It was an enriching experience to get to know a group of scholars from the UK as well as from America. After encountering some bright research scholars, supported by Edward, and listening to their interesting presentations, I requested him to support such a scholar, or Visiting Fellow, who would be based at the United College of the Ascension and agreed and appointed a scholar from America for three years. She was analyzing the popular film *Bend It Like Beckham* identifying inter-cultural interaction and elements of implicit religion in Britain. The college was enormously benefitted by her presence and input and Edward visited the college from time to time for monitoring and reviewing.

While the presentations in Denton were research-based academic papers, on Sunday mornings all were welcome for the 8. 00 am Holy Communion in the 17th century local parish church. In fact, a considerable number of participants and presenters were Anglicans, friends and colleagues of Edward. Statistics of Churches and members in Britain have been regularly presented. Therefore, it was not difficult to realize that Christian concerns were not divorced from the pursuits of implicit religion. Then, quite spontaneously, I asked the question, 'Is study of implicit religion applicable to India, particularly Indian theological colleges and seminaries?' I had conversations with Edward and we planned the following.

With fond memories of his earlier stay in Bangalore and recognizing resources at the United Theological College, in collaboration with UTC, we organized a consultation held on 17-19 March 2005. In preparation, the basic books on implicit religion and copies of the Journal were sent. However, there was no evidence that the UTC faculty and the resource personnel had known or understood the specific parameters of implicit religion. Bailey's paper set out the background of the continuing struggle to define and understand the nature of religion in the West. Drawing from his own journey in this connection, he gave three pointers 'towards a reality that needed to be studied before it could be described, and might, by definition, be incapable of definition.' The three pointers forming a cluster are commitment(s), integrating foci and intensive concerns with extensive effects. From studies of the manifestation of religion in mysterious ways, he identified two near-synonyms – *invisible religion* and *implicit religion* – and two non-synonyms – *folk religion* and *popular religion*. 'Implicit religion directs our attention to expressions of commitment etc. that at present tend not to be seen in religious terms.' It asks whether there might be some aspects of a religious character in the returning procession of an Olympic gold medalist or in the emotional attraction of a shopping mall at Christmas. Similar or parallel activities would include the returning procession in a Corpus Christi fiesta and ritual compulsion to go away on holiday, where 'sacrifice' and 'devotion' is involved. Obviously, the language and context of the thinking was European, particularly British. Then there were other presenters, mainly Hindu and Muslim. They were pointing out the spiritual values of their tradition such as tolerance and hospitality and positive attitudes to the secular polity of India. (For a full report, see my "Editorial: The Quest for Spirituality in the Secular-Multi-faith Context of India", *Jounal of Implicit Religion*, 8/2, July 2005, 101-117). Edward made use of this opportunity to visit my village and had a first-hand experience of the development project he supported.

I was still keenly aware of the distinctive nature of Indian secularism which exists side by side with religious pluralism with the predominant presence of Hindus with their impressive temples, worships and colourful celebrations of festivals. I sounded out Edward about the possibility of conscientising the theological teachers of the Protestant seminaries in India, persuading them towards, or informing them of, our ideas. Coincidently, I was made the president of the Association of Theological Teachers in India in the Triennial General Body held in September 2013 in Mangalore. Members of the new General Body and I were determined to revive ATTI with programmes of relevance. We recognized that the last substantial publication of ATTI had been the papers presented in a national consultation in 1981, i.e., *Theological Education and Development* (ed. by Gnana Robinson, Henry Wilson and Christopher Duraisingh, Bangalore, ATTI, 1984). We had to seek resources. Edward Bailey came forward to raise a grant and give the keynote address. And Packiam Samuel, the Director of the Henry Martyn Institute Hyderabad, agreed to collaborate and host. I happened to be in England in March-June 2015 and was discussing with Edward the practicalities and preparations for Hyderabad at the Denton Conference in the second week-end of May. But unexpectedly, I received the message that Edward Bailey had died on 22 April. At the same time, once again I admired the greatness of the man when his wife Joanna informed me that before his death he had mentioned the grant for the conference in Hyderabad and that the promise should be respected. Denton in May was not the same without Edward. Everybody missed his friendship, scholarly interaction and multiple responsibilities including checking the registrations and distributing copies of the papers. The trustees further reaffirmed their commitment to the Hyderabad conference and agreed to my suggestion that I would present his paper, arrange the papers for publication and dedicate it into his memory. Later, the annual conference of Implicit Religion was shifted from Denton Hall to Serum College in Salisbury. In the recent reshuffling of trustees, although offering to step down, I have been persuaded to stay on.

The Conference at HMI Hyderabad was held on 4-6 August, 2016 and there were about thirty delegates apart from those who attended locally. Realizing the usefulness of the conference, representatives from the North-East India asked for a supplementary conference and that was held on 12-14 November, 2016 in the CBCNEI compound, Guwahati. About 25 teachers of the NEI region including two additional resource persons attended. There was an overwhelming plea to continue such consultations in the context of many challenges, particularly growing nationalism with fascist tendencies on the one hand, and stubborn denominationalism, conservatism and fundamentalism in the Churches in India.

Implicit Religion without Boundary

Bailey was keen to retain the name 'implicit religion' and he was always open to clarify its uniqueness in relation to its seeming synonyms. It certainly helps to study phenomena such as personality cult, particularly celebrity cult. But if one goes through the Denton papers and articles of the *Journal of Implicit Religion* one may easily come to the conclusion that this branch of study is without boundaries. Particularly, it touches on aspects of the philosophy of religion, sociology of religion and phenomenology of religion. Even the way implicit religion is defined in terms of one or a cluster of the three pointers, namely, commitment(s), integrating foci and intensive concerns with extensive effects may be elaborated. There is great scope to unpack and explain each of these and their varied expressions. I could not help connecting it to the observations of theologians such as Karl Barth and Henrik Kraemer that humans have the incredible capacity to create gods and religions of their wish, which is in contravention to the divine revelation in Christ. Perhaps the basis is that they are created in God's image with capacity to imagine and make images. But if such pursuits do not give a sense of meaning in life why should cults in their variety still flourish? Is there room for applying a critical analysis to such phenomena? The Indian scholars of religion(s) and theology have before them numerous avenues to explore, the most obvious of which are nationalism, personality cult, celebrity cult and secularism. They will share insights with their western counter-parts while presenting unique insights into the Indian situation.

Acknowledgements

Many deserve my immense gratitude and most notably, Edward Baily, his wife Joanna and daughter Catherine; the trustees of the CSIRCS; Packiam Samuel and his staff team who were involved in administering and hosting the Conference; paper presenters and participants; the members of the Executive Committee of ATTI, (H.G. Mithra, the Secretary, Limasangla Lemtur the Vice – President, Praveen Perumalla, the Treasurer, Alias, K.V., Royce Victor, Haokip, K. Sagar Sundar Raj, and Idan Topno) for their counsel and support; particularly Mithra, who looked after the organization of the conferences and presented Bailey's paper in Guwahati; Sunil Caleb who presented it in Hyderabad and offered the Foreword; and Eric Jones, a member of the Evesham Methodist Church in England and expert in communication who has been through the draft making corrections and suggestions.

The publishers, *Christian World Imprints*, deserve appreciation for their enthusiasm, interest and efficiency. Mr. Sudhanshu Kanda's prompt communication with courtesy and openness is commendable!

It is my hope that this book will stimulate those who struggle to understand different manifestations of religion or religiosity and who feel frustrated in the pursuit of making their religion appealing to people of different segments of society, socio-political ideologies and religions. The stimulation may lead to encourage and undertake new studies and researches into untrekked paths and untreated avenues. Where there is no vision, openness, critical thinking and commitment, religions will prove to be invalid in the long run.

Israel Selvanayagam

10 March 2017 Evesham, England

1

Is Implicit Religion and Secular Spirituality only a Western Concept and Experience?

A Keynote Presentation

Edward Bailey

(Prof. Edward Bailey was very much looking forward to be present at the conference in Hyderabad, or at least addressing the audience via Skype. Very sadly he passed away on 22nd April 2015. Respecting his enthusiasm and acknowledging his support for the conference the Trustees of the CSIRCS accepted a suggestion that Dr. Bailey's key ideas of implicit religion and secular spirituality should be presented by someone in Hyderabad and Gauhati. Edward's family asked Dr. Israel Selvanayagam to put together the basic ideas using the materials sent by them.)

Religion and its Variety

In whatever way perceived and interpreted it is obvious from history that human being is a religious animal although today some may not like to be labelled as religious. It used to be the case for centuries that religion meant the explicit religious practice including myths, rituals, experience, social formation and ethical codes. In the nineteenth century, while Christian missionaries were encountering the world religions, there were pioneering efforts to translate and edit the 'Sacred Books of the East.' Making use of the facilities provided by the colonial governments, scholars went far and wide and studied the exotic cultures and religious behaviour of human communities in islands, hill tribes and so on. Soon – and inevitably? - one question raised was about the origin of religion. The answers included magic, *mana* or sacred power, idea of holy as both fascinating and terrifying, and so on. Different methodological approaches were emerging, and among them most popular have been the historical, psychological, philosophical, sociological, anthropological and the phenomenological. Departments of the study of religion with different names – Comparative Religion, Religious Studies, Divinity School, History of Religion, Phenomenology of Religion, etc., were established in all the major universities in the West. Researches with high sophistication and a mass of outcome of findings, suggestions and interpretations, present a stunning variety but keep=alive the question of a convincing definition of religion.

While the definitions and details of the visible religion continued to be analyzed, in the twentieth century new forms of religion were observed. For example, the recognition of what was termed as 'quasi religion' was found necessary for a theology of correlation (Tillich). Thus nationalism, fascism, communism, etc., were pointed out with reference to their visions and rituals. Then came in usage names such as folk religion, popular religion, invisible religion and civil religion. One can study profitably the connotations and applications of each of such term. While being aware of all these, based on study and observation, I raised the question of whether there is some kind of inherent religiosity in the secular domain. I proposed the term implicit religion which changes the conventional distinction between the sacred and the secular. I tried to test this change in the church, in schools where religious education is compulsory and public houses such as a pub. Subsequently, a Centre for the Study of Implicit Religion and Contemporary Spirituality was established in a British university context, study and research fellowships in different institutions established, an annual international conference held and publications including (now) a quarterly Journal produced. As those who are associated with this venture would realize, even implicit religion and secular spirituality, has gone beyond a simple concept. As the papers presented in the conference and essays in the Journal show, there is no discipline of formal study, departments of public service and popular displays of human talents such as sports that cannot be related to implicit religion. More usually, the parameters of philosophy, sociology and psychology border with implicit religion. However, at the beginning of this important conference I limit myself to explain as clearly as possible the definition(s) of implicit religion and its application to various areas of life and work.

What is Implicit Religion?

The concept of implicit religion took shape as a way of encapsulating the question, what does one stand for or what makes one tick? It is the sort of question we may ask when someone dies: it may help us understand people better (from their inside, so to speak) if we ask it sooner, rather than later.

The possibility, and importance, of this quest began to take shape in two pastoral contexts during the 1960s: it was a grass-roots corrective to some academic and ecclesiastical attitudes that were prevalent at the time. Simple observation, as an assistant curate in a parish with an influential liturgical tradition, showed that it would fly in the face of obvious human reality, to suggest that religion was always epiphenomenal, a veil obscuring some other reality, such as a form of psychological escapism or of sociological ideology. One didn't have to agree with or approve of a particular form of religion, but it would be impossible to understand, at least for some people, if one ignored this part of their empirical intentionality.

Then, as an assistant chaplain in a boarding school, I realised that something similar was true of at least some of, those colleagues on the staff, or among the pupils, who would have declined a 'religious' label. They had their own 'secular', if you like, but after a year's study, I changed it to 'implicit', religion. Now a fairly accepted even obvious idea, at the time it was novel, and disruptive of conventional categories, with their assumptions and practical consequences. However, meeting in 1968, almost by chance, probably the only person in this country who felt similarly at that time, I retired from my then position, and tested the hunch in three empirical studies: through open-ended interviews, starting with 'What do you enjoy most in life?', and ending with, 'Who are you?'; then as an assistant barman in a public house; and finally as Rector, for 36 years, of a parish of 6,000 people in the suburb of Bristol in England.

As it happened, each of my three formal 'definitions' of the concept ('descriptions' would be a better term) applied, in turn, to the data resulting from these studies. The implicit religion of individuals could be described in terms of their *commitment(s)*; the life of a public house in terms of *integrating foci;* and a residential community, in terms of *intensive concerns, with extensive effects*. The first of these definitions, *commitments*, describes people's "psychology", stretching all the way 'up' from their subconscious, through their conscious, to those moments of heightened awareness that we could call 'surconscious'. The second definition, *integrating foci,* describes the more 'lateral' processes of their integration, both inwardly, within themselves, and outwardly, with others. The third definition, intensive concerns with extensive effects, reflects the characteristically English understanding of religion, as in sayings such as, 'I read the papers religiously', meaning 'regularly, but deliberately', 'habitually, but voluntarily'; it is, in other words, 'my *chosen* rule, or way of life'; 'I do it, because I believe in it.'

The concept of Implicit Religion invites us to consider whether talk of people's 'devotion' to their children, the 'sacrifices' they make in order to 'better' themselves, or the 'spiritual' benefits of undergoing the 'rituals' of a health centre, might be closer to what is conventionally called religious, than we may sometimes think. We ask whether there might be a religious dimension to ordinary life (even if the religion is of a kind we've never met before), in order to enhance our overall understanding, both of others and of ourselves.

At this juncture, I want to acknowledge criticisms against the idea of implicit religion and its own limitations. There are two questions raised: first, if implicit religion requires a study of whatever a person or group happens to be committed to at some particular time and place, how can we provide materials to equip the researcher? I would answer saying that this may be the case for every study of something new. However, materials on the basis of the past experiences and openness for the new experience do help. What is needed is an adjustment of thinking and addition of a language. Second, as the concept of implicit religion hypothesizes that in advance of empirical study, may it be possible to state what form the implicit religion of any individual or group will take? In answer, let me note that for anthropologists anything is found to be religious or sacred in some context or other. But this position can't impinge on other sciences. 'If everything is religious the word is meaningless.' This may rule out new, specific happening and studying it with interest.

As limitations, the following acknowledgements are in order. The three-fold description – commitments, integrating foci and intensive concern with extensive effects – may not be sufficient. Other descriptions such as 'human depths' have occasionally come to my mind. However, the three are sufficient to give confirmation, demonstrate overlap, and provide a point of intersection. Even multiplicity of terms are not adequate to recapture the original intuition and conceptualization. In fact the study of implicit religion concerns not only non-verbal behaviour. One may characterize behaviour religiously implicit but not taking the behaviour itself. For instance, someone obsessed with secularism may not be able to discern in secularism a kind of religion. In the light of the above discussion, it may be reasonably suggested that the concept of implicit religion offers a precision to the meaning of religion and coherence to the religious phenomena studied both of its historical origin and popular usage.

Pluralism and Implicit Religion

***Moral Foundation*:** Something of the moral foundation of the pluralism that is practiced in everyday life is captured in a series of Interview Responses. The following is a bare summary: In human relationships the root problem is communication. When it does not happen in a clear manner emotions may run high. Similarly, persons want to be treated with respect irrespective of their race and colour. Also in everyday life, when suddenly something clicks and a person emerges and says something to another that he means, as an equal person. What one person does not like in another is lack of humility, arrogance, and insensitivity to the opinions of others and the refusal to recognise that there's a grain of truth in other people's views. One hates people to be unnatural—to be bombastic, or have snobbish ideas—that does strain one's tolerance.

Does one ever feel that there is anything lacking in one's life? The answers include more contact with their parents, sharing concerns but without arguing as their views are different on everything they discuss—religion, politics, everything. People are unique individuals and each one has the right to believe what s/he is convinced of.

The commentary on these reported interviews speaks of the Self as 'the primary, given, reality in the interviewees' worldview', and of its evaluation as 'both human (i.e. fallible) *and* sacred' and describes it as 'the basis of a solidarity.' This 'solidarity' paraphrases, it may be suggested, what current commentators, such as sociologists and politicians (optimistically, perhaps), call 'communities'; what Durkheim described as the consequence of 'effervescence'; what the Hebrew scriptures saw as Spirit (that which *joins*); and which we are labelling 'pluralism.'

Thus, although at that time it was more likely to have been seen as linked to the concept and ideal of 'democracy,' which was itself seen as an attempt to institutionalize the virtues of 'liberty, equality, fraternity, may now be offered as the empirical (albeit subjective) and existential (phenomenological, even) essence of Pluralism. Therefore, as the Self overcomes its ineffability and becomes available for discussion, in a relatively relaxed or 'profane' (better, *secular*) way, through the concept of 'human' i.e., imperfect nature,' so it becomes available in a manner more demanding of respect, through the concept of beliefs. The sacredness that is attributed to them is wholly unrelated to any abstract quality of objective truth. It derives entirely from their closeness to the self. They are its property (almost in an Aristotelian sense), chosen and possessed by the individual, and yet obligatory and possessive of him, revelatory of his inner being and of his judgment upon himself. Pluralism, then, may be seen as one stage in the 're-discovery' (by an insular and cerebral world) of this ancient assumption.

The kind of social psychology present in the interviews goes well beyond Hobbes's struggle of all against all, or Locke's marriage of mutual convenience. It is, however, social, rather than corporate: each (individual) depends upon others, and each may become 'party to' (a limited number of) others; but neither the whole, nor any of its parts, is dependent upon either the individual or the totality, for its existence and identity. The order of the day, according to this widespread, yet private, wisdom, is neither corporatism nor individualism (each of the poles being an imaginary abstraction), but, to coin a word, 'societism.' Thus, sociology has come into its own, because it studies, neither society *tout simple*, nor any particular society as a whole, but an entity of indeterminate boundary, which is yet large enough to comprehend all these particular experienced relationships.

The second research exercise (in the pub), as it happens, likewise conducted without benefit of this particular expression, indicates the presence of the same kinds of practices and ideals. The context was the life of a public house, in Bristol. An anecdotal occurrence, and the lessons drawn by a particular 'regular' from another anecdotal occurrence, together speak volumes about Pluralism in practice, certainly in Britain, at the time (1970): One of the first conversations of depth, between the observer and this customer, arose from the behaviour of a certain visitor (to the pub).This new customer hailed from Lancashire, but was working temporarily in Bristol, came to the pub daily for a fortnight, and offended against the *mores* by both drinking and talking too much. (The regular) found this behaviour so irritating that he transferred himself, complete with his glass and book, round to the other (the 'public') side, until such time as the visitor ceased to visit the lounge. When the visitor (whose anti-Bristolian comments also failed to endear him) transferred himself to the public side (from whence the

Manager - virtually uniquely, in 400 hours of observation - soon expelled him) the regular returned to his accustomed place by the lounge bar. He described to the (research student) barman, by means of an autobiographical parable, the usual and proper way of introducing yourself to a pub and possibly any other small community (whether residential, or an interest - group) in England, certainly (but not only) in the recent past.

One winter, he said, he had been staying in a Butlin's (holiday camp) chalet near Maidenhead, and used to go each evening to a pub in the nearest village, which he said was some miles away. He always greeted the locals, who were farmers and labourers, as he entered, but, after ordering his drink, talked only with his wife or the landlord.

Eventually there came an evening when the 'locals' (i.e., the regulars of the 'local'), being short of a player, asked if he could play 'Spoof' (*sic*): the point being, that 'they had seen I could hold my own' (without seeking to dominate others). By way of contrast, the man from Bury in Lancashire had been constantly buying drinks for other people in the Bristol pub, and glibly introducing himself all round (putting them in his 'debt,' and so 'down'). It was not hard to envisage the self-effacing reply (probably, that, Yes, he did know the rules) that he would have given the locals near Maidenhead. Indeed, as he claimed he won the game that evening, it is even more certain that he would have disclaimed any skill, beyond the barest familiarity with the rules. But as a consequence, of course, he and the players had become the best of friends, with invitations for him to shoot where he liked, and to call at their farmhouse for lunch any day he was in their vicinity. Again, by way of contrast, he said other visitors 'walked into the pub, bought them all drinks (it is difficult to credit this as happening frequently, especially at that time, despite some possible degree of influence from the nearby capital city), and then were ignored.'

The report on the period of observation in the public house finds that the customers can be typologised by age, or by the type of beer-glass preferred ('handles' or 'sleevers'). However, while each of those two "ideal types" relate to more characteristics, and suggests more unity between them, than such stand-by's as gender, education, income, self-assigned class, and so on, neither is nearly as revealing as a pair that were invented for this context, the second of which might be seen as a precursor of Pluralism.

In a pub in my case my position was a mono-man. Poly-people, on the other hand, see culture, like personality, as an inevitably variegated phenomenon, in a world that includes more than one nation-state-society, or religion-culture-race. No single culture can therefore be capitalized, for none is normative; with the paradoxical consequence (as in Hinduism, or the Roman Empire) that tolerance becomes *de rigeur*. Following, significantly, the academic anthropological example culture becomes a non-normative, generic category, with a plural reference: everybody has their own culture(s), music(s), etc; and, a theorist of implicit religion might add, their own religion(s), implicit and explicit; but to that we will return.

***Pluralism and Contextual Factors*:** The third field of research, i.e., a sub-urban parish church of the Church of England was long and ongoing. Peoples' experiences and expressions were checked against the secularism debate nationally and internationally. The concept of implicit religion seemed as though it might have been a substitute for, or a successor to, 'secularization,' which no longer enjoyed the status it had held in those circles for most of the twentieth century. On the one hand, there was an obvious 'return to religion,' at least in the public sphere; or, to be more precise, there was a renewed recognition, in the public sphere in the 'West,' of the place of religion in both public and private life around the globe. On the other hand, there was a blurring of the then assumed (by academics) division, in most areas of thought and life, between the religious and the secular. While students of religion had not yet quite reached the stage of asking themselves what on earth religion could possibly be about, if it was *not* about the secular, at least the boundary was increasingly being seen as permeable, and hence 'fuzzy.' Thirdly, this increasing prominence of religion, combined with the increasing recognition of its practical relevance (at least in the lives of others), may well have been two of the many factors behind the gradual, and it would appear virtually invincible, rise to the surface of 'spirituality,' as concept, value, and practice.

'Pluralism' was not only more accurate, but also less value-laden, then 'secularity' or 'secularism,' as a term for referring to a world in which religion was still both relatively conspicuous and important, and in which spirituality was everywhere invoked, not least where previously it had been unexpected: in sales, sport and sex, for instance.

Sometimes, though, it carried its own hint of a value system, and one that was positive, to boot. For there seemed to be some kind of assumption, not only that the societies in which these conferences were being held, in North America and in Europe, were unusually or even uniquely pluralistic, but also that this was somehow to their credit. One was put in mind of Ninian Smart's (1968) enquiry: now that the West had lost its Empires, did it see its secularism as another way of claiming a new hegemony, based on historical priority?

However, if those were the underlying assumptions, might it not be the case that the nation-state-societies bordering the North Atlantic might not themselves be the laggards; or be in danger of imitating the man who discovered he been speaking in prose all his life? So far as history was concerned, could any of them match the diversity of the Silk Road, or eighth-century Baghdad, or any major medieval city with its 'quarters'? So far as the contemporary world was concerned, could they equal the sight of a Jain monk (wearing a face-mask, to avoid harming a germ or a fly), walking past a Moslem butcher's stall, in the bazaar in Bangalore, the IT capital of a Hindu society? Or (as in a 1961 photograph, taken at Srinagar airport), porters from (Buddhist) Ladakh, loading a (secular) Indian Airlines plane, with the luggage of Moslems going on Hajj to Mecca? Or, applying *un peu d'ethnographie* to (probably) any of the sixteen thousand Church of England parishes into which the country is divided, the daily experience of any Anglican minister, during an afternoon's traditional home visiting, of millionaires and paupers?

Indeed, it is noteworthy to have so many foreign-born citizens in Toronto or London or Sydney; to have more Jews in New York than in Jerusalem; or to have 59 mother-tongues at a school in Oxford; as it was to have more scientists alive in the twentieth century than in all previous centuries combined. But such claims to excessively 'exceptional' status also need to bear in mind the contemporary rural immigration into Chinese cities (and Stalin's all-too-numerous, total ethnic removals); or the size of New York's population compared to Israel's; and that 59 first-languages is relatively un-remarkable (some UK schools have a hundred); or that there were also more martyrs, as well as scientists, in the twentieth century (however either 'martyrs' or 'scientists' is defined).

However, more significant perhaps than these numbers games (with their competitive moral edge: 'We are more varied than thou'), is the existential content of this, (apparently) prized, Pluralism. The term could legitimately be applied to a contiguous collection of "silos" (in management jargon); 'diversity' could be used to describe a bird's eye view of a gaggle of ghettoes. In this sense, the Hindu caste system, the former South African system of racial *Apartheid*, the English class system, old-style segregation in the US, the continuing grudging 'tolerance' of 'gypsies' throughout Europe, 'reserves' for First Nations throughout the Americas, Australasia, India and elsewhere, all occur in societies that are 'pluralistic,' in that they are composed of diverse components. But, as an ideal (and it is an ideal, as the consideration of its motivation has demonstrated), Pluralism proper strives for Equality, Liberty, and *Fraternity*, for a Democracy of the spirit as well as the letter, for communication, and hence a sense of *comm*-unity.

This, however, involves emotions, and is an emotive issue; which has made it a political issue, not only in all the countries just mentioned, but also in many more (perhaps all). If all (not just the underdog) venture out of their ghetto, and enter into relationship with the Other(s), change follows: do we seek assimilation (in whatever direction), resulting in homogenization, or reciprocity of influence and inspiration (whether *or not* that also results in homogeneity)? Politically, the question pits the poly-people against the Mono-man (which gives the observer, however dedicated to 'objectivity,' a certain *frisson*: sociology morphs into advocacy).

No doubt this political dimension is also one of the reasons for the growing popularity of Pluralism in our supermarket trolley of sociological concepts. It is, however, more effect, than cause. The driving force is the previously mentioned moral imperative, universalised now through modern media of communication, as well as ever as Weber pointed out through trade. For trade, and (what is now usually called) religion, were 'glocal' (both local and global), and hence already plural, in the days of "the beaker people" (1800 BCE).

Advantages of an 'implicit-religious' understanding of Pluralism: Once upon a time, some people? seem to have interpreted the decrees of the Early Church's ecumenical councils simply as the fruit of the work of the Divine Spirit. (In fairness, they probably saw the Holy Spirit as having worked upon and therefore through the Councils' Episcopal members). Any who took that peculiarly detached (and un-Incarnational) view, were no doubt surprised when it was suggested that the Decrees also owed something to political motives and psychological processes. Most have long since accepted that neither the religious-theological-divine, nor the secular-scientific-human, necessarily excludes the other: *both-and* is at least as likely to be the case, as *either/or*.

The 'Implicit Religion' hypothesis can be seen as taking a similar (not identical: the spiritual-divine-theological are, strictly speaking, adjectival, and lack the initial capital letter) approach to the empirical, in this case to the facts and theories that are labelled as Pluralism. The 'religious' (in this case, 'secular-religious') does not replace the simply 'secular' understanding of psychology, politics etc: it is simply another string in the violin, waiting to be played upon, to produce a more rounded and mature symphony of understanding.

One advantage of using this 'religious' string is the considerable number of further issues and lines of enquiry that it encourages. For instance, (and they have not been followed up in this introduction, but could be, in sustained research), to what extent is Pluralism a creed, an ontology, and/or an ethic? Are rituals involved in its practice, or espousal? What are the characteristics—and what is the actual *character*—of its solidary (solid? Not quite sure about solidary) base? Is it an alliance, or party, or a communion? Is there a canon, whether literary or oral? Does it ever excommunicate any individual, group or practice? What does it stand *for*? Hope for? Look for? What can it *not* speak about? And if it cannot, is that because it is too sacred, or too abominable, to be mentioned? And so on.

The secular (or so the implicit religion hypothesis wishes to suggest) is far too significant, worthy and venerable to be interpreted simply as a secular phenomenon, and through secular approaches, alone. Whether or not it has divine implications, it does have religious import; on those grounds, it should be appraised by every method available.

Application: Three British Examples

1. Princess Diana was killed in a road accident on 31 August 1997. The whole nation was shocked by the loss of a charming, down to earth and charitable member of the British royal family. Soon streets were filled with milling crowds, with flowers and candles. Churches were unprecedentedly filled with people in tears and spontaneously praying. One pertinent question raised

was: what made a nominally Christian but phenomenally secular British people instantly religious? More questions were raised: Was there a feeling in the subconscious which was pushed to burst out by this tragedy? Does a great princess had to die in such a tragic manner for people to become religious or spiritual for a while? Number of studies have been done on this phenomenon.

2. The most popular and public creed in England is 'Football is our religion.' For newcomers to football matches the hymn-singing may remind them of a service of worship in a cathedral or open ground. Dimensions of religion such as ritual, mythical, social and experiential can be identified in football. The celebrities become not only fascinating figures of public attention and respect but also are taken as new trend setters of culture and models of values. With talent, training and media projection they seem to evoke a kind of transcendence in the minds of their fans. For many of them football is more than life and death. Of course, this would apply to other sports as well. Statues of certain sports stars have almost become cult centres. The style of organization, contents of hymns, traits of personalities, the role of the media and what exactly happen in the stadium have been studied from the perspective of implicit religion.
3. In South West England there is a village with a large field called 'Glastonbury'. The annual Glastonbury Festival attracts thousands of people who live in tents, share food and enjoy exotic music and dance. Most of them appear to belong to a sub-culture. But those who have observed the different elements of the festival point out vitality, love and regeneration of life. Their life and activities may appear to fall into the category of a folk religion. However, the observation of implicit religion cannot be invalid.

The above three British examples may illustrate the fields of research and experiences of implicit religion. There are many more examples as studies, publications and papers presented in the Denton Conference and essays published in the journal. Over the years, the concerns and interest have become international and varied.

Application to India?

After receiving my degree and before training for ordination I spent two years in Bangalore (1959-1961) on a World Council of Churches Scholarship at the Christian Institute for the Study of Religion and Society under M.M. Thomas who was doing research under his mentor P.D. Devanandan, the founder-director of CISRS. Later he succeeded his mentor as the Director of the CISRS. His contribution to the ecumenical movement qualified him to become the Chair of the Central Committee of the WCC in 70s. His prophetic writings during the time of Emergency in mid-70s was recognized by an alternative government of

India when he was made the Governor of the North-Eastern State of Nagaland in the 90s.

While interfaith dialogue was pioneered by CISRS, M.M. Thomas was primarily engaged in a study of secular ideologies and particularly in dialogue with Marxists. Consequently, he managed to write on the 'secular meaning of the gospel.' His ideas of sacred fellowship outside the church and Christ-centred syncretism were provoking. And in the fifth General Assembly of the WCC held in Nairobi (1975), in the context of discussion on injustices like racism, he introduced the phrase 'spirituality for combat.' Thomas' ideas and experiments continue to be studied and in them one can find resonance of the concept of implicit religion. With this background, we organized a consultation on spirituality at the United Theological College, Bangalore, in March 2005. It was obvious that some hard work and thinking was needed to grasp the implications of M.M. Thomas' vision and to unlock 'spirituality' from the traditional boxes of explicit religion.

Hinduism seems to be a double-edged sword. On the one hand, as a kaleidoscopic and encyclopedic religious tradition, it has been influenced by secular thinking although the basic beliefs in the power of the Vedic ritual and karma and transmigration of the soul continue. It seems to be the generosity of the Hindu majority who have allowed India to become the socialist, secular, democratic, republic. But on the other hand, there has been a tension between revivalist Hindus and secular thinkers. It is important to explore the ideals of equality and justice and realize them in public life. The position of a majority may be one of arrogance and stubbornness or of creating a space initiating dialogue with the minorities. One may expect a common religiosity and shared values while continuing the journey.

Conclusion

The concept and study of implicit religion has a long journey yet to go. Its distinctive place in the science of religions or the study of religion should be stabilized and developed. Interfaith dialogue, if pursued with all earnestness, has a great deal to contribute and refine. It is my firm conviction and hope that participants in this conference will grow gaining newer insights and thinking and able to see their religious and spiritual life as well as others' in a new light. And their dialogue with members of secular movements will be further enlightening.

Finally, let me finish with one of the observations I have noted in my Editorial for the last issue of *Implicit Religion* (18/1 2015): 'I suspect that any idea that has ever occurred, or any course of action I have proposed, has always been improved, in and by the process of discussion.'

2

Defining Religion in 'Hindu' India
A Review of Major Attempts

Israel Selvanayagam

An Introductory Observation

It is almost a miracle that India, with more than 1.3 billion people, a few ancient civilizations, hundreds of languages and dialects as well as a composite culture, is multireligious with a secular polity. It may be astonishing that the 'Christian countries' in the West are crudely secular in outlook and behaviour whereas India as a 'Socialist, Secular, Democratic Republic' is intensely and explicitly religious. The opening words of the preamble to India's Constitution read as follows:

> WE, THE PEOPLE OF INDIA, having solemnly resolved to constitute India into a SOVEREIGN SOCIALIST SECULAR DEMOCRATIC REPUBLIC and to secure to all its citizens:
>
> **JUSTICE**, social, economical and political;
>
> **LIBERTY** of thought, expression, belief, faith and worship;
>
> **EQUALITY** of status and of opportunity; and to promote among them all
>
> **FRATERNITY** assuring the dignity of the individual and the unity and integrity of the Nation.

We are not going to analyze whether it is good or bad but to observe that with a majority of population (more than 80%) being identified as Hindu it seems to be very difficult, if not impossible, to achieve the ideals of secularism – justice, liberty, equality and fraternity. What is known as Hinduism is a multifarious tradition, with poly-paradigmatic or poly-centric visions (Vedic, yogic, devotional, cultic, etc), values and traditions, cannot be defined easily. Attempts to identify different traditions, strands and communities with caste orientation have been tacitly thwarted.[1] Therefore, it is understandable that scholarly studies undertaken by westerners are generally confined to a particular aspect or tradition. At the same time, there are efforts to unite all traditions within one umbrella but are done primarily by the proponents of the Hindutva movement or political Hinduism. There have been proposals to remove the words 'secular' and 'socialist' from the preamble to the Constitution with both supporting and opposing arguments.[2] Even in this seemingly chaotic and unpredictable situation discussions are on the nature of secularism in India. Those who hold the secular vision with its ideals of equality, freedom, justice, rational thinking, etc., argue that Hinduism is incompatible with secularism and in response such critics are termed as pseudo-secularists with a claim that Hinduism is generous, all absorbent, hospitable and profoundly secular.

Although, the Indian religious traditions have supplied fodder for the everincreasing industry of religious studies from its inception, the academic study of religions in India is yet to gain traction. Indeed, the academic disciplines variously called in the west the History of Religion, Comparative Religion, the Science of Religion, Divinity, and the Phenomenology of Religion are virtually nonexistent. But there are departments of Indian philosophy, text books and new materials in which the traditional interpretations and arguments are repeated without much imagination of their appeal to the society around them which is marred by poverty, corruption and untouchability. Few universities recognize 'value education' provided by some autonomous colleges and departments of Islam, Christianity and Sikhism. One would wish for activities of interaction between these departments but the 'secular university ethos' hardly encourages and provides space for such creative interaction.

Defining religion or recognizing the difficulty of or difficulties in defining religion is patently a starting point in studies of religion across the world. Also, the definitions provided betray certain approaches or perspectives such as historical, socio-analytical, sociological, anthropological, psychological, philosophical, phenomenological, theological and so on. In the west classical definitions include the following: religion as 'instinct for reality' (Plato), 'the perception of the infinite under such manifestations as are able to influence the moral character of (wo) man' (M. Muller), 'the sigh of the oppressed creature, the heart of a heartless world…the opium of the people' (K. Marx), 'unbelief, a human rebellion against God' (K. Barth), 'the feeling of absolute dependence' (Schleiermacher), 'what the individual does in his (her) solitariness' (A.N. Whitehead), 'ultimate concern' (P. Tillich), 'a unified system of beliefs and practices relative to sacred things…set apart or forbidden which unite into one single moral community' (E. Durkheim),

1 For a concise and objective treatment by a former Census Commissioner and Registrar General of India, see M. Vijayanunni, "Where is the Caste Data?," *The Hindu*, 15 July 2015, 14.

2 For example, some reactions from across the nation, see Raksha Kumar, "What's all the fuss about?," *The Hindu Magazine*, 15 February, 2015, 2.

'the serious and social attitude of individuals or communities toward the power or powers which they conceive as having ultimate control over their interests and destinies' (J. Pratt), 'response to an inscrutable mystery' (A. Lang), 'belief in an impersonal (sacred) power' (Van der Leeuw), 'fascinating and mysterious sense of holiness' (R. Otto), 'the feelings, acts, and experiences of individual men (and women) in their solitude, so far as they apprehend themselves to stand in relation to whatever they consider divine' (W. James), 'projection of infantile dependencies upon imagined super human beings' (S. Freud), 'collective unconscious which handles the overpowering and destructive *anima* and helps to explore the immemorial treasures of myths and symbols' (C. Jung).[1] Definitions of religion continue to be taken seriously in the study of religion at different levels.[2] With often boring overlap, more recently, again not without favoured perspectives, some comprehensive definitions are provided.[3] The search and formulations continue.

There have been attempts to introduce western methods including a discussion on the definition of religion. For example, Eric Lott, a western scholar who encountered the Indian religious traditions with passionate involvement, has suggested a tool for approaching India's religious traditions. After giving a warning about any claim of an absolute definition, he provisionally suggests a definition that might be 'both sufficiently inclusive and sufficiently focused to be of some methodological use':

> Religion is the way humans experience and relate to some sacred Focus (or foci). It is an experience transmitted as a community tradition with sacred symbols, places, times, people and (sometimes) scriptures; it is expressed in rituals, myths, doctrines, and ethical-cultural values; by participating in this constantly adapting tradition perceived human limitations and threats to existence are experienced as overcome or transcended.[4]

It is revealing that western tools developed in the fields of sociology of religion, psychology of religion and structuralism are introduced in the context of the study of Indian religious traditions. Imaginative reconstructions of the bhakti experiences and traditions is phenomenal. Some scholars in India who have grasped these tools have made attempts. However, pride of preserving the heritage without asking any critical questions seem to dominate the religious practices and studies.

---

1 Eric Sharpe, *Comparative Religion – A History*, London: Duckworth, 1975, 39-114; gleaned from more detailed descriptions.

2 E.g. see Nancy Ring *et al*, *Introduction to the Study of Religion*, Maryknoll: Orbis Books, 1998, 61-63.

3 Alan Richardson, *Religion in Contemporary Debate*, London: SCM, 1968, 16; George Lindbeck, *The Nature of Doctrine*, London: SPCK, 1984, 33f.

4 Eric J. Lott, "Approaching a Religious Tradition" in *Religious Traditions of India*, ed. by P. S. Daniel, David C. Scott and G.R. Singh, Senate of Serampore College: Indian Theological Library, 1988, 2.

At the same time, the emphasis on 'experience' in Lott's definition is very relevant in the Indian context, as we shall see, where, even in study circles, experience is repeatedly emphasized as the essence of religious life without taking any effort to analyse the nature of that experience. In one of the few attempts to bring together Indian approaches to the study of religion, the participants of the project categorically maintain that experience is the essential core of religious life. It is either re-experiencing an ancient spirituality based on certain sacred acts, or experiencing afresh the fountains of life, which would transcend all logic. There is an assertion that no one can understand religion if one has not had a religious experience oneself.[1] Then it is unrealistic to expect rigorous studies of the 'varieties of religious experience' as done in the West. In due course, however, the same author (Lott) moved from struggling to give a formal definition to identifying different dimensions of religious life.

Indian thinkers seem to call for a different approach not only because of the specific nature of the religious traditions cradled in the sub-continent, but also because of peculiar ways of trying to amalgamate conflicting differences into a single framework such as life-soul, transcendence, supreme reality or absolute mystery. Such a rigorous and detailed study of religion, including carefully defining religion, is not evident in India. But Indian religious traditions, particularly Hinduism, have been studied comprehensively over the centuries starting from the Orientalists and continuing with a host of western scholars. Along with them and beside them Indian scholars have studied the Indian religious tradition mainly from a sociological perspective. Names such as M.N. Srinivas, S.C. Dube, Leela Dube and their son Saurabh Dube come to mind.

Indian Definitions of Religions

We will illustrate the positions of five well-known and recent Indian thinkers, most of whom are also Hindu apologists. One can easily decipher the typical Hindu emphasis on experience punctuated with certain philosophical or ideological positions.

Swami Vivekananda (1863 – 1902) who interpreted Hindu Vedantic thought for the reformation of Indian society and who founded the Ramakrishna Mission, had a view of universal religion based on the divinity endowed in every human being.

> Each soul is potentially divine. The goal is to manifest this divinity within by controlling nature, external and internal. Do this either by work or worship or psychic control or philosophy – by one or more or all of these – and be free. This is the whole of religion. Doctrines

1 See the essays in *Approaches to the Study of Religion*, ed. by Harbans Singh, Patiala: Guru Gobind Singh Department of Religious Studies, n.d.

or dogmas or rituals or books or temples or forms are but secondary details.[1]

Through the experience of transcendental meditation one can see the unity in all multiplicity. That is the test of true knowledge as well. At the level of personal devotion, Vivekananda held that God is the absolute truth and that truth can be judged by truth alone.

Rabindranath Tagore (1861 – 1941) as a poet, artist and thinker, as well as the only one who wrote a book on Religion, *The Religion of Man: The Hibbert Lectures of 1930*, saw religion as a constant struggle for balance in the spiritual arena of human beings. For him religion in essence is a harmonious whole which cannot be exhausted by its partial manifestations or dimensions. The Vedic orientation and the Bengali Vaishnava tradition helped him to see the ultimate harmony of religious life that includes intense form of devotion.

Religion is 'the creative principle of unity, the divine mystery of existence.'[2] God is the Supreme Being in whom all things human, knowledge, will and action, are comprehended and who is the Ultimate Goal. Self-realisation and devotion are fundamental means to achieve this goal. Obviously, Tagore's assessment of the Vedic vision and life is partial, idealist and unscholarly. Later we will illustrate this with the most popularized Vedic dictum of 'one truth and different names.'

M.K. Gandhi (1869 – 1948) combined his religious vision with an additional vision OR one of political independence and a just economic structure. For him Hinduism with its essential message of *ahimsa* or non-violence was the most glorious religion. By means of non-violence only one can attain the goal that is God or Truth. Truth cannot be confined to a perceived fact, accuracy, and veracity of statements or logical truth reached by deduction from accepted premises. 'Truth is the sovereign principle which includes numerous other principles. This truth is not only truthfulness in word, but truthfulness in thought also and not only the relative truth of our conception but the absolute Truth, the Eternal principle, that is God.'[3] Ahimsa is not only abstaining from harming but also engaging in loving action and is not only the essence of Hinduism but also the essence of all true religion. It is the supreme manifestation of Truth. Again, there is an imagined Hinduism as the most glorious, but hiding the complexity, struggle and degradation. This is not to deny that every religious tradition suffers from a tragic difference between the ideal and the actual. It is a hermeneutical irony that Gandhi stood for non-violence and his assassin for violence for the noble cause of restoring an ancient dharma.

---

1 *What Religion is in the Words of Swami Vivekananda*, ed. by Swami Vidyatmananda, Calcutta: Advaita Ashrama, 1998.

2 R.Tagore, *The Religion of Man*, Boston: Beacon Press, 1961, 14f.

3 M.K. Gandhi, *Autobiography: Or the Story of My Experiments with Truth,* Ahmedabad: Navajivan Trust, 1927/1991, xi.

Aurobindo Ghose (1872 – 1950), a spiritual hero and political activist, interpreted religion in terms of 'integral yoga.' He based his ideas on the Upanishadic teaching of Brahman, the transcendental unity and stability lying behind the phenomenal variety and flux. Growing self-awareness with constant recognition of the Supreme Self permeates all areas of life. 'We acknowledge that nothing is likely to become a universal and master impulse in India which is not identified with religion. The obvious course is to recognise that politics is religion and infuse it with the spirit of religion; for that is the true patriotism which sees God as the Mother in our country, God as *sakti* in the mass of our country (wo) men, and religiously devotes itself to their service and their liberation from present suffering and servitude.'[1] Integral yoga helps one to achieve a supreme consciousness of oneself and the Supreme Self in the evolutional path towards the Super Mind.

S. Radhakrishnan (1888 – 1975), a Hindu philosopher and apologetic, who held the Spalding Chair of Comparative Religion in Oxford and a former president of India, saw religion as the soul of civilization. For him, 'Religion has been from the beginning the bearer of human culture. It is the supreme achievement of (wo)man's profound experience. It is the deepest kind of life reflecting the different phases, complex and conflicting, of human living. Millions of minds, their thoughts and dreams, go to make a religion. A large part of the world received its religious education from India. Despite continuous struggle with superstition and theological baggage, India has held fast for centuries to the ideals of spirit.'[2] These words are seminal which are explained and interpreted voluminously. Radhakrishnan claims that Hinduism represents best the essence of a world religion with its complex variety yet leading to the concrete spirit or the Absolute real. For him the non-dualist world-view and experience provide most authentic framework for a unified spirituality and universal religion. His 'Religion of the Concrete Spirit' is not much different from that of Paul Tillich.

All these five Hindu thinkers have viewed religion from the perspective of the 'pan-mythic' Hinduism or religious traditions of India which, in their view, culminate in the mystical experience of oneness with the supreme reality. They do not show any interest in studying the nature and phenomenal variety of religious experience around the world as well as in India itself. One may argue that the main reason for these thinkers holding tightly the Vedantic view of ultimate unity was to counter the claims of Islam and Christianity for 'one truth-one religion' in their distinctive ways. The framework of one truth-many religions is most popular among people of the sub-continent ranging from illiterate masses to educated thinkers. This provides no motivation to understand not only the

---

1 Sri Aurobindo, *Birth Centenary Library*, Pondicherry: Sri Aurobindo Ashram Trust, 1971, Vol. 1, 235.

2 S. Radhakrishnan, *Eastern Religions and Western Thought*, New Delhi: Oxford University Press, 2000 (ninth impression), 116.

distinctiveness of other religious traditions but also the very nature of religion in its various dimensions. We will come back to the question of 'one and many' within Hinduism, and its power and usefulness for realizing or resisting 'Hindu India' to become fully secular. And, to be sure, a tiny spray of post-modernity, growing sense of modernity and majority living with primitive conditions and beliefs roll together in India and this makes it unique from any other country in the world.

Defining Hinduism: An Objective Attempt

Jawaharlal Nehru (1889-1964), freedom fighter and the first Prime Minister of the independent India, wrote his famous book *The Discovery of India* while he was in jail. It combines his autobiographical notes, political journals and perceptions of India, past, present and future. Though he was not a practicing adherent of any religious tradition (some would say agnostic), the notes on Hinduism he has provided in consultation with his jail-mates and friends cannot be said as unscholarly. He points out that the first reference of the word 'Hindu' in an 18th century *Tantric* work where it means 'a people and not the followers of a particular religion.' But the word is used in the Avesta and in old Persian, as derived from the Sanskrit term Sindhu, the Indian name for the river Indus. 'From this Sindhu came the words Hindu and Hindustan, as well as Indus and India.'[1] He refers to the 7th century Chinese traveler I-tsing who mentions these terms but adds Noble Land (*Aryadesha*) as the most suitable name. Nehru also notes that the use of the word 'Hindu' in connection with a particular religion is of very late occurrence and this goes well with scholarly opinions although there is no end to arguments and elaborations.[2]

From these clues, Nehru generalizes about religion in India. According to him,

> The old inclusive term for religion in India was *Arya dharma*. Dharma really means something more than religion. It is a root word which means to hold together; it is the innermost constitution of a thing, the law of its inner being. It is an ethical concept which includes the moral code, righteousness, and the whole range of (hu)man's duties and responsibilities. Arya dharma would include all the faiths (Vedic and non-Vedic) that originated in India; it was used by Buddhists and Jains as well as by those who accepted the Vedas. Buddha always called his way to salvation the 'Aryan Path.'[3]

He also mentions the names 'Vedic dharma' (all those philosophies, moral teachings, ritual and practices, derived from the Vedas), 'Sanatana dharma' (ancient

---

1 J. Nehru, *The Discovery of India*, London: Meridian Books, 1951, 58.

2 E.g. For a detailed suggestions, assertions and emphases, see Julius Lipner, *Hindus: Their Religious Beliefs and Practices*, London: Routledge, 2010, 1-23.

3 Nehru, Op. cit., 58.

religion including Buddhism and Jainism, 'the expression has been more or less monopolized to-day by some orthodox sections among the Hindus who claim to follow the ancient faith'). It is important to note that Nehru does not acknowledge the fierce challenge of Buddha, Jaina and other renouncers' movements and their impact on the Vedic dharma, which in turn created vigorous debates on the vision, authority and message of the Vedas.

At the same time, Nehru has acknowledged the conglomerate and complex nature of the Hindu religious tradition(s) in his own way. For instance, he writes:

> Hinduism, as a faith, is vague, amorphous, many sided, all things to all (wo)men. It is hardly possible to define it, or indeed to say definitely whether it is a religion or not, in the usual sense of the word. In its present form, and even in the past, it embraces many beliefs and practices, from the highest to the lowest, often opposed to or contradicting each other. It's essential spirit seems to be to live and let live...(*after referring to Gandhi's assertion as Truth and non-violence as essence of Hinduism*) but many and undoubted Hindus say that non-violence as Gandhi understood it, is no essential part of the Hindu creed. We thus have truth left by itself as the distinguishing mark of Hinduism. That, of course, is no definition at all.[1]

In the following lines Nehru further clarifies that the ancient way of life with faith and philosophy was largely synonymous with Indian culture and it is incorrect to identify as Hindu culture. Faith communities from outside such as Muslims and Christians were Indianized without changing their faith and in turn contributed to a composite culture.

Nehru does not go into scriptures, but in order to indicate one aspect of the glory of the ancient India he refers to the Vedas, 'the first spoken word.' He reproduces the dedicatory line of the Rigveda: 'To the seers, our ancestors, the first path-finders.' He refers to Tagore's description of the Vedic hymns as

> the poetic testament of a people's collective reaction to the wonder and awe of existence. A people of vigorous and unsophisticated imagination awakened at the very dawn of civilization to a sense of the inexhaustible mystery that is implicit in life. It was a simple faith of theirs that attributed divinity to every element and force of nature, but it was a brave and joyous one, in which the sense of mystery only gave enchantment to life, without weighing it down with bafflement – the faith of a race unburdened with intellectual brooding on the conflicting diversity of the objective universe, though now and again

1 Ibid., 59.

illumined by intuitive experience as 'Truth is one: (though) the wise call it by various names.'[1]

No other verse has been quoted more frequently than RV I. 164. 46, that on 'one truth-many names' particularly in connection with discussions of multifaith context and interfaith dialogue. For those who are versed in proper exegetical exercise it can be most irritating, even annoying! Does this verse talk about an undefined and metaphysical truth or God? Let us look at the verse in the context of its occurrence: the object of the query is a bird-shaped altar of the *Pravargya* ceremony in preparation for the Soma sacrifice. 'They say it is Indra, Mitra, Varuna, and Agni, and also it is the winged, well-feathered (bird) of heaven (= the Sun).'[2] Arguably, the central truth of Vedic religion is its power generating ritual engine, extravagant and expensive. Even after its rejection and refutation by the renouncers, certain Vedantins and thinkers, this ritual continues to be the life-force in Hindu temples and even the icons or images of the supreme Gods (Shiva, Vishnu, etc) depend on its infusing life, giving the impression that God and ritual remain as parallel powers in Hindu worship. Today the 'meaningless' rituals involving gallons of milk, oil, clarified butter etc are projected on the mass media. To be sure, Vedic/Hindu ritual is unique and its value is intrinsic, not instrumental. One may detect behind all the talk about the ancient glory and spirituality of Hinduism that the interests of the priestly class are tightly protected.

When certain definitions of religion appeared not convincing in the scientific study of religion, scholars started identifying dimensions of religion – ritual, ethical, experiential, social, etc. As we have noted above, ritual in its unique nature and belief is kept silent in definitions in 'Hindu' India. Another important dimension is social. While there are relentless and repetitive lists of ethical qualities with illustrative stories the possibility of establishing a community based on them is hardly questioned. Even where these qualities are integrated with profound articulations of visions and values, particularly by the Vedantic proponents, the communities did not go out of the esoteric circles. For instance, in the advaitic vision of Sankara a liberated person is supposed to be seeing all beings equally. For Ramanuja such a person is supposed to see him/herself as part of realizing the one supreme Self of all. Madhva too insisted unity in devotion. But none of them experimented with a community of equals of all castes and outcasts with a sharing of resources. If such an experiment is done in earnest it may attract or correct the minority religious communities in India.

1 J. Nehru, *The Discovery of India*, London: Meridian Books, 1951, 63.

2 Rigveda I.164.46; translated by Jamison & Brereton, *The Rigveda*, Oxford: Oxford University Press, 2014 in 3 volumes. For a discussion with some detail see I. Selvanayagam, *The Dynamics of Hindu Traditions*, Bangalore: Asian Trading Corporation, 1996, 98ff.

As was the custom in his time, Nehru confined himself to Vedic/brahminic traditions to define religion in Hindu India. Others added to the sense that Hinduism was Vedanta and Vedanta was advaita Vedanta. Several bhakti traditions in different regions, primal traditions and popular diverse cults in numerous varieties are clubbed together with the name Hindu. Recently some traditions such as the dalit have demanded separate recognition. So far, such voices are either ignored or stifled. As we noted earlier, details of religious traditions and caste groups are yet to come up in national census data. But at the same time a kind of 'sanskritization' has been going on bringing independent local cults under the Vedic umbrella. This process still continues.[1] This is an important area for research, particularly in relation to the strategy followed, money spent and local people's understanding.

Single Majority Religion in Secular India: Promises and Challenges

So long as one does not scratch the bundle of the Vedic dharma, Hinduism is extremely absorbent, elastic, tolerant and generous. The question, 'if another country in the world had more than 80 percent of the population belonging to one religion, would that faith not be declared as the state religion?' seems to be reasonable. Equally reasonable is the historical fact that different, even conflicting, regions and religious traditions needed a secular framework to be brought under one umbrella. One may argue that the secular polity in India was a Hindu necessity to accommodate disparate and contradicting traditions. At the same time, one marvels at the elastic framework of Hinduism to be able to contain an extraordinary variety which includes atheism, agnosticism, polytheism, theism with the claims of one tradition claiming superiority over the other, philosophical schools in constant debate, sectarian cults transcending theirs in joining swelling crowds of pilgrims from other cults and so on. In such a situation, can we believe the vigorous claim of the Hindutva leaders that Hinduism is essentially and profoundly open to accommodate differences and provides political support, safety and development for all people? Here we point out some challenges.

First, communal historiography was evidenced in connection with the pulling down of a 450 year old Babri Masjid in the temple town Ayodhya in Utter Pradesh in 1992. Riots and killings apart, there were claims and counter-claims about whether the mosque was built over a demolished Ram temple. There are, in fact, numerous spots claimed to be the birthplace of Ram in the town with innumerable temples and shrines. Ayodhya and related issues continue to be burning.

Another related historiographic issue has been noted by the most respected Indian historian, Romila Thapar.

1 B. Kolappan, "Bringing folk deities into Vedic fold: Structure and rituals of temples for Sudalaimadan, Mutharamman in Vedic tradition," *The Hindu*, 14 July 2015, 7.

> Some are now propagating an interpretation of Indian history based on Hindu nationalism and what has come to be called the Hindutva ideology. Since the early twentieth century, this view has gradually shifted from supporting the theory of an invasion to denying such an event, now arguing that the Aryans and their language Sanskrit, were indigenous to India, The amended theory became axiomatic to their belief that those for whom the subcontinent was not the land of their ancestors and the land where their religion originated were aliens.[1]

Second, India's External Affairs Minister Sushma Swaraj, addressing a crowd with some passion and with claims of personal discovery, has suggested 'we make the Gita (our) national scripture.'[2] Interestingly, few years ago (2011-12), in the heat of a controversy over a Russian translation of the Bhagavad Gita, one of her predecessors, S.M. Krishna, declared that the Gita was India's national book! Within scholarly and interreligious circles, this was regarded as an insensitive declaration, as a specifically Vaishnava scripture such as the Gita cannot represent even the multi-scriptural and multi-traditional Hindu community, let alone the non-Hindu communities.

The success of the Vishva Hindu Parishad's popular programme aiming to ensure every Hindu home has a copy of the Gita should be evaluated through an empirical study. Similar questionable events have taken place in politically higher places. At the beginning of September (2014), during his visit to Japan, Prime Minister Narendra Modi presented two copies of the Gita to the Japanese government (in 2004 a copy of *Ramayana*), saying that there could be no greater gift from India. Since then he has been doing the same during his other foreign trips. The peculiar tolerance of the Indian religious community was evident as there was no hue and cry about such events. However, there have been voices from some moderate Hindus and secular thinkers about the threat to secularism in India where the Constitution is the common Bible of all Indians.

Third, the first International Yoga Day (21 June 2105) gained remarkable worldwide attention through mass media. The display of practising yoga by groups, great and small, was phenomenal and fascinating. There were many discussions and writings before and after the event and they cover the history, types and benefits of yoga. Though the Muslim community did not join the euphoria, as it was projected as a Hindu contribution to the international community, no one denied that for those who can bend their body, stretch their limbs and control their breath, yoga contributes to wellness and wellbeing. But what was not mentioned was practical interpretations with application. For example, Sri Aurobindo Ghosh's 'integral yoga' combines meditation, devotion and political action. Swami Vivekananda developed action-oriented yoga to address the plight

1 Romila Thapar, *The Penguin History of Early India: From the Origins to AD 1300*. New Delhi: Penguin Books India, 2002, 14.

2 *The Hindu,* 8 December 2014, 12.

of the poor masses of India whose skeleton frames appeared in his meditative mind-screen. He perceived God in the form of the poor and called him Daridra Narayaṇa and launched a mission for the poor. For these new types of yoga they claimed that the inspiration came from the Gita.

Fourth, western scholarly contribution to the study of Hinduism for more than three centuries has been phenomenal. But today any reference to historical facts that would hurt brahmanic sentiments is reacted to very strongly. For example, Wendy Doniger brought out a remarkable book entitled *The Hindus: An Alternative History*[1] and without making a scholarly response to some of her studied observations she was personally attacked and by attacking the author's publisher in New Delhi (Penguin) the extremists tried to ban the circulation of the book.[2]

Fifth, Hindutva politicians, missionary gurus and the flourishing and influential Hindu Diaspora in the West try very hard to give a glorious picture about 'Hindu' India. Globalization of caste and practice of untouchability in their country of domicile is never acknowledged; similarly, poverty and destruction of the environment. Most recently, researchers in the areas of environment, human rights, poverty, starvation etc coming from outside have been banned.[3]

At the level of public life in secular India, number of questions may be raised. For example, can the photographs of gods and goddesses be mounted in government offices? What is the control over encroachment of road space for building shrines? Can the authorities allow ceremonies and rituals at occasions such as groundbreaking for building and opening the shutters in damns by ministers? Can they allow spectacular public performances of ritual sacrifices and prayers in solidarity with 'convicts'? Another example: following the judgment of a trial court in Karnataka state on J. Jeyalalitha, the late actor-turned politician and chief minister of Tamilnadu, was sent to jail with a heavy fine in her eighteen year old disproportionate assets case. For her return from the jail, the Vedic ritual Sri Satha Chandi Mahayagam was performed in the temple town Madurai with 108 sacrificial pits and 150 priests, preceded by 10,000 women distributing pongal (rice-gram mix), complimented by pujas and prayers across the state, and attended by several government ministers including the chief minister.[4] There was widespread criticism about such display in a secular country, and more significantly, by other factions of the Dravidian Front that a government with the word 'Dravidian' in its title for the glaring act of alliance with the Aryan revival. Of course, subsequently the High Court, dismissed the previous

1 London: Penguin Books 2010.

2 See report in *Hindustan Times*, 2 March, 2014.

3 See the article "For Foreign Scholars, Home Ministry acts as tough guide" by Anuradha Raman, *The Hindu*, 3 July 2015, 1; the author notes in passing, 'Foreigners contribute substantially to research work undertaken by reputable NGOs.'

4 L. Srikrishna, "Mahayagam for Jeyalalitha," *The Hindu*, 5 March 2015, 6.

judgment and released Jayalalitha who was re-instated as chief minister, though, recently, after her death, the Supreme Court of India upheld the judgment of the Trial Court.

Perhaps we need to revisit the positions and promises of secular visionaries in the heat of India gaining Independence. Let us take the most obvious example. Nehru argued for total separation between state and religion. He wanted to move on single mindedly with his 'sacred development' agenda without allowing himself to be hampered by religious and superstitious notions. Gandhi, on the contrary, voiced for the continued moral force of religions in politics. He also proposed the dictum 'equal respect to all religions.' Not only representing Nehru's concerns, even otherwise, looking back from the perspective of the experience of nearly seven decades of Independent India, one may raise some prickly questions. For example, can we really have equal respect uncritically? May equal respect for every religion not be construed equal respect for every superstition? Is tolerance, respect and even acceptance of other persons possible without subscribing equal respect for all their beliefs and practices? Is the State in a position to distinguish between meaningful practices despite all limitations and ambiguities, and unmeaning, degrading and inhuman practices? Any effort to define religion in 'Hindu' India needs to take such questions seriously.

Common Human Affection: A Concluding Note

Explicit religion and secular spirituality is the unique situation of India and it requires engaging observation and social experience. For outsiders, it may be difficult to understand the cultural bond which is stronger than religious adherence and caste affinity. It is not uncommon to encounter persons who are part of a crowd at a temple in connection with festival or sacrifice along with their family and relatives but not participating in the ritual or cultic activities. They have no problem in identifying with the worshippers but at the same time being secular with certain cultural affinity. While strong and ancient traditions hardly move, there have been reformers and secular thinkers whose thinking has made some impact. There is scope to move further if there is a willingness. For example, Gandhi's assertion that Truth is God and truth and non-violence constitutes the essence of Hinduism, the experiment and exploration he started must continue with periodic assessment of its outcome in concrete issues like equality for all – caste, class, gender and religion. Moreover, the Hindu government seems to be promising to 'Clean India' not only the sacred rivers like the Ganges but also all areas of life including the bureaucracy. Defining religion in India may become easier when such changes happen with the coincidence of gaining clarity of religious vision and practice.

However, one aspect of 'Hindu' India is fascinating from a common human viewpoint. We have both experienced and heard stories of instant hospitality, quick friendship in travel and work places; in the context of communal conflicts and riots persons of one religion have provided shelter to strangers from another religion at great personal risk; there are those who rehabilitate victims of injustice and exploitation for education and employment without asking about their religion; and so on. Such acts reveal not only simple common human affinity but common human affection. Where do they come from?

3

North East Indian Secular Spirituality? An Exploration towards *Sacred-secular* Spirituality

Songram Basumatary

At the outset, it must be made clear that the topic 'secular spirituality' is not yet popular in the North East Indian academic discourses in general and in the theological discourses in particular. Perhaps, it is not much of a welcome talk. The reasons may be of two. First, the institutional religion-centric spirituality is very strong. Secondly, people in general have less or even no idea about the secular due to the fact that the concept secular is absent in the traditional worldviews of various tribes in NEI. The latter reason is very well expressed in the theological discourses within Tribal Theology in recent times. The tribal theological discourses are overwhelmed with expressions and arguments that there is no dichotomy between sacred and secular in the traditional worldviews and the life-worlds. It is even claimed that there is nothing called secular. Everything is sacred and everything is spiritual.

However, the strong distinction and separation maintained between religion in general and the Church in particular with State and political affairs in NEI shows that there is strong sense of both secular and spiritual. Also, the recent socio-economic consciousness and political wakening reveals that there is emerging a trend of secular quest of the meaning in life among various tribes or ethnic groups. There is a growing attempt to relate religiosity or spirituality in general and the message of salvation in Christ in particular, with the human quest for existence. The search for the meaning of religion struggles on, and the quest/search for people's dignity, identity, and justice and peace in the society steadily grows. There is a "common quest for a new humanism" through religious and secular frameworks in which people of all religious traditions and of no religion struggle together to enrich life. In this, the religious answers to the questions of life and the quest for meaning in life appear insufficient. People, particularly the younger generation are unconvinced of mere religionist spirituality. They are not in favour of the isolationist pietistic spirituality that has nothing to do with the realities of the public squares. There is a rising quest for, what M.M. Thomas called, the "spirituality of combat."

This scenario certainly calls for a deconstruction of the existing understanding of spirituality and and re-imagining of a more viable spirituality which is holistic in nature and inclusive of both sacred spirituality and secularist spirituality.

Therefore, with much hesitation and careful thought I intend, in this paper, to explore a possibility of something called – unhyphenated in-between spirituality called – "Sacredsecular Spirituality" rather than trying to import and implant the predominantly Western idea of "secular spirituality" or somehow digging out secular spirituality from within the life-worlds of diverse NE Indian tribes. The paper is divided into three major sections. The first is the conceptual note on "Idea of Sacred and Secular." The second is "Sacred and Secular Spirituality" where an attempt is made to highlight a few key non-separable concepts, notions, belief and practices of various tribes with brief conceptual notes on spirituality. The final section is an exploration towards the alternative possibility of an un-hyphenated in-between spirituality, which is of neither religious nor secular in the strict sense of the term.

1. Ideas of Sacred and Secular

Dictionaries define 'sacred' as something pertaining to or connected with religion that is opposed to the secular or profane. It is derived from the Latin *sacrare* meaning 'holy.' In contrast, the term 'secular' is defined as something of, or relating to, worldly things or to things that are opposed to sacred things or not concerned with or related to religion. It comes from Latin term – ***saecularis*** which means "of a generation, belonging to an age" or worldly or temporal and its adjective form 'secularity' denotes a state of being separate from religion, or not being exclusively allied with or against any religion.

In philosophical and theological interpretations, realities and attributes beyond the natural realm such as transcendent, ultimate, eternal, divine, holy, purity, etc., are considered the sacred domain.[1] In religion, such conceptualizations of realities beyond are considered to be at the core of existence and to have a transformative effect on lives and destinies of human beings. The Christian doctrines are framed in the overarching notion that God exists outside of time and space or the realms of phenomenal realities. This has created the

1 There are quite a number of literary works that speak on the primacy of religion/sacred over the secular. For instance, Rudolf Otto, *The Idea of the Holy* (1923); Max F. Scheler, *On the Eternal in Man* (1960); Nathan Soderblom, "Holiness," *Encyclopedia of Religion and Ethics* (1928, reprinted 1955); W. Brede Kristensen, *The Meaning of Religion* (1960); Gerardus van der Leeuw, *Religion in Essence and Manifestation* (1963); Mircea Eliade, *The Myth of the Eternal Return* (1954), *Myth and Reality* (1963); *Patterns in Comparative Religion* (1958); *The Sacred and the Profane: The Nature of Religion* (1959).

medieval Western idea of *secular* to indicate separation from religious affairs and involvement in temporal affairs – a complete separation between Church and State. Secularism got its meaning (with the idea that?) religion has no place in the public arena and religious issues should not be the basis of non-religious institutions. All non-religious organizations or government institutions and their representatives should remain separate from religious institutions, their beliefs, and their authorities. As a result, what is called the secular society refers to all aspects of society that are not synagogue, church and temple.

Such a dichotomic concept of reality, particularly in Christianity, in fact, raises some pertinent questions as to "what is sacred about religious symbols and practices?" or "what is secularity in what is called secular?" To concentrate our minds, for example, on water and bathing/drinking, food and eating are secular things and activities. And there is nothing religious about them. However, when it comes to sacraments such as Baptism and Lord's Supper, all these are symbolically considered to be sacred elements and activities. Paradoxically, the water of baptism is holy, but the same water in the well or river is not; the bread in the Communion is holy, but not the bread in the bakery. Similarly, a house for worship is not called a building, villa or palace but a Temple, a sacred space. Even institutions of learning such as a school, seminary or university where sacred things are taught are not sacred, but only the Church or chapel. The Bibles kept in a Church alters or street shrines are adored as sacred, but not the Bibles kept in the libraries or book selves. This is so, not only at a conceptual and symbolic level, but at a practical level as well. Asking or praying to God for daily bread are considered as sacred acts or even acts of spirituality, but if somebody asks or prays for the same thing from another person that is a secular act, literally – begging. And if the person gets the thing he/she asked for from somebody the next day, the act of giving from the giver is less sacred or spiritual than the act of praying by the one who prays. The former is considered as merely social service, not a spiritual act.

2. Sacred and Secular Spirituality

'Spiritual' is derived from the Latin word – *spiritus* meaning, breath. Hence, spiritual or spirituality has something to do with the essence of living as breathing is an essential element of human life. The cognate words with this common root include *inspire*, *aspire* and to *conspire* which means to breathe together.[1] Similarly, the word 'religion' comes from the Latin *religare* meaning, "to bind" or "to tie." Interestingly, the term *ligature*, meaning suture, also is derived from the same Latin root. These derivations give us a clue to the original intention of religion and spirituality, which was to reconnect the parts to the whole. This is the essence

1 Interestingly, alcohol in Latin also is *spiritus*. The same term is used both for the highest religious experience and the most depraving poison. The helpful formula constructed is therefore "*spiritus contra spiritum*" signifying the high spirit against low spirit where the highest form of religious experience counters the most depraving poison.

of spirituality. However, the meaning of the word spirituality is replaced, in the passing of time, with piety due to irreconcilable dualistic sacred and secular worldviews and religious doctrinaires.

The idea of secular spirituality, perhaps, emerged more as a kind of an anti-religious or an atheistic or non-theistic spirituality. The humanists, philosophical naturalists, and non-theists are often frustrated about religion bound spirituality and desert religions in search for connections, community, and a sense of purpose and meaning in life. There are numerous writings that attempt to connect and contextualize human beings among one another and in the world rather than alone with the divine.[1] Therefore, "secular spirituality" is understood and expressed to be the pursuit of spirituality having no formal affiliation to any of the religious organizations or institutions. In other words, it simply means an adherence to a spiritual ideology that has no connection with any religious beliefs. This is a spirituality that applies specifically in the context of temporal affairs which emphasizes inner peace within and around an individual rather than peace in relationship with the divine.

Philosophically, the question has been raised as to whether there is an innate spiritual impulse independent of the fear of death and of religion itself. And it is argued that there is indeed a lack of or sense of incompleteness in every human person that always gives rise to a longing for something beyond the known, which cannot be put into words as human beings are always under *the cloud of unknowing*.[2] The flow of longing into an awareness of belonging and back into longing again is the original and naked human impulse. Perhaps, it has been common to all human beings throughout human history. This perhaps does not need belief of any kind. It has nothing to do with thinking or believing. One might justly call it an authentic expression of the human spirit; and as such it is the source of spirituality, unbound by any religion of any kind. Such impulse, intuition or inner feeling gives rise to secular humanism and a personal and secular form of spirituality independent of external beliefs. As with any other religious inspiration, it is concerned with compassionate action in this world and not with rewards in some hypothetical afterlife. Such extraordinary accomplishments of the human spirit surely add up to a more lasting good done in the service of humanity than all the religions of the world together.

Therefore, the proponents of secular spirituality make a case for a form of secular spirituality in which the motivation is to live happily and/or to help others.[3] Rather than spirituality requiring a supernatural being, spirituality can

---

1 For instance like A. Comte-Sponville, *The Little Book of Atheist Spirituality*; Steve Antinoff, *Spiritual Atheism*; Robert Solomon, *Spirituality for the Skeptic*; Jeaneane Fowler, *Humanism: Beliefs & Practices*; Peter Van Ness ed., *Spirituality and the Secular Quest*; David Cortesi, *Secular Wholeness* an many more.

2 By an anonymous 14th century English writer.

3 Tony Wilkinson, *The Lost Art of Being Happy: Spirituality for Sceptics* (Findhorn Press, 2007).

also be experienced through a secular or non-religious world view. According to Robert C. Solomon, "Spirituality is co-existent with religion and it is not incompatible with or opposed to science or the scientific outlook. Naturalized spirituality is spirituality without any need for the 'other-worldly.' Spirituality is one of the goals, perhaps the ultimate goal, of philosophy."[1] The Dalai Lama also has expounded the view that secular spirituality emphasizes humanistic qualities such as love, compassion, patience, forgiveness, responsibility, harmony and a concern for others.[2] The proponents also go to the extent of saying that spiritual practices such as mindfulness and meditation can be experienced as beneficial or even necessary for human fulfillment without any supernatural interpretation or explanation. Spirituality in this context may be a matter of nurturing thoughts, emotions, words and actions that are in harmony with a belief that everything in the universe is mutually dependent.

Such ideas of secular spirituality, perhaps, go along very well with many of the traditional NE Indian worldviews and life-worlds.

3. Sacred-Secular Worldviews and Life-worlds among NE Indian Tribes

In traditional worldviews and life-worlds of NE Indian tribes, religion is not a faith statement, but a way of life in its entirety where any action and activity of a person is considered religious or spiritual. They believe there is something divine in everything and so live accordingly as spirit-conscious beings. The sphere of life is permeated by the presence of spirits or supernatural forces and so they live in the constant consciousness of a divine presence in everything and their life is governed by that consciousness. Due to this, there is nothing secular for them as far as the common meaning of the term secular is concerned. The following lines give us explicit descriptions of the understanding of such non-secularity in reality.

- [...] no distinction can be made between sacred and secular, between natural and supernatural, for Nature, man (*sic*) and the unseen are inseparably involved in one another in a total community.[3]
- ...tribal worldview often...transcends the secular-sacred which is so much a part of the thinking of the West. It may be at one and the same time sacred *and* secular. It is preoccupied with gods, spirits, and ghosts, but it is patently anthropocentric (and ethnocentric) in most cases. It brings nature and supernature together in a curious amalgam. It brings space and time together in an inextricable mix. It cements this world

1 Robert C. Solomon, *Spirituality for the Skeptic: The Thoughtful Love of Life* (Oxford Scholarship Online, 2003), 8.

2 Dalai Lama, *Ethics for the New Millennium* (NY: Riverhead Books, 1999), 22.

3 John V. Taylor, *The Primal Vision: Christian Presence amid African Religion* (London: SCM Press Ltd., 1963), 72.

and the other world together in a single system. This unity is not that of monism or pantheism, however. It is rather the unity of a continuum on which boundaries between deities, spirits, animals, [hu]men, and natural phenomena are more or less obscure and always shifting.[1]

- In it [the tribal vision] there is the vision of the spiritual continuum with which the dead and the living, natural objects, spirits and gods, the individual, clan and tribe, animals, plants, minerals and humans form an unbroken hierarchical (*sic*) unity of spiritual forces; and the human self is not an individual self but an extended universal self present and actively participating in an all parts of the totality.[2]

These are the expressions of tribal belief and a vision of cosmic oneness,[3] common-ness and interdependent-ness. Such worldviews and life worlds of harmony with creation and awareness of being one with the whole of creation is the spiritual foundation.[4] What is conceptualised in Tribal Theology as "God-human-nature continuum" – a philosophy and principle, is the sources of spirituality. This is the spirituality of cosmic harmony, a "total harmony" among all beings.[5] Commitment and dedication to the harmony of creation springs from love, nurture, care and acceptance. The indigenous spirituality is built on the concepts and reality of the non-differentiated and non-independent

1 David J. Hesselgrave, *Communicating Christ Cross Culturally* (Allahabad: St. Paul Publications, 1981), 149.

2 M.M. Thomas, "Primal Vision and Modernization," a paper presented in The National Seminar on Theological Implications of the Primal Vision, sponsored by BTESSC/GLTC, September 9-12, 1993 at Gurukul Theological College and Research Institute, Madras, 2. As cited in Yangkahao Vashum, "Theology of Land: A Naga Perspective," in *The Tribal Worldview and Ecology*, ed. A. Wati Longchar and Yangkahao Vashum (Jorhat, Assam: Tribal Study Centre, ETC, 1998), 70.

3 Such worldviews, in fact, are very much present in Hindu religious traditions, mainly in *Vaishnava* traditions. For instance, according to Ramanuja's *Vedantic* Approach to God, "God's inseparable relationship, a triadic relationship embraces souls and nature under the "Inner Controller," the Great Self of all beings." See Eric Lott, "The Ecological Body: An Epiphanic Image for Mission", in *Mission with the Marginalised*, ed. Samuel Meshack (Thiruvilla: Christava Sahitya Samithi, 2007), 324-45[341]. The element like ecstasy of devotion, a drawing in a feeling of love for God and of being loved by God is found both in tribal life of devotion and in primal Hindu religious world. However, Eric Lott strongly argues that much of the elements of *Sanskritic* culture are derived from and adaptation of more primal cultural roots. See Eric Lott, *Religious Faith, Human Identity: Dangerous Dynamics in Global and Indian Life* (Bangalore: Asian Trading Corporation/United Theological College, 2005), 14. Hence, it is derivative that the old religion of the indigenous people may furnish a splendid basis for Christianity.

4 Cf. George E. Tinker, "The Integrity of Creation: Restoring Trinitarian Balance," *Ecumenical Review* 41/4 (October, 1989): 535.

5 John V. Taylor, *The Primal Vision: Christian Presence amid African Religion* (London: SCM Press Ltd., 1963), 72.

connectedness of all entities[1] even calling earth 'mother,' animals 'brothers and sisters.'[2] This, in fact, is a handy principle that can counter the predominant three main religious foci: the object of religion, the subject of religion and their reciprocal relation where the direction and relationship is in terms of descending and ascending order.[3]

There may be a counter argument that though nothing is secular in tribal worldviews and beliefs, everything is not sacred, both in concepts and practices. Or if at all everything is sacred and the entire living - world is governed by non-dichotomic worldviews and its resultant spirituality, then why are there so many disrespectful and violent social practices between human-nature, human-creatures and human-human among various tribes? Are these worldviews and life-worlds present reality or a distant past, or an imaginary future?

Perhaps, this fact is true that the "Rich was the tribal culture; big is the gap between that culture and the present culture." Number of issues and questions arises from this fact. Probably, the idea of being secular being absent from people's perception and experience is either due to close intimacy or fear of spirits. And the traditional spirituality perhaps might have been the mere appeasement of malevolent spirits rather than a spontaneous spirituality of individuals and community.

One other fact is that being ritualistically religious is not necessarily the marks of spirituality and a condition for being spiritual. Instead, spirituality finds its meaning in person or community's existence in the secular. Here, the idea of secular spirituality is not to be confused with the idea of "secular society" by the way. Perhaps, human existence is itself secular to the extent that it is undertaken as per the conceptions of the world and self which are not directly indebted to religion. Which, moreover, promotes the organization of society in ways that permit its participants to pursue both religious and non-religious paths to have fulfilment in life. Referring to the distant past worldviews and lifeworlds of the tribes of NEI, it implies that there are ways of understanding the world as a

---

1 See M.M. Thomas, "Modernisation of Traditional Societies and Struggle for new Cultural Ethos," *Ecumenical Review* XVIII/4 (Oct., 1966), 429. There are distinctions between the entities, but there is a mutual interpenetration, including God. This is implicitly expressed even by Moltmann. He writes, "If the Creator is himself (*sic*) present in his creation by virtue of the Spirit, then his relationship to creation must rather be viewed as an intricate web of unilateral, reciprocal, and many-sided relationships..., relationships of mutuality which describe a cosmic community of living between God the Spirit and all his created beings."Jurgen Moltmann, *God in Creation: A New Theology of Creation and the Spirit of God* (San Francisco: Harper & Row, 1985), 14.

2 Cf. Sitakant Mahapatra, "Invocation: Rites of Propitiation in Tribal Societies," in *Indigenous Vision*, ed. Geeti Sen (New Delhi: Sage Publications, 1992), 64.

3 Gerardus van der Leeuw, *Religion in Essence and Manifestation* (Princeton University Press, 1992).

cosmic whole and the self as an enduring agent that are not directly indebted to any religion.

This gives us a clue that there is an alternative!

4. Sacredsecular Spirituality

As discussed above, there seems no clear-cut distinction between sacred and secular in the traditional worldview and the life-world of various tribes in NEI. What is sacred does not go against what is thought to be secular and what is thought to be secular does not go against the sacred. In other words, the sacred is never against the secular and secular is never against the sacred. Rather both mutually penetrate each other. However, because of the extreme dichotomic sacred secular understanding of reality fed by religious superspiritualism and hyper Christian spirituality people have failed to see the sacred in a secular and secular in a sacred. The Christian missionaries have somehow convincingly planted a notion and a mindset among the tribal elite in the region that just being spiritual or religious without belonging to one of the "religions" lacks civilisation. "Such a mindset," according to Miri, "led the tribal population, either hurriedly to associate themselves with any one of the doctrinaire religions, particularly Christianity, or to work hard at building up a system of its own to counteract the other theologies."[1] At worst, though they are inherently religious without being in any doctrinaire religions; people of the region were demeaned and denigrated as people without religion or God by the western missionaries and colonizers due to their reverence for all creation and their belief in the primacy of the larger community rather than the individual.[2]

Therefore, the signs of the time demand that we help the separated prodigal children to meet at 'sacredsucular' and provide an alternative spirituality as way to live in harmony and live life in fullness not only with fellow human beings but also with all creation. The components of this religion-less spirituality are traditional beliefs, values and virtues such as cosmocentric worldview, veneration of nature and love for creatures, nature-friendly living, communitarian life, a sense of moral sanctity, truthfulness, gentleness, integrity, honesty, innocence, tolerance, simplicity, generosity, hospitality, sharing and caring, concern for others, respect for elders, humor and merrymaking, etc. Besides, there are numerous communitarian practices that express the very meaning of the sacred, religious and spiritual in its true sense. For example, hunting, fishing, farming, harvesting, constructing houses, dams, roads, singing, dancing and many such others are all very much inspiring, bonding and life giving practices.

By the way, the proposed "sacredsecular spirituality" is not an anti-religion or anti-gospel, but the true essence of religion and the Christian gospel. Perhaps,

1 See Sujata Miri, "Religions and Being Religious," in *Religion and Society of North-East India*, ed. Sujata Miri (New Delhi: Vikas Publishing House Pvt. Ltd., 1980), 28.

2 Vashum, "Emerging Vision of Indigenous/Tribal Theology," 22.

secularity of this kind can best be understood not as being 'anti-religious' or 'anti-gospel,' but as being "sacredly secular and secularly sacred." For nothing is sacred and nothing is secular in an absolute sense as many symbols and activities in religious rites are secular themselves and none of the secularity inherent in them lead to irreligiosity.[1]

Therefore, a daunting challenge and task is to question the pseudo-spirituality all around in religious circles, which is merely an inner-peace oriented and self-righteous spirituality, but sociologically unsound and irrelevant.[2] For, such pseudo-spirituality has nourished individualism against the idea of community and solidarity. It has also encouraged other-worldliness against social, economic and political dimensions of the gospel among various Christian communities in NEI. It has, in addition, set a wrong mindset that does not believe in reasoning or rational action. One needs to acknowledge the fact that what is secular may be secularly sacred and what is sacred may be sacredly secular. The time has come to find sacred in a secular and secular in a sacred and replace the pietistic spirituality with sacred secularistic spirituality, because spirituality that has nothing to do with the socio-cultural, economic and political realities is certainly not sacred. Spirituality that challenges the forces of injustice, oppression, exploitation and rampant moral deterioration, though not, in itself, sacred, reveals everything sacred.

The attempt in this new spirituality is to transcend the other worldly unrealistic religious worldviews or ideologies and the one-sided pietistic narrow religious spirituality. It seeks to offer a new dimension and understanding of spirituality in relation to a wider human community. The imagined vision in this spirituality is a "Common Humanity" that places the function of religion as building a common human community. For, what the Christian faith and gospel values bring is the fullness of life and a community of life. Its function is deliverance from the bondage of human will or conscience, and the depriving and oppressive belief systems and religious structures.

For spirituality to be the fulfilment of both religion and secular quests, one needs to bring one's religionist individualist soul oriented spirituality into the altar of common spirituality for common humanity. This move perhaps may not be welcome as it confronts and challenges all people with the twin tasks of redeeming spirituality from the other-worldly pietism on the one hand and self-centered spiritualism on the other. But such debate and dialogue is the way forward for such a vision of spirituality for common humanity in one world and under one God. It is my prayer and hope that the "sacredsecular spirituality" would serve as

---

1 See Jack David Eller, "What Is Atheism?," in Phil Zuckerman, *Atheism and Secularity, vol. 1: Issues, Concepts, Definitions* (Praeger, 2010), 12-13.

2 Cf. H. Vanlalauva "Mizo Christian Spirituality," in Tochhawng, Rosiamliana, K. Lalrinmawia, and L.H. Rawsea, eds. *Groundworks for Tribal Theology in Mizo Context* (Delhi: ISPCK, 2007), 154-59.

a corrective measure to both the extremity of secularised world where doctrinaire religion has little role to play and to the extremity of highly spiritualised world where secular ideologies have no role to play.

Let there be quasi-spirituality rather than a pseudo-spirituality!

4

Religion and Secular Spirituality in India
An Islamic Perspective

Mohd Fahim Akhtar

India has always been a land of different religions. One can experience a small world in India. Several religions were born here, and from here they spread to different parts of the world. Major world religions have been in India, and their followers exist in a large number in this country. Thus, India is a special country having its unique identity in matters of religion. Additionally, of course, it is India's strength, beauty and pride.

Diversity of Religions

India has a long history of religious diversity. The reason behind this is its secular nature. A secular sprit has always existed very deep inside this land. India cannot be imagined without its secular characteristics. It is very clear from its history that India was a preferred place to where nation after nation migrated in the past. Different religions came and settled here. None of them was forced to exile completely. Judaism came here and to the present day its followers have cohabited in this land. Christianity is welcomed here and a sizeable population of Christian people lives in different parts of this country. It is the same with Zoroastrianism.

As far as Islam is concerned, this religion reached this land as early as it came into existence in sixth century AD, along the costal parts of India, with the traders who had been coming to India for a long period before that time. And soon Islam spread amongst the native people and they embraced this religion. It is very important to note that in early thirteen century CE, when Muslim rule was established here with its capital at Delhi, this Delhi Sultanate ruled over the width and breadth of this country for more than three centuries, followed by the Mughal rule of almost same length of time. In these six hundred and fifty years of rule from 1206 to 1857, Islam remained a minority religion among a huge majority of non-Muslims. All major and well-known religions which are here today were also present at that time. And no major incident of religious persecution occurred between that times. How did this happen? Could it have been simply because of the secular fabric of this respectful land and secular nature of its inhabitants?

In Secular India

We must say that India is a secular country by its nature, and its strength lies in its being and remaining secular. This was the reason that when India gained independence, it was declared to be a Sovereign, Socialist, Secular, Democratic Republic, assuring its citizens justice, liberty and equality. Articles 25-28 of the Constitution of India provide the Right to freedom of religion for all citizens of India to profess, practice and propagate any religion of their choice. The State would have no religion of its own. It would be neutral in the matter of religion and no religion would be given preference over any other. The state would protect all religions and treat them equally. It would ensure that none of its citizens would be discriminated against on the grounds of religion.

This is the concept of secularism in India. The state cannot prefer one religion to other, nor will it represent any specific religion. It does not mean that a secular state is considered as an irreligious or atheistic state. It would be completely wrong to act against religion in order to be secular. Rather to facilitate all religions, to treat them equally, to give equal space to all religions and to provide all rights to all adherents of every religion, is the correct meaning of secularism. This is a clear understanding of the Constitution of India.

From this point of view, and taking the advantages of the right to freedom of religion in the Constitution, Indian society witnessed in both the past and present several phenomena in the matter of religion. First of which is freedom of choice of religion. This was guaranteed by the constitution and should be guarded by the Indian courts. Every citizen of this country has the right to embrace any religion of his or her choice. This conversion has continued in Indian society as an accepted phenomenon, both socially and legally. The second aspect is that different religions or different forms of religious trends have been invented and surfaced in the society. Some of them are religions as is the case with Sikhism, while some others are forms of spirituality. Though these forms in the second category have in their basic appearance associated with one or any particular religion, they are not considered or claimed to be as a separate religion. For this category suits the name of spirituality.

Spirituality

Spirituality is a small component of a religion. It could be in one form or another. It doesn't follow any specific religious system and adhere to its fixed rituals and rules. So, the spirituality is an individual choice of his or her religious desire according to his or her own way of thinking. This type of spirituality can be named secular spirituality, which reveals that the person associated with any form of his or her choice of spirituality, is not governed by any set rules or attached to any organized system. It also concludes that spirituality can hardly be defined. One can attribute number of good characteristics to a specific form of spirituality, but it would not be considered to be equivalent to a religion. It means that there are differences between them both. While religion is an organized system and a of way of life, governed by set rules and rituals, spirituality has a loose type of attachment with some forms of meditation or self-styled activities.

Religion in Islamic Texts

Islam has a specific concept for religion, which has been described and elaborated in its two basic sources of guidance, i.e., the *Quran* and the *Sunnah. Quran* is the Book of Almighty Allah, revealed with its Words in Arabic to the Prophet Mohammad (Peace Be upon Him), and *Sunnah* is the Sayings and Deeds of His Messenger Mohammad (PBUH). These two cannot be ignored in any explanation or conceptualization pertaining to religion.

Below are listed some basic characteristics of religion in the Islamic perspective.

1. Oneness of Religion

The Quran, the first Islamic source, emphasizes that there was and is only one religion sent to mankind from Almighty Allah. All His Messengers throughout the ages, right from the first Prophet Adam, followed by number of Prophets such as Noah, Hud, Saleh, Abraham, Jacob, Joseph, Moses, Jesus, to last Prophet Mohammad (Peace Be Upon Them), brought the same religion. There was no difference in its basic teachings and rules. The only differences were in details and forms of rituals. Following are the Quranic texts in this regard:

> God has ordained for you the same religion which He enjoined on Noah, and which We have revealed to you, and which We enjoined upon Abraham and Moses and Jesus, so that you should remain steadfast in religion and not become divided in it.[1]
>
> We have sent revelation to you as We did to Noah and the prophets who came after him, to Abraham, Ishmael, Isaac, Jacob, and the Tribes, to Jesus, Job, Jonah, Aaron, and Solomon and David, to whom We gave the Psalms.[2]
>
> To every one of you We have ordained a law and a way.[3]

2. Revealed Religion

Religion in Islam is one which is being revealed from Almighty Allah. The Quran says that it is Almighty Allah who has sent His orders, rules and guidance to His

---

1 Al-Quran, 42:13.

2 Al-Quran, 4:163.

3 Al-Quran, 5:48.

Prophets in every human society and every nation, and that is the Religion. The Quran says:

> Go down, all of you, from here: then when guidance comes to you from Me, anyone who follows My guidance will have no fear, nor will they grieve.[1]
>
> We have sent you with the truth as a bearer of good news and a warning – there is no community to which a warner warning? has not come.[2]
>
> … and Abraham enjoined his sons to do the same, as did Jacob, 'My sons, God has chosen this religion for you; so do not let death overtake you, except when you are in a state of submission.[3]

Thus, the religion in Islam is God-made. It is not a man-made system. Man has nothing to do with the formulation of religion, its rules and rituals. No ritual or rule could be termed religious if it is not revealed as evident in the Quranic text. So, Religion is revealed by Almighty Allah. The Quran declares:

> The only religion in God's sight is complete submission to God.[4]
>
> Today I have completed your religion for you and completed My blessing upon you. I have chosen for you Islam (complete submission) as your religion.[5]

3. No Amendments

The essential parts of religion cannot be changed by anyone at any time. No amendment can be made in the basics of the religion. No such right has been given to any person or any group whatever position or status he or they might have. The Quran clearly mentions that this right of amendment was not given even to the Prophet Mohammad (PBUH):

> When Our clear revelations are recited to them, those who do not expect to meet Us say, 'Bring us a different Quran, or make some changes in it.' Say, 'It is not for me to change it of my own accord. I follow only what is revealed to me. I fear, if I were to disobey my Lord, the punishment on a Dreadful Day.[6]
>
> … nor does he speak out of his own desire. It is nothing but revelation sent down to him.[7]

---

1 Al-Quran, 2:39.

2 Al-Quran, 35:24.

3 Al-Quran, 2:132.

4 Al-Quran, 3:19.

5 Al-Quran, 5:3.

6 Al-Quran, 10:15.

7 Al-Quran, 53:3.

Keeping this point in mind, it is worthy to note that Islamic teachings, laws and rituals are of two types: one part is of basic teachings, firm laws and fixed ways of *Ibadat*. This part is small and limited, but very firm, established and unchangeable. They are basically some duties, some prohibitions and directives. In this category come five pillars of Islam (*i.e. (i) declaration of faith [Shahadah], (ii) daily five prayers [Salah], (iii) one month Ramadan fasting [Saum], (iv) annual Alms [Zakat] on rich to be given to needy people and (v) pilgrimage to Kabain Makkah once in life, if able to do so [Hajj]*; also, basic laws pertaining to family matters, limited prohibitions in food, beverage, dress and financial transactions and directive principles for whole life. The vast range of different activities in life like business, dressing, food items, sports, education, research, international relations, governance and other day to day matters is an open field for the framing of rules as per the requirements of a changing world in every age, provided that it is within the tenets of, and not in contradiction to Islamic principles. This would be done only by the experts in Islamic sources, i.e. *The Quran* and *Sunnah*. This process is called *Ijtehad,* which has been practiced throughout the ages and is still practiced today all over the world.

The first one of these two types of Islamic rules and teachings has been instrumental in preserving the originality, real characteristics and the original face of Islam. Therefore, one can see that Islam has remained intact in its features throughout the fourteen centuries of time, and in different cultures and customs in the world. The second type, which is major part, paved the way for Islam to play its leadership role in guiding the followers in this everchanging world by the tool of *Ijtehad*. This *Ijtehad* is basic principle approved by the authentic texts of *The Quran* and *Sunnah*.

4. Belief in All Prophets

Religion in Islam is incomplete without having belief in all the Prophets of Almighty. One has to have belief in every Prophet of Allah, as one has belief in the last Prophet Mohammad (PBUH). Islam doesn't differentiate between one Prophet and another. The Quran says:

> We do not differentiate between any of His messengers[1]

As per the Quranic texts there were Prophets in every nation and human society in every age. The Quran has narrated the life and story of some of them, and stated that none of the societies remained deprived of getting revealed guidance by Prophets sent by Almighty Allah. The Quran says:

> Before your time, We sent other messengers; of them there are some whose story We have related to you, and some whose story We have not related to you.[2]

1 Al-Quran, 2:285.

2 Al-Quran, 40:78.

Thus, the approach here is inclusive in the matter of religion. If a follower of Islam denies any prophet, be it Moses or Jesus or any other prophet for that matter, he could not be accepted as a Muslim or as having faith in belonging to Islam. Similar belief and respect must be shown to all the Almighty's Prophets by a Muslim and any follower of the Religion of Islam.

5. Belief in All Revealed Books

It is also essential for Religion in Islam to have belief in all Books Revealed by Almighty Allah, similar to the belief in The Quran. Quranic texts mention some names of Books revealed earlier than the Quran, such as *Tawrat* (*Torah), Zuboor (Psalms), Injeel (Gospel)* and *Sohuf-e-Abraham and Moses (Books of Abraham and Moses).* These Books have been mentioned in different verses of The Quran. There might be some other Revealed Books also which we do not know about them because of non-availability of information. To have belief in all Revealed Books is compulsory for having faith in Religion as per Islamic teachings. The Quran says:

> They all believe in God and His angles, His scriptures and His messengers.[1]
>
> This is the Book; there is no doubt in it, It is a guide for those who are mindful of God, who believe in the unseen, and are steadfast in prayer, and spend out of what We have provided them with; those who believe in the revelation sent down to you and in what was sent before you.[2]

6. No Compulsion

The last basic characteristic of religion in Islam is that it gives freedom of choice of religion to every individual. It doesn't impose its belief upon any person. Islamic texts are very clear that the matter of accepting a specific religion is at the individual's discretion. The very existence of belief cannot occur without having conviction in the depth of one's heart. The expression of faith in words or in chanting sacred sentences is a later stage of having faith in a religion. If a person doesn't have that conviction and acceptance in his heart, then mere expression does not serve the purpose and such a person would not be considered to be a follower of that religion. This is the Islamic perspective of being a faith bearer of a Religion.

Therefore, the *Eiman,* i.e., the Faith is defined in Islam as: 1. conviction by heart, 2. expression by tongue and 3. action accordingly by bodily parts. These are the three components of *Eiman* or Faith. And they are to be genuine with concrete expressions. Thus says the Quranic:

1 Al-Quran, 2:258.

2 Al-Quran, 2:2-3.

> The Arabs of the desert say, 'We have believed.' Say to them, 'You have not believed yet; say rather, "we have submitted" for faith has not yet entered into your hearts.'[1]

The Quran terms such people with the name of Hypocrites.

> When the hypocrites come to you, they say, 'We witness that you are indeed the Messenger of God.' God knows that you are indeed His Messenger, but God bears witness that the hypocrites are surely liars.[2]

Since all people could not have the same conviction towards a particular religion, it does ultimately result in adopting religious tolerance and accepting the followers of different beliefs. This constitutes the basis for religious diversity and peaceful co-existence.

This point also reveals that Islam has a secular approach towards other religions. Indeed, Islam is a preaching religion. It demands from its followers that they propagate and preach the message of Islam and the message of The Quran to all human beings, only because this message is the treasure of humanity. Only Muslims don't have the monopoly upon the Holy Book of Almighty Allah. The Quran repeatedly describes that it has been revealed to all mankind. E.g.:

> The month of Ramadan is the month when the Quran was sent down as guidance for mankind with clear proof of guidance and the criterion by which to distinguish right from wrong.[3]

Therefore, The Quran addressed in several verses to the whole of mankind besides addressing the believers in some verses. But this preaching will be limited to convey the message in a better way and portray the beauty of religion in practice. No force is allowed to be adopted for preaching, because it cannot be turned into conviction by heart which is absolutely essential for accepting faith. The Quran is categorical:

> There shall be no compulsion in religion.[4]

These six points are the characteristics of Religion in Islam. So, as per Islamic concept, any form of spirituality or religious activities for that matter, cannot be termed Religion if it doesn't have the above-mentioned features. Also, no one can make amendments in its features. But it is also clear that Islam recognizes other religions and welcomes religious pluralism. Islam also accepts different forms of spirituality, clearly because Islam doesn't impose its belief upon others. In other

1 Al-Quran, 49:14.
2 Al-Quran, 63:1.
3 Al-Quran, 2:185.
4 Al-Quran, 2:256.

words, Islam has a secular approach towards other religions and spiritual forms of faith.

7. Religion in Society

The above discussion presents one dimension of Religion, which describes the concept of religion in Islam and its characteristics and features. There is another dimension of religion, which is also very important to look into, and identify its characteristics. This dimension will examine the applicability of religion in practical life and its role in resolving the challenges it throws up.

Below are some points of this aspect:

1. Islam as a religion is a complete system for life. It claims to be comprehensive and to encompass every nook and corner of human society. Islamic teachings cover the whole span of life beginning from the birth of a person to his death, and from his individual life to his life in diverse fields of the society. It doesn't differentiate between private and social life in terms of being governed by the rules and regulations of Islamic teachings. There is no vacuum or absence of guidance in any matter of life. One cannot have the feeling of being left without mile stones at any stage of one's life journey, nor can the society face the same situation and suffer from a similar crisis in such matters, be they social issues, medical questions, political affairs or economic challenges.

   The basis for this claim is the availability of comprehensive guidance in The Quran, the complete Book of Almighty Allah, and in Sunnah, the detailed recording of sayings and deeds of the Prophet Mohammad (PBUH), which provides guidance both on a micro and macro level in life. And these two sources are easily accessible for the whole of mankind.

   This claim has been made by the The Quran itself in several verses. For example:

   > Today I have completed your religion for you.[1]
   > We have left out nothing in the Book.[2]
   > And we have explained everything in detail.[3]
   > We have sent down the Book to you to make everything clear,
   > a guidance, and a mercy, and glad tiding for those who submit
   > to God.[4]

1 Al-Quran, 5:3.

2 Al-Quran, 6:38.

3 Al-Quran, 17:12.

4 Al-Quran, 16:89.

This is not merely a claim which is unsupported by practical evidence. The history of Islam in different parts of the world bears testimony to this claim. No Muslim society in any period of time or within any geographical boundary remained without having Islamic guidance for their various problems and situations.

2. The religion of Islam instills scientific temperament in the minds of people. The quest for knowledge is not only required but is mandatory for every individual, irrespective of gender, cast, class and colour. One can imagine the importance of knowledge in Islam with the fact that the revelation of The Quran starts with the very first word of 'Read.' These are the first revealed verses:

> Read! In the name of your Lord, who created: created man from a clot [of blood]. Read! Your Lord is the Most Bountiful One who taught by the pen, taught man what he did not know. Yet man behaves arrogantly, because he thinks himself self-sufficient: truly, all will return to your Lord.[1]

The word 'Read' occurs twice in these initial verses, pen is named once along with knowledge, while learning and knowing is mentioned three times. From this can be judged how strong the relationship is between Islam and knowledge, reading, learning and with the pen.

Perhaps Allah has, in this verse, expressed significance of the pen for writing. The verse says:

> Nun. By the pen, and all that they write![2]

Verse after verse the Quran talks about the importance of knowledge, urges on promotion of knowledge and describes the high position of those who have knowledge. There are hundreds of verses in the Quran which ask man to use his wisdom and intellect, and think in the world around him and also in the world inside him, and study the universe. E.g.:

> Say, 'Are those who know equal to those who do not know?' truly, only those endowed with understanding will take heed.[3]
>
> So, question the people of Zikr, i.e., those who know it, if you do not know.[4]

---

1 Al-Quran, 96:1-8.

2 Al-Quran, 68:1-2.

3 Al-Quran, 39:9.

4 Al-Quran, 16:43.

> And say, 'My Lord, increase my knowledge.[1]
>
> Have they not looked into the realms of the heavens and the earth and all that God created?[2]

Besides, Prophet Mohammad (PBUH) said in one tradition:

> Quest for knowledge is a duty of all Muslims.[3]
> The word Knowledge is the lost capital of the believer; he is more rightful to obtain it wherever he finds.[4]
> Seek knowledge even if it is (available) in China.[5]

It is clear from these verses and traditions that there is no place in Islam for ignorance and superstition. One has to use one's wisdom and apply one's mind in everything around. That was the reason behind the educational revolution the world witnessed in seventh century AD. The vast spread of knowledge occurred in Muslim society in the early era of Islam, not only in the field of religious sciences, but also in the fields of what today we call modern sciences. A well-known institution by name of *Bait-ul-Hikmah* (*Center for Wisdom*) was established by the famous Abbasid emperor Haroon Al-Rasheed in Baghdad in the eight century AD. This institution was instrumental in transferring Greek knowledge and philosophy to contemporary generations at that time, by translating them into the Arabic language, and creating number of Muslim scholars who not only gained mastery, but made highly valuable additions to modern sciences like medicine, mathematics, astronomy, physics, chemistry, botany, zoology, geography and philosophy, etc.

3. Nature and natural resources are the treasure and divine gift to humanity. It is their source of life. Among these natural resources and wealth human society exists. So, the environment around man is of dual relations, the relation with fellow human beings and his relation with each and every part of his surroundings. The wellbeing of humanity and its good fortune depend upon the quality of this relationship. Therefore, for the goodness of human society, a good relationship with both is of the utmost importance.

---

1 Al-Quran, 20:114.

2 Al-Quran, 7:185.

3 (Khateeb, Mohd bin Abdullah. 2001, *Mishkat-ul-Masabeeh*, Hadees No. 218; DaroIhya Al Turas Al-Arabi, Beirut.

4 Tirmizi, Mohd bin Saurah, 2004, *Jame Al-Tirmidhi*, Hadees No. 2687; Maktaba Nizar Mustafa Al-Baz, Makkah.

5 Ajlooni, Isma'il bin Mohd. 2001, *Kashful Khfa' waMuzeelulIlbas*, p. 124; Darul Kitab Al-'Ilmiyya, Beirut.

Our country as well as the whole world today, faces number of serious problems in terms of human relations with fellow beings and with nature as well. This crisis has resulted in multi-faceted miseries and griefs. The situation on earth today is exactly what the Quran predicted in this verse:

> Evil has appeared on land and sea because of what the hands of men have earned.[1]

Islam, in its teachings, has given due care to the environmental discourse. It has, first divided the whole of human affairs into two categories. One belongs to Almighty Allah and called *Hoqooq Allah* which means Almighty's rights, like the details of prayer and worship.

The second category relates to one's fellow human beings, which is called *Hoqooq Al-Ebaad*, which means people's rights. This deals with all the affairs of human beings together.

Islam says that Almighty Allah will not forgive if there is any oppression upon any other human being. The settlement can only be between the concerned and affected individuals, either here or in the hereafter. This concept compels each person to make clear his affairs pertaining to other fellows, and got them settled.

As for as relations with the surroundings are concerned, the Quran mentions in detail the beauty, diversity, sequence, value and utility of different types of nature. It says that a complete system of nature has been put in place by Almighty Allah. Human beings should respect this system, in order to gain continued benefits. This is called in the Quran *Mizaan* which means balance.

> And the heaven He has raised high, and He has set up the Balance. In order that you may not transgress due balance.[2]

At the same time, the Quran says that Almighty Allah has sent down this wealth of nature in a limited quantity and will continue sending as per need:

> And there is not a thing, but with Us are the stores thereof. And We send it not down except in a known measure.[3]

---

1 Al-Quran, 30:41.

2 Al-Quran, 55:7-8.

3 Al-Quran, 15:21.

We have created everything in due measure.[1]

To avoid the disturbance in this measurement, the Quran has suggested and ordered the following:

a. Extravagance to be avoided:
   And eat and drink but waste not by extravagance, certainly He likes not those who waste by extravagance.[2]

   Yet do not spend extravagantly, spendthrifts are the brothers of Satan, and Satan is ever ungrateful to his Lord.[3]

b. Accountability to be maintained:
   On that Day, people will come forward in separate groups to be shown their deeds: whoever has done the smallest particle of good will see it; while whoever has done the smallest particle of evil will see it.[4]
   Then on that Day you shall be questioned about your worldly favours.[5]

   Greed to be eschewed:

   Greed for more and more distracted you [from God] till you reached the grave.[6]

8. Secularism and Muslims in the Indian Context

Muslims in India have a very clear idea about secularism, on the basis of what has been elaborated above. They should understand that it is secularism which can keep the people of India united. Therefore, Indian Muslims are expected to try their best, through their organizations, institutions and writings, to preserve and strengthen secularism and the secular fabric of Indian society. If understood clearly, there may not be a contradiction between the personal laws of different Indian communities and secularism. Secularism doesn't come between the freedom of people to practice their personal laws within their respective communities. Rather it provides them satisfaction and a feeling of pride in being citizens of a great secular India.

Much against the present government's proposal, the prevailing perception among Indian Muslims demonstrates that a uniform civil code (replacing the existing faith-based personal laws) doesn't suit the fabric of Indian society. Since

1 Al-Quran, 54:49.

2 Al-Quran, 7:31.

3 Al-Quran, 17:26-27.

4 Al-Quran, 99:6-8.

5 Al-Quran, 102:8.

6 Al-Quran, 102:1.

there are several personal laws, customary laws, ritual practices and belief systems among various communities, it seems to be impossible to implement a uniform civil code. And there is no guarantee that such civil code would create communal harmony among people of different faiths. Rather, true secular polity should provide safe and creative space for different religious communities to grow in self-understanding, understanding other religious communities while maintaining peace and striving for common welfare.

The problem arises for religious minorities when some forms of worship are adopted in the name of national culture. As per Islam, worship is allowed only for Almighty Allah. We can name Him God or Ishwar or Lord. But only He will be worshiped. But giving respect is a different thing. One can respect one's elders, one's country and national symbols, but they should not be worshiped. We have to differentiate between different types of cultural phenomena and worship. The saluting of the tri-color flag, singing the national anthem and secular songs are practiced in Muslim communities in India, and there is no problem with them. Great Poet Iqbal's song "*Sare Jahan Se Accha Hindustan Hamara*" is always being sung in Muslim educational institutions and Madrasas.

There is clear difference between Mother India and Mother Goddess but the government seems to confuse them. India is the Mother land for its citizens, and to preserving its unity, integrity, glory and greatness should be a duty and desire of every Indian citizen. But it doesn't mean that the portraint of mother or land should be worshiped to express the respect. In a country where belief in one God or Supreme Reality has been held for ages, and while still that continues among different religious traditions, the position that no secondary reality deserves worship needs to be respected.

Finally, the answer to the question given in the background paper, sent to the presenters in the conference at Hyderabad ('*Can there be a secularity with a sense of the sacred but not tied with a particular religious tradition*?') is YES. In the unique context of religious plurality in India, basically secularity is all about being fair and neutral with all religions. However, the ways of non-religious expressions of the sense of sacred or transcendent awareness in the complex Indian situation needs to be explored. What we have pointed out in this paper with Quranic quotes suggests that Muslims need not be averse to such explorations while they are deeply committed to their faith and tradition.

5

Islamic Spirituality in Secular India
Some Modern Thinkers

M. M. Abraham

Introduction

The first Islamic State was established in Madeenah. The Prophet Muhammad was given the temporal and spiritual leadership of the newly emerged Islamic community. The spiritual life of the community under the leadership of the Prophet equipped them to bring up an Islamic *Ummah*, based on justice and equality.

When Islam spread throughout Arabia and beyond, it had to encounter numerous other religions and cultures. Most of the established Muslim nations had never shared their power with any minority groups. But the large number of Muslims living in India for centuries belonged to minority religious groups and had to face many challenges and problems from time to time. The multi-religious and secular India had thrown up many questions for Islam and Muslims in India. When we analyze the reactions to these questions, we realize that there are different understandings and dimensions of the Islamic spirituality. A discussion of the different approaches of a few Indian Muslim thinkers and leaders would help us understand their diversified views and attitudes to secularism and to a secular India.

Islamic Spirituality

The fundamental faith and practices are the core basis of Islamic spirituality. The uncompromising belief in and total surrender to the Almighty God is the essential content of faith and the underlying principle of all religious practices in Islam. The belief in the Quran as the revealed scripture of Islam binds all Muslims together into one believing community. All Muslims believe that Muhammad is the Prophet and transmitter of the truth of the Islamic faith.

The Islamic mysticism called Sufism introduced a more devotional and mystical dimension to Islam and became very popular as Islam spread beyond the Arabian confines. Its greatness is to be appreciated in view of its contribution to Islamic society, civilization and spirituality. The Prophet Muhammad himself must be considered as the first Sufi.

We find in the Quranic assertion that God is nearer to us than our own jugular vein (50:16). We read how he created each person from the tiniest particles of matter (75:37) and how the angels praised God and confessed that he had taught them all they knew (2:23). In contemplating the above verses Muslims are reminded that God is indeed the source of all life and all knowledge, and that he bestows these and other spiritual gifts on an undeserving humanity.

Secularism and Islam

Secularism emerged in the west in the wave of renaissance and enlightenment in protest against religious authority and domination. In due course, a secular society has been seen as a non-religious society. It seems highly doubtful whether such concept of secularization is applicable to the Indian context.[1]

Islam does not admit any distinction between religious and secular. Secularism as an ideology has not only certain historical associations in its very origin but has also acquired certain ideological implications in modern times. So, it should never be used simply, in a generalized manner. Islam is an all pervasive phenomenon which contains within itself religion and state, society and culture. It is absolute by its very nature, to which nothing can be added and from which nothing can be subtracted.[2]

But the philosopher-poet Muhammad Iqbal (1876-1938) rejected any relation between secularism and Islam. He suggested that secularism was a negative force, that it is mechanical, deprived of intuition as well as of an awareness of religious experiences. In Iqbal's view, Islam – including its faith, culture, and historical tradition – was worth living, worth dying for. Iqbal also believed that secularism would dehumanize Muslims and would be a great obstacle to the emergence of a great nation.

Iqbal never took any note of the tolerance, understanding and faith in diversity implied in the concept of secularism. Iqbal's emphasis on the cultural role of Islam and Muslim communal identity lacked "spiritual" motives.[3] He was more concerned with political solidarity which in practice meant a separate electorate and organization of the Muslims. It ruled out any possibility of joint political participation. This led to political communalism, Muslim nationalism, and ultimately the partition of the country. Iqbal's interpretation of Islam and

1 Sam V. Bhajjan, *Understanding Islam*, Mumbai: GLS Publishing, 2011, 50.

2 Ibid., 51.

3 Moin Shakir, *Politics of Minorities*, Delhi: Ajanta Publications, 1980, 147ff.

Islamic tradition was completely unsecular. But it caught the imagination of common Muslims.

The old Iqbal was radically different from the young Iqbal who had once adored his country and had sung songs of love and unity.[1] People still remembered his 'Indian Anthem' in which he had said: "The best in the world is our Hindustan. We are her nightingales. She is our rose garden." That was at the time when Iqbal regarded "each particle of the dust of his motherland as a god." But that was before he left for Europe. When he returned from there in 1908 he was a changed man.

Like Iqbal, Maulana Maududi (1903-1979) also rejected the idea of secularism and said: "In an Islamic State, non-Muslims would have no voice in making the law, no right to hold public office, no right to be employed in the army, judiciary, ministry or any post."[2] This statement was made while he was appearing before the *Munirs* commission appointed by the Government of Pakistan.

Yet another Islamic scholar, Mushirul Haq, saw no contradiction between his religion and secularism. He said that in the common sphere of life, Muslims are willing to let secularism prevail, but their personal life, their thought, is their own, and must be governed by the rules of the religion which they follow.[3]

The fundamentalists consider the personal law to be an essential part of their religion and therefore voice their support for status quo. According to them, any attempt made by 'outsiders' to influence Muslim personal law would amount to revoking the *Shariah.* The secularists first started their campaign with a demand for 'reform' in Muslim personal law. According to Mushirul Haq, a secular state should not be partisan in matters of religion and should give religious freedom to every citizen. This concept of secularism is not alien to the Muslim and therefore he finds no difficulty in accepting it.

Islam in Secular India

In India, different people understood and interpreted the Indian brand of secularism to mean different things in different situations. Only a small minority really understood what was really meant by secularism. No one ever made a bold statement to tell the truth and say that secularism did not mean neutrality towards religion.[4]

Some intellectuals, immediately after independence, thought secularism in India, should also mean indifference to religion. Even Jawaharlal Nehru had this view. But soon he realized that it may not work in India and defined Indian secularism as equal protection of all religions by the state. Asghar Ali Engineer

1 Mushirul Haq, *Muslims Politics in Modern India,* Meerut: Meenakshi Prakashan, 1970, 106.

2 Qamar Hasan, *Muslims in India,* New Delhi: Northern Book Centre, 1998, 51.

3 Sam.V. Bhajjan, *op.cit.,* 63.

4 Brahm Datt Bharti, *Indian Secularism,* New Delhi: Era books, 1988, 31.

says that in India religion has always been centre stage.[1] Thus, secularism here was never conceived as indifference, much less antagonism, to religion. Secularism was conceived as a philosophy giving equal respect to all religions including regional faith traditions. Thus, our secularism works more in a multi religious context. Our country has always had a rich experience of religious pluralism while the west has come to know religious pluralism and multi-culturalism only since the Second World War.

By quoting from *Al-Hilal* of Maulana Azad, the historian Mushrirul Hasan said:

> Islam does not commend narrow mindedness and racial and religious prejudice. It does not make the recognition of merit and virtue, of human benevolence, mercy and love dependent upon and subject to distinctions of religion and race. It teaches us to respect every man who is good, whatever be his or her religion, to let ourselves be drawn towards merits and virtues, whatever the religion or the race of the person who possesses them… Islam teaches us that the purpose of the creation of humankind is that he or she should represent God on earth; keep burning the torch of truth and light.[2]

Islamic Spirituality in Secular India

The Indian Muslim leaders disagreed on their approach to Indian secularism and democracy. During the pre-Independent and post Independent periods they formulated policies based on their religious convictions as the true followers of Islam. A statement of Maulana Azad shows this: 'There will be nothing left with us if we separate politics from religion.'[3] Azad's Islam asserted patriotism rather than communal action. It also breathed a universal spirit.

A Muslim reformer Sir Sayyid Ahmed Khan (1817-1898) was indifferent to politics. He asked the Muslims to abstain from active politics. He reasoned that since Muslims were backward in the field of education, they would be unable to receive their full share of government administration without the patronage of the British Government. He did not, however, say that participation in politics was religiously forbidden.[4]

A majority of conservative Muslim leaders at that time thought that India under British rule had ceased to be *Dar-ul-Islam* (the land of Islam or peace) and had become *Dar-ul-Harb* (the land of *kafir* or non-believer); so to receive western education was to become a *kafir*, or infidel. But Syed Ahmad said the policy of religious toleration adopted by the government justified India being regarded as

1 Asghar Ali Engineer, *Muslim Minority*, New Delhi: Gyan Publishing House, 2008, 51ff.

2 Mushirul Hasan, *Islam in the Sub-Continent*, New Delhi: Manohar Publishers and Distributors, 2002, 158.

3 Raj Mohan Gandhi, *Understanding the Muslim Mind,* New Delhi: Penguin Books, 1987, 222ff.

4 Mushirul Haq, *op.cit.,* 132.

Dar-ul-Islam.[1] The movement started by Syed Ahmad proved his statement and produced tremendous results among the Muslims in India.

Syed's active opposition to the Indian National Congress did not begin until Badral-din-Tayyibji was elected its president (1887).[2] From Syed's point of view this was the beginning of erosion in Muslims' political solidarity which would be disastrous for the future of the Muslim community. Accordingly, Muslims were numerically much smaller than the Hindu population, educationally backward, politically immature, and in economic resources and enterprise far behind the others.

All Muslims were not in agreement with the Aligarh strategy of separatism. There were those among the western educated Muslims, who believed in Hindu-Muslim co-operation. Another group which resisted Aligarh separatism was the *Ulama* best represented by the Deoband School. As scholars and custodians of Islamic doctrine and law, the *Ulama* had always felt deeply threatened by the secular and westernizing trends associated with British rule and thus offered unremitting opposition to those tendencies. The *Ulama* were unwilling to make common cause with Aligarh, viewed with skepticism the policy of loyalism to the British, and endorsed Hindu-Muslim co-operation.

Abul Kalam Azad (1888-1958) never accepted the views of Sir Syed. He was a religious person by birth, by education and by social classification. He decided upon secularism as his goal of public life. He could never get rid of religion as the final authority in his own arguments for secularism. Through his journal *'Al-Hilal'* published from Calcutta, Azad influenced the Muslims of India in favor of national politics. Before Azad, politics had been a taboo for the Indian Muslims. A section of the *Ulama* were satisfied with the existing situation so long as they had religious freedom. Azad launched a campaign with his pen saying that religious freedom was meaningless without political emancipation.[3] Azad also realized that the Muslim masses would not participate wholeheartedly in the struggle unless the *Ulama* would come out of their seclusion. Azad was successful in his effort. The *Ulama* broke their tradition and threw themselves into politics. Now the political struggle had become a religious duty for every Muslim.

Azad said very often that for the Hindus, patriotism must be a secular obligation but for the Muslims it was a religious duty. Azad had always tried to present the *Khilafat* issue to the Muslims more in the interest of India's freedom than that of the *Khilafat* in Turkey.[4] Azad said that it ~~is~~ was a question of the victory or defeat of our own country. He asserted that unless you succeed in your

1 Abdul Sabahuddin, *Indian Nationalism and Islamic Politics,* New Delhi: Global Vision Publishing House, 2006, 20.

2 Raj Mohan Gandhi, *op.cit.,* 37.

3 Mushirul Haq, *op.cit.,* 132.

4 Ibid., 101.

own country, success will not greet you elsewhere. Therefore, India is the first goal of the *Khilafat* movement.

Azad was the president of the Indian National Congress for number of years and was an uncompromising opponent of the Muslim league's demand for partition. Azad warned that history would never forgive the congress leaders if they agreed to partition. In his book, *India wins Freedom,* he reflects his deep sorrow that he could not prevent India's partition. For that, Azad blames Nehru and Patel, and was unsparing in his criticism of them.[1]

Both Azad and Gandhi were men of religion and wanted spiritualization of politics through their respective religions. Gandhi and Azad were also deeply secular: for Azad, it was unorthodox Islam, for Gandhi it was liberal Hinduism. Both were themselves liberated from the stronghold of orthodoxy. Azad shared Gandhi's conviction that without Hindu-Muslim unity *Purna Swaraj* was not possible. In 1923 Azad declared:

> If an angel descends today from the clouds and announces standing on the top of the Qutab Minar of Delhi, that India will get her independence provided she gives up the desire for Hindu-Muslim unity. I shall certainly refuse to accept independence and keep on preaching for unity. If independence is delayed, it will be a loss only for India, but if our unity is gone that will be the loss to humanity.[2]

Azad's commentary on the Qur'an shows him to be a Muslim deeply concerned with the future of his co-religionists, and of India in general; and it is useful to read part of a speech which he made in 1942, at a time when the germs of partition were growing rapidly among the Indian Muslims:

> I am a Muslim and this thought fills me with pride. The traditions of Islam during its career of thirteen centuries ago to form my heritage, I am not willing to give up an iota of this portion. Islamic education, Islamic history, Islamic arts, Islamic sciences and Islamic culture constitute the elements of my wealth and as a Muslim; it is my duty to preserve it... But in addition to these feelings, I am also the possessor of another feeling, which has been created by the stark realities of my eternal life. The soul of Islam is not a barrier to this belief; in fact it guides me in this path. I am proud to be an Indian. I am an integral part of this unified and impartible nation. The glory of this nation is incomplete without this valuable component. I am an essential factor in its composition and I shall never give up this claim... we gave this country the most precious of our possessions and one which was greatly needed by it. We gave it the message of democracy and equality.[3]

1 Maulana Abdul Kalam Azad, *India Wins Freedom*, New Delhi: Orient Longmans, 1959, 184ff.

2 Mushiral Haq, *op.cit.,* 81.

3 Annemarie Schimmel, *Islam in the Indian Subcontinent*, Leiden: E.J. Brill, 1980, 235.

After the Independence and partition, the pained Azad said:

> India gained her freedom but lost her unity. The only result of the creation of Pakistan was to weaken the position of the Muslims in the subcontinent of India. If we had remained steadfast and refused to accept partition, I am confident that a safer and more glorious future would have been awaited. The basis of partition was enmity between Hindus and Muslims. The creation of Pakistan gave it a permanent constitutional form and made it as much more difficult of as a solution.[1]

Until the end of his life, Azad propagated communal harmony, religious broad-mindedness, cultural cosmopolitanism and the relevance of religion to public life. What emerges is that Azad's fundamental religious vision, which centered on a belief in *Wahdat-i din* or the essential oneness of all religions, was formulated by 1910 and remained unchanged throughout his life. In a speech to the Bengal *Khilafat* conference in 1920 Azad said:

> The tragedy is that the world worships words instead of meanings... If one day the veils of 'externals and names' can be lifted so that truth and reality (*Haqiqat*) come before all unveiled, then, at once, all quarrels of the word will end, and all who quarrel will see that what we all seek is one and the same.[2]

With regard to the approach to secularism and composite nationalism, Muhammad Iqbal and Muhammad Ali Jinnah (1876-1948) had different opinions when compared to Abul Kalam Azad. In the last years of Iqbal's life, just before his death in 1938, there was a fascinating interaction between him and Jinnah. Iqbal gave Jinnah an entirely new dimension to his understanding of Islam. Jinnah took up Iqbal's notion of a separate Muslim homeland, of the discovery of Islamic identity, of the construction of an Islamic destiny and of pride in Muslim tradition and culture. Jinnah was predicting and promoting an Islamic bloc years before it became a reality promising to liberate first the Muslims of India and then the Muslims of the world.

In spite of all the orthodox Muslim propaganda against him that he was not sufficiently a practising Muslim, that he could not even say his prayers properly in Arabic, that his actions were un-Islamic, that he could not speak Urdu, Jinnah came to be acknowledged by his followers as the *Quaid-i Azam* (the great leader). Iqbal the thinker had passed the flame to Jinnah the man of action. The result was a formidable combination of ideas and action. Nothing would stop the Muslims now. In his presidential address at the 1940 Lahore session of the Muslim league, Jinnah declared that it was a common mistake to assume that the Muslims were a minority. They were not; they were a 'nation by any definition!' Islam and Hinduism were not religions in the strict sense of the term but were different and

---

1 Abul Kalam Azad, *op.cit.*, 225ff.

2 Francis Robinson, *op.cit.*, 287.

distinct social orders, and that it was futile to expect that India would ever be able to evolve a common nationality. The separatist idea of Jinnah existed among a section of the Indian Muslims. In 1940, Jinnah prophesied that democracy of the kind that the congress favoured would mean the complete destruction of what is most precious to Islam.[1]

Maududi opposed the positions taken by Azad and Jinnah. He founded *Jamaat-i Islami* in 1941. According to Maududi, secularism, nationalism and democracy are the roots of all the calamities. He dreamt of a theocracy, or rather a Theo-democracy where the Kingdom of God- the only legislator is administered by the whole community of Muslims. A country that has a Muslim majority should accept the *Shariah* as the law of the land. He wrote:

> The sun, the moon and the stars are thus all ... 'Muslims' this is Islam. The natural religion of man not associated with a people or country. In any age, in any country, among any people, God – knowing the truth- loving men believed and lived this very religion. They were all Muslims, whether or not was this religion termed in their language 'Islam.' He said that there is no virtue in righteousness apart from correct Muslim faith.[2]

The newly established Jinnah's Pakistan rejected Maududi's idea of theocracy. Jinnah established Pakistan as a secular Islamic state. Later on, after the death of Jinnah, Pakistan transformed itself into an Islamic state more or less on the line of *Jamaat-i Islami*. Maududi presented theocracy as the first and foremost objective of the revelation of the Quran and of the preaching of Muhammad. He conceived everything else as being clearly subordinated to this.

Maulana Abul Hasan Ali Nadwi (1914-1999) condemned the theocratic approach of Maududi. He feared that by the influence of this ideology a whole class of Muslims were being misled into conceiving Islam as primarily an effective socio-political organization geared towards bringing about theocracy. For Nadwi, the tradition of the great reformers clearly showed that the duty of establishing religion (*ikhamat-i din*) has always been conceived as consisting of a comprehensive effort to 'please God' 'follow the prophet,' to make the *din-i haqq* prevail, to 'erect pillars of Islam,' to 'revive the religious science,' and 'to ordain good and forbid evil.' The *caliphate* and Muslim political powers were established to serve all these purposes.[3] Nadwi argued that Maududi's view of the religious history of Islam is too narrow and pessimistic.

There had been in all ages true renovators of Islam, individuals who, out of a deep religious commitment, have made remarkable efforts towards establishing

1 Abdul Sabahuddin, *op.cit.*, 35.

2 Annemarie Schimmel, *op.cit.*, 237.

3 Christian W. Troll (Ed*), Islam in India,* vol. 1, New Delhi: Vikas Publishing House, 1982, 172.

Din-i-Islam in its various aspects, always employing practical wisdom (*hikmat-i amali).*[1]

Like Abul Kalam Azad and few others, Muslim leaders were associated with the secular movement. Budruddin Tyabji and M.A. Ansari served as congress presidents. Tyabji held the view that he would act from within rather than outside and advance the general progress of India and at the same time safeguard the interests of the Muslims. Ansari took initiative for the Hindu-Muslim unity. Till his end, Ansari did not allow his faith come in the way of achieving Hindu-Muslim unity. When Gandhiji started the Salt Satyagraha in 1930's, Ansari thought that the main issue confronting the country was the achievement of unity among Hindus and Muslims. To Mahatma Gandhi, Ansari was the true symbol of Hindu-Muslim unity. Rafi Ahmed Kidwai, M. Mujeeb, Fakhrudhin Ali Ahmad and Zakir Hussain also supported secularism, Indian Nationalism and communal Harmony. Fakhrudhin Ali Ahmad, Dr. Zakir Hussain and Dr. A.P. J. Abdul Kalam also served as the Presidents of the Indian Union. Zakir Hussain once stated that, "Indian Muslims... would not accept the complete loss of their cultural identity. They would like to be good Muslims as well as good Indians."[2]

Conclusion

Indian Muslim leaders had no uniform approach to Indian secularism, nationalism and democracy. Few like Abul Kalam Azad strongly supported secularism and Indian Nationalism. He considered this attitude as a religious and spiritual responsibility. Muslim thinkers like Maulana Maududi severely opposed Indian Nationalism and secular democracy. He had advocated for the implementation of the theocratic rule, on the basis of the Muslim *Shariah*. He claimed that he had put forward his principles as a true follower of the Islam. Sir Sayyed had rejected Azad's secular democracy and Maududi's Islamic theocracy. These diversified views show that it is very hard to define Islamic spirituality in a secular India. The majority of the Indian Muslims now follow secularism and democracy. They are also part of the secular political movements. But a small section of Indian Muslims still follow the ideas of Maulana Maududi. The strong Muslim community of India can further strengthen the Indian secularism and democracy as India has the second largest Muslim population in the world. If secularism and democracy are deeply rooted among the Indian Muslims as their religious and spiritual responsibility, it will not only be a blessing for India but also for the entire world.

1 Ibid. 172.

2 Annemarie Schimmel, *op.cit.*, 223.

6

Secular Spirituality from an Ao Naga Tribal Woman Perspective

Asangla Lemtur

Introduction

Secular spirituality decolonizes the Western concept of Christianity that colonizes the tribal Christian women. According to David C. Scott, "the subject of women has been greatly distorted by the editorial lens of history which has been largely written by men…That is due to androcentric methodologies, biases, and values in reporting, organizing and interpreting the materials."[1] The socio-cultural traditions of the Ao Nagas maintain the dignity of every citizen in a community. Though it also consists of oppressive elements in social practices that de-humanize women, I understand that a re-reading of the ancient Ao Naga folk tales, legends, stories and culture would work towards recovering the rights that women enjoyed in the past. The ancient Ao Naga folklore contains ethical and moral principles that governed the ancient Naga society. However, these ethical and moral values were subsumed by patriarchal modernity and Christianity.

The Ao's had only oral traditions which were the source of people's literature, social customs, religion and history, and which evolved into a comprehensive and integrated network of indigenous knowledge systems, incorporating art with reality, history with imagination, and the ideal with the practical. According to Temsula, the tradition constitutes for the Ao's the world of their origin, as well as the idiom of their continuance within the world.[2] A re-reading of the Ao Naga tribal folklores, stories and myths points towards freedom and autonomy that woman enjoyed in the past.

---

1 David C. Scott, "Women and Patriarchy in World Religions" in *A Reader in Feminist Theology*. Series 2. ed. Prassana Kumari, Madras: Gurukul, 1993, 42.

2 Temsula Ao, *TheAo-Naga Oral Tradition,* Baroda: Bhasha Publications, 1999, 174.

Human Rights in the Ao Naga Cultural Tradition

The cultural traditions of the Ao Nagas speak very loudly about the rich ethical teachings of the people on human rights. The Ao's, 'culture' or *'sobaliba'* is the determining factor of the practices of human rights, because it is the culture that gives them an identity as a person and as a community. An individual alone cannot talk of his/her identity unless being a part of the community. Therefore, for the Ao Nagas, collective or community identity plays the most prominent role in the understanding of human rights. Every individual is a part of the larger community in the form of a clan, village, or a tribe. The identity of a person emerges from the land he/she belongs, and hence the concept of human rights goes beyond human to the land and nature.

Myths about Human Origin

There are legends, myths and stories in the traditional Ao Naga worldview which tell of the emergence of the human being and project them into evolving beings. The Ao's in their animistic religion gave paramount importance to their belief in the folklore that their ancestors emerged out of the earth at *Lungterok.*[1] The Ao myth records that out of the six stones emerged three males named Longpok, Tongpok, and Longjakrep, and the other three were females named Longkakpokla, Yongmenala and Elongse.[2] First to emerge was Tongpok (penetrated out of) with Longkakpokla; the second was Longpok (burst out of stone) with Yongmenala; and the third was Longjakrep (stone break) with Elongse. They represented three different clans where intermarriage was practiced. The different clans among the Ao's trace their respective origins to one of these stones.[3]

In a re-reading of the myth of the origin, we understand that both men and women came into being together as equal beings. The three women came out of the *lungterok* along with men. This describes the beautiful myth of men and women coming into existence together. A reconstruction of the myth of human origin enables us to discover the original concept of human rights. In this

1 *Lungterok* literally means six stones (*long* means stone, *trok* means six). N. Talitemjen Jamir, *Ao-Naga Cultural Heritage* (Mokokchung: The Author, 1997), 1. Some of these stones are to be seen above a village called *Chungliyimti* on the South bank of the river Dikhu. Temsula Ao, *The Ao-Naga Oral Tradition, 1.* Also see, Purtongzuk Longchar, *Historical Development of the Ao Nagas in Nagaland,* Dimapur: The Author, 2002, 44.

2 J.H. Hutton recounts seeing these stones on 6th November, 1923. By his account, he saw only three of these stones standing, of which two were male and one female. The biggest one, a female was reported to have been destroyed by a Christian missionary who, however, suffered 'well deserved' misfortunes for his act of sacrilege. J.P. Mills, *The Ao-Nagas*, London: Macmillan and Co. Ltd., 1926, 6.

3 For example, the teller of the story maybe a *Chungli* speaker and even though the main discourse may be delivered in his dialect, when he wishes to authenticate his narration with the ballads of old, these are presented in the *Mongsen* dialect. Temsula Ao, *The Ao-Naga Oral Tradition,* 2.

reconstruction of the myth, both men and women are seen to be playing equal roles as evolving beings in equal partnership. It is said that "they learned stage by stage refining themselves in all aspects of life."[1] They developed together as equal partners into full-blown human beings with coverings, though it cannot be proved that they were transformed from stone to human beings. Yet, the stone from which they are believed to have emerged is still lying today in the village of Chungliyimti, which looks like a woman lying flat on the ground facing the sky.[2] Hence, this paradigm shift in the re-reading of the myth of human origin declares aloud the equal rights and dignity of women in human development.

An Egalitarian Society

The Aos live in a well-defined and seemingly egalitarian society. Their concept of society is enshrined in the word *loktiliba*, which means 'way of life of the people.' The traditions and norms encoded in this term therefore determine the conduct of every Ao in life, and position in Society is judged according to the measure of their contribution. *Sobaliba* plays the most important role among the Ao Nagas in imparting the knowledge of how to live in a community. Every individual in the community was important in an Ao Naga society and therefore all individuals and community were looked upon with great love and respect. By nature, the people were ready to help the needy, destitute, aged and strangers. They were willing to share their belongings with their neighbours and friends in need, like sharing land with the landless and lending crops for sowing. They were very hospitable, respected elders, parents and village leaders and they abstained from the things that degraded a human being like committing adultery, killing, torturing living beings, false witness, stealing and cheating.[3] They lived together for the welfare of their community by even sacrificing their lives, and not seeking for power and self-glorification. They were taught to rear their children in the right path, to be honest, to be sociable and cheerful, to preserve the environment, skilled in handicrafts or weaving, hardworking and were willing to participate in all community activities like singing and dancing. They were also taught to have commitment, dedication and co-operation in everything they do individually or as a community. They observed all community norms, customs and religious ceremonies. The Aos believed that such practices would make a human community more human and humane.[4]

The sense of community was an important value, which was extended to every member of the society whether male or female. So, no individual member

1 Nungshitula, *The Naga Images of the Human Being*, 52.

2 Ibid., 53.

3 In an Ao Community, one of the most shameful and resentful action is stealing. A person who steals has the trademark of a thief and this stigma will affect the lineage. Nungshitula, *The Naga Images of the Human Being*, 55.

4 Nungshitula, *The Naga Images of the Human Being*, 56.

was left out or neglected in the village.[1] Women and men worked together, ate together and danced and rejoiced together. One of the important aspects was the 'Community Work.' In the Ao Naga villages most of the important works are done by the community with free labour. For instance, the community voluntarily constructs a bachelor's house (*Arju*), roads and village gates, wells, houses, foot-paths, churches, etc. On these occasions, everybody is involved without consideration of their social status. Even a minister is found working with a poor farmer, singing together the same chorus. Hence, much of the works are done by group, both men and women exchanging labour known as "*Yangtep.*"[2]

'Ongangla' *Arasentsur*[3] a Political and Religious Leader

Ongangla was a diviner, seer, prophetess, a medium or *arasentsur* who was a wise woman.[4] According to Wati Longchar, "She is the only diviner who is remembered till today by the Aos."[5] These diviners were sought on all important occasions to ascertain the divine will, particularly when a person became sick. It was believed that the soul of the sick person was imprisoned by a spirit, and the family members would approach one of the *arasentsur* to identify the spirit. A careful re-reading of the Ao Naga tribal culture shows that on some occasions women played a more significant role as for instance, in the feast of merit, the women tasted meat and wine before serving and said the prayer of sanctification and God's blessings.[6] Like many other Naga tribes, the Aos were not rigid in their approach towards women's participation in private and family sacrifices. Hence, according to the need of the hour women too performed the rites and rituals. In case of sickness sometimes women were allowed to do the duty of an *anpong.*[7] Women also played the role of Shamans, diviner and medicine men, who were known as seer, prophet, medium and mediator. Among the Aos there were many '*arasentsur*' who played vital roles in the religious life of the people, for example, the diviner 'Ongangla.'[8] In most

1 O. Alem Ao, *Tsungremology: Ao Naga Christian Theology*, Bangalore: Clark Theological College, 1994, 6.

2 A. Lanunungsang Ao, *Rural Development in Nagaland*, 218.

3 '*arasentsur*' means 'diviners', 'seer', and 'prophetees.' The term literally means the one who bites out or removes *Ara* (diseases).

4 She was commonly known *as Arasentsur* or *Aosangmongpi.* N. Limala Lkr, "Rediscovering Women's role and status in society" in *Tribal Study Series* No. 3, 81.

5 Wati Longchar, "Creation Poem of the Ao-Naga: A Theological Exploration" in *Doing Theology with the Poetic Tradition of India: Focus on Dalit and Tribal Poems.* Ed. Joseph Patmury, Bangalore: PTCA/SATHRI, 1996, 116.

6 Sashi Kechutzar, "The Role of Women in the Indigenous People's Religion of the North East India" in NarolaImchen ed., *Women's Issues in the 21st Century*, Women's Study Series No. 1, Jorhat, Assam: ETC, 2001, 92.

7 Ibid., 96.

8 Sashi Kechutzar, "The Role of Women in the Indigenous People's Religion of the North East India" in NarolaImchen ed., *Women's Issues in the 21st Century*, Women's Study Series No. 1,

of the private and family sacrifices, the mother officiated during the sacrifices in the absence of father. Despite of the rigid patriarchal set up, it is quite evident that certain rituals were always performed by women. There are also tales of wise and potential women in the Ao tradition which were often suppressed and neglected.[1]

The *Arasentsur* was a healer, a religious functionary who could be either a male or a female. Since, diseases were believed to be caused by the displeasure of the deities, the *Arasentsur* remove these diseases' by her healing powers. A person was not chosen for this position. It was regarded as a gift.[2] The *Arasentsur* could diagnose sickness by means of divination or by performing magical rites, after which, they performed an operation on the patient by bitting out the *Ara* and getting healed. They were regarded as priests because their function was regarded as religious - faith-healers who performed sacrifices and other religious rites for healing. They were also considered to be prophets and prophetesses who could predict the course of future events by divination or visions or by going into trances during which they talked with the deities and the spirits of people who had died, about future events, the coming of rains, etc. They played the role of a counselor, who was consulted regarding individual or public affairs like building a house or cutting the forest for cultivation, head hunting, making a war drum, construction of *morung*, holding of public festivals, to discover lost or stolen properties, etc. They were regarded as spiritual persons who act as mediators between the super natural and the human and who were able to communicate with the super natural beings- gods, angels, spirits, dead persons, etc.[3] Among the patrilineal societies, priesthood is mainly confined to males, and yet, we also find instances of women exercising priestly functions.

Ongangla's story can be traced back only in some songs where fragmented stories of her role is mentioned. In one of the Ao songs her role is depicted in this way.

O Chungliyimti Kong nung
Mongdangayimer
Arrsalang pang nung
Nutsungtemangsendenang ne
Nutsungtemangsendener
TsungremkumerOngangla dang jagi
Amdokamsui wane
Tsusentsubokkulemang to

Jorhat, Assam: ETC, 2001, 107.

1 Nungshitula, *The Naga Images of the Human Being*, 94.

2 NarolaImchen, *Women in Church and Society. The Story of Ao Naga Women*, Jorhat, Assam: Eastern Theological College, 2001, 33.

3 Ibid., 34 & 35.

Tsusentsubokulemtetayur
Qrungsakuagi
Yimrong song sang tuden none.[1]

Translation:
Oh, in the range of Chungliyimti
Called a village meeting
In the platform of warriors assembled all the people.
Having all people assembled,
They decided to go to Ongangla, a woman of God
Who told them to worship the new spring well
And having worshipped the new spring well
to erect the head-tree
and to administer ceremonies to the village head-tree.[2]

This song talks about the origin of worship and sacrifice in the Ao religious system. The people knew about the existence of a Supreme Being who is the Creator and Giver of all blessings, yet they did not know how to offer their sacrifices. Ongangla is considered to be the one who taught the people how to worship God. The men learned how to worship through her teachings. She laid the foundation of the Ao religious tradition and so she is called as the mother of Ao religion. But in the passing of time, religious functions were confined to only male priests.[3]

Another important role that Ongangla played was that, she instructed the men to erect the head-tree at the center of the village, which was regarded as the holy place by the Aos. People hung heads in this place as an offering to the Supreme Being for blessings in the field, cattle, family, and village.[4]

Earth as the Mother

According to Wati Longchar, the Ao Naga culture perceives the earth as mother. The mother earth is conceived as the symbol of unity and life for all living creatures, human beings, including the Supreme Being.[5] Yangkahao Vashum also states that the Nagas hold the belief that the land is the mother earth and is considered as the generous mother who gives birth to them and also nurtures and sustains them by the produce of the land. Since the earth with her natural bounty is the source

1 N. Talitemjen Jamir, Asen Sobalibaren, Mokokchung: Ao Socio Cultural & Literary Society, 1992, 14.

2 N. Limala Lkr, "Rediscovering Women's Role and Status in Society" in Tribal Series No. 3, 80.

3 Ibid., 82.

4 Ibid.

5 A. Wati Longchar, "A Liberated Woman in Captivity" in NarolaImchen ed., *Women's Issues in the 21st Century*, Women's Study Series No. 1, Jorhat, Assam: ETC, 2001, 115.

of their life and sustenance, the mother earth is deeply respected and honoured.[1] Hence, in th Ao Naga tribal understanding of the earth, we see the feminine principles as of valueing and nurturing the earth, that consists of conservation and nurturing of life. We need to call upon eminine values like caring, compassion and non-violence, for building a better world without any destructive tendencies. Eisler rightly states: "Let us reaffirm our ancient covenant, our sacred bond with our mother, the goddess of the nature and spirituality."[2]

Conclusion

Deconstruction helps to rediscover our lost stories from the biased interpretation of myths and folklores that de-humanize and subordinate women. It rediscovers the important roles played by women as leaders, diviners, prophetesses and advisers in the family, community and village. The invaders who came in the form of foreign rulers, Western Christianity and education, came with the colonial agenda which supported the already existing patriarchal structures to rule and domination.

A deconstructive reading of the tribal culture, folklores, stories and myths brings back the lost tribal values of human dignity and rights intrinsic to all creatures including nature. It rediscovers the cultural practices of women's equal rights, their status in the society and the stories of successful women who were leaders of both men and women. Hence, re-affirming of women's dignity should come to the forefront, and not just remain as a sub-text as is found in today's patriarchal Christianity.

1 Yangkahao Vashum, "Theology of land: A Naga Perspective" in *The Tribal Worldview and Ecology*, ed. A. Wati Longchar, Tribal Study Series No. 2, Jorhat, Assam: Tribal Study Centre, 1998, 74 & 75.

2 R. Eisler. "The Gaia tradition and the partnership future: an ecofeminist manifesto" in *Reweaving the World: The Emergence of Ecofeminism*, 24.

7

Religion and Secular Spirituality in Tribal Traditions of NEI
A Feminist Perspective

T. Vanlaltlani

Introduction

It was in 1987 at the ATTI General Conference at Leonard Theological College, Jabalpur, that I, by chance, presented a paper on 'Theology by the People- Mizo Perspective' (while I was a B.D degree holder) and it is a good feeling that today in Guwahati that I speak about Religion and Secular Spirituality in Tribal Traditions of NEI - A Feminist Perspective. I would like to start by saying that North East India (NEI) is the region consisting of eight states namely, Arunachal, Assam, Manipur, Meghalaya, Mizoram, Nagaland, Sikkim and Tripura where majority of the citizens follow tribal culture and custom. It would be unjust to talk about religion in NEI without starting with primal religion (in NEI background today the word 'tribal' has been used as one and the same with 'primal') because it is the oldest of religions, and many people in the NEI area have been practicing primal religion up to the present time. Thus, while some may say that India has been the cradle of at least four world religions like Hinduism, Buddhism, Jainism and Sikhism[1] and the spirituality of the followers of these religions, an NEI religionist would have said that the most senior religion of India is Primal religion such as that which was practiced earlier than the formation of Hinduism and is being practiced to this date in the area of NEI. But this paper, due to practical reasons from the writer's side, is limited by focusing more on tribal religious tradition especially in relation to some examples selected, experience and secular spirituality of the people in Mizoram.

1 Israel Selvanayagam, "Religion: Its Complexity and Variety" in Background Paper for Paper presenters in the Conference held at Henry Martin Islamic Institute, Hyderabad, 4-6 August, 2015, 1.

1. Religion in North East India and Secular Spirituality

As mentioned above there are eight states in the NEI and the inhabitants follow different religions. Among the variety of religions followed there are some who practice Hinduism and others following Islam; a fewer number of people are followers of Buddhism, Jainism and Sikhism. Many other people, especially those who are mainly in hilly areas, follow Primal/Tribal religion (we will continue to use the term Tribal religion) and their day-to-day life is closely attached to their religious beliefs and practices. For the tribal people in the NEI nature means a lot and natural resources are the root of their life, belief, actions, and their ritual performances and practices (This is not to negate the creative action of God who created the earth, the nature, the universe and all that dwell in it). The tribal religious elements and characteristics like their belief in a Supreme God, gods and goddesses, spirits (both benevolent and malevolent ones), animism, animatism, mana, omen, taboo, fetishism, lycantrophy, and others are rooted in natural resources and phenomena. Their domesticated animals are also meant for religious ritual sacrifices and economic dependence. This means that their religion is none other than the integration of their socio-cultural and economic understanding and their interdependence. Similarly, their social and political identities are very much integrated with their religious and cultural elements. Their religion is a lived religion which cannot be separated from their society, economy, culture and life experiences as affirmed by Paulus Kulu who wrote the followings:

> We can say that tribal religion is nothing other than beliefs expressed culturally. In the same way regarding tribal culture we can say it is nothing but beliefs lived out, or in one word ... religion in practice. Thus, we come to the conclusion that from the tribal point of view religion and culture are constitutively related like two faces of the same coin.[1]

Many of the NEI tribals have maintained their traditional religious belief which is lived out in their practical life and actions. Hence, their religiosity and their secular spirituality go hand in hand and are manifested through their lived action rather than theoretical and philosophical expressions.

At this juncture, let me add a feminist comment on tribal religion in general. Tribal religion and most of its implied activities, performances and celebrations are put into practice by men and women. They worship the Supreme God together, gods and goddesses, spirits willingly or unwillingly. Together, they constantly hold the sacredness of animism, animatism, mana, omen, taboo, fetishism, lycantrophy, and others rooted in the natural resources and phenomena. Their domesticated animals, mainly reared by women, are also meant for religious ritual sacrifices and economic dependence. In all, these women and men practice their religion together. Hence, tribal spirituality, intentionally or unintentionally, is

1 Paulus Kulu, "Tribal Culture" in *Sevartham*, No. 18, 1993, 15.

gender inclusive because tribal religion is the integration of their socio-cultural and economic understanding and of their interdependence. Tribal religion rounds up and deals with the whole life of the tribal people and the ideas of sacred and secular are not separated in their life. It is tribal religion that really pervades all sides and points out their life irrespective of the secular or religious, socio economic, culture or politics. Hence, tribal spirituality may be interpreted as both religious and secular, or their religious spirituality is secular or their secular spirituality is religious.

2. Nature Religion of the Tribals and their Agro-Economic Secular Spirituality

The religion of hilly tribal people in the NEI can be described as nature religion because natural phenomena and resources are meant for their economic survival and religious heritage. Trees, plants, rocks, rivers, waters, plants, bamboos, flowers, aquatic animals and wild animals, etc., have religio-cultural values because they all are means of their socio-economic and political survival. Nature and its products are made use of for creating peace of mind within oneself as well as for creating kinship and social relationship with the purpose of having a harmonious life in tribal society. Although, tribal religion has contained the strong concept of a Supreme God, their daily life is more attached to spirits whom they believe to be both benevolent and malevolent in their interference in their life. This results in them neglecting their relationship with the Supreme God in whom they believe. Since there is a belief that the Supreme God is not treating them badly and is not a malevolent one causing them bad luck or bringing misfortune upon them they give less attention to the Supreme God. Rather their agricultural economy and daily affairs are attached to nature and its resources. Since, tribal society and culture are community centre conditioned many of the tribal community members give devoted attention to the community land ownership for their equal sharing of land, and all members have a strong sense of ownership and responsibility for security and the protection of land.

The nature religion of the tribals is not systemtized or institutionalized with the support of written scriptures like the church of today. Rather, their religion and spirituality are manifested and expressed in their secular life and activities. It is not, for them, necessary to separate their religiosity as implicit religion (Edward Bailey's term) or explicit because the coverage of their religious spirituality is holistic in nature. There cannot be any margin separating their religious life and the secular world in which they live as social as well as religious beings. For the tribal people a religion having no implication and significance to the day-to-day social life of its adherents has no meaning for them, it is, rather, a meaningless religiosity. A living religion must be relevant to its followers' daily life, activity and practices by guiding one's mindset, thoughtforms, theoretical formulations, ritual performances and festive celebrations to become integrated both secularly and religiously.

Let me add a feminist reflection to the point. Women play important roles in an agricultural community especially in the activities of shifting jhum cultivation. They are the ones who are constant partners in all walks and works of an agricultural economy through their active cooperation with their male partners. There is no agricultural work done and completed without the activity of women. Here we quote, "They (women) sow, plant, weed, raise seedlings, harvest, thresh, and store agricultural products."[1] They are working together with their males for clearing of wild plants and weeds for proper growth of a paddy and other plantations. Their daily domestic and agricultural activity is closely attached to nature and its products. When it comes to religious sacrificial activity women are those who collect sacrificial materials like water, firewood, agricultural production, harvested vegetables, cereals, etc., for the purpose of ritual sacrifice. They prepare their home-made special alcohols (*Zu* in Mizo and *Arauh* in Bru languages) for ritual sacrifice as well as for sharing such special drinks while making sacrifice. Therefore, in a tribal society in which nature religion and agricultural economy walk hand in hand women and men play active roles in the practice and formation of religion and secular spirituality. Women are more attached to the details of agricultural economic activity and secular spirituality whereas their males are more apparent when it comes to priestly performance and leadership. Perhaps this is the main factor leading even tribal theologians to have opinions and make decision resulting in a gender biased and exclusively male leadership in the church and her hierarchical administration. Women in agricultural society maintain their spirituality in their day-to-day life and and practice their spirituality in their agricultural fields by fully participating in giving respect and care to nature and its products. But, the rituals and their performances mostly cagtegorized as religion and its spirituality are restrictively attached to men; consequently, women are excluded from such things whereas they are very much spiritual in all their religio-secular lives and activities. Therefore, men's spirituality is more confined to a narrow-minded religion while women's spirituality is more inclusive and wider in their outlook and concern. Hence, secular spirituality is another way of saying women's spirituality in tribal society of North East India.

3. Respect for Life in Tribal Tradition

In tribal traditional life, although there can be inter-village and inter-tribal warfare, homicides are rare due to the respect they have for human life. Due to the care and respect for life, abortion, foeticide and infanticide are almost non-existent. Although, there is no such law to prohibit murder, intentional killing of a fellow

1 Lalrinawmi, "A Feminist Critique of Land Holding Patterns in Mizoram" in *Theologizing Tribal Heritage: A Critical Rellook*, ed. Hrangthan Chhungi, Delhi: CWM/ISET-ECC/PCI/ISPCK, 237.

human, for whatver reason, is condemned in the strongest terms, as if with a curse. Long life is regarded as a divine blessing and a short life a curse. Blessing, therefore, is well understood as the reward of those who are morally good whereas death during one's youth or in the prime of one's life is viewed as a curse. In other cases, it is believed as a punishment for one's cruel acts and words. For this very reason, of respect for human life, there is also provision for protecting those who have killed fellow humans accidentally. The practice of seeking refuge to avoid death is called *lal sutpuivawn* in Mizo society. For instance, if a man has accidentally killed his friend by mistaking him for game during a hunting trip, the man would run fast to the village chief's house and embrace the main pillar of the house, which is called *sutpui*, in order to avoid the impending revenge from the relatives of the deceased. Once he embraces this pillar, it becomes a taboo to kill him. Thus, in tribal Mizo culture, in as much as it is rare to hear homicide, revenge killing is also very rare.

Since everything revolves around human life, it is believed that malevolent spirits always try to destroy human life. Thus, misfortune in life and ill health are viewed as the work of these spirits. Therefore, in order to propitiate these spirits, prescribed sacrifices are offered to them. For this reason, there are numerous and different levels of sacrifices performed by the tribal people in order to please the spirits so that the latter may not kill their loved ones. There are also different sacrifices offered to the benevolent spirits for blessings in life, especially good harvests, success in hunting and good health. Religious sacrifices and performances do not spell it out in words but spirituality outside the the function of religious worship and priestly performance promotes life sustaining and psychological healing to the one who is searching for continuity of life in the midst of fear of brutal death. Hence, tribal spirituality functions beyond religious realm, programme and coverage.

Tribal traditional respect and care for life deserve special appreciation from feminine perspective. Since there is sex preference from the parents' (preferring boys?) side there is socio-religious security and protection for girl children and all women. Women's roles and their function in tribal agricultural society for the preparation of ritual sacrifice to the spirits, for the healthcare and healthy living, is appreciated, except in the priestly performance, it is strongly and positively noted that God's creation of both sexes as equal is well recognized and accepted in tribal tradition. Women's contribution in life-bearing, life-caring and life-sustaining is beyond human comprehension. In tribal traditional society, it is extremely rare to hear about a murder committed by woman.

4. Tribal Communitarian Nature and Sharing Mentality

One of the most significant elements of tribal religious lifestyle is its communitarian nature and character. Community is above the individual. A wise saying of Mizo, which is often recited is '*sem sem dam dam, ei bil thi thi,*' which roughly means:

'One who shares (with others) will live while those who eat by themselves will die.' The saying teaches that, while those who are generous and hospitable will live long, those who are selfish and therefore do not want to share what they have with others will die soon. This saying contains a socio-ethical implication in the life of the Mizo community motivating them not to become selfish but to be a generous and hospitable people who would share what they have with others. For this reason, people shy away from a selfish and greedy person, while a generous and hospitable person is highly regarded and honored. For instance, a hunter who follows '*sem sem dam dam, ei bil thi thi*' principle will not keep the game for his family alone. The game meat would be cut into small pieces (approximately about 50 grams per piece) and distributed to the neighbouring families if the game is small, and to the whole village if the game is big. The present author too used to witness such sharing practices during her childhood life in the village. Even a new harvest of vegetables and crops were shared with neighbours on this very same principle of '*sem sem dam dam, ei bil thi thi*.'

There are also many other teachings for the benefit of the community. For instance, when doing open-air toilet, the advice is to pass stool at the far and upward slope side of the path and urine to the down slope side of the path (*Kawng chhakah e la, kawng thlangah zung rawh).* One can appreciate this saying if one knows the topography of Mizoram. Being hilly and slopy land, if one does his/her stool business at the upward slope side of the path, people will not be tormented by the smell. This clearly teaches how the Mizo society put the community interest above individual benefit and convenience. Another saying, '*Lampui changkhatah mi an be chhe ngai love*,' teaches us that one must not speak unkind words to people even once, be it a stranger or a person known to you. Positively put, we must speak kind words to everyone at any time, in any place and under any circumstances. This teaches that kind words are imperative for community living. We must not hurt each other by our words. Every community member must be surrounded by kind words of care and concern. This principle also goes beyond one's immediate community. In a larger context, any member of human society and the community deserves attention, care and good words.

Land ownership is another example that vividly exhibits the communitarian life of tribal society. In tribal areas, land collectively belongs to the whole community. Permanent ownership of the land by individuals is almost unheard of owing to the belief that the land is a gift of the creator who gives it collectively to the whole community. The creator of the land is the creator of the community. To some extent, this belief and practice remains in many tribal societies even after they may have embraced Christianity, Hinduism or other religions. However, this eco-friendly community land ownership has begun to experience change in the recent pasts owing to an industrialized and globalized economy and developments that commercialize the land. Such a process is negatively affecting tribal community lands causing deforestation and limitless exploitation of the land. This makes many tribal people landless in their own lands.

Communitarian nature and sharing in a tribal society is mainly maintained by the women of that society. Women, being mainly in charge of the daily family economy, are more responsible in the implementation of the principle of the traditional ethics of communitarian nature and sharing. Although, they are such true practitioners of spirituality, women, are the ones who have been marginalized and excluded wherever and whenever religion is institutionalized with the systematized layers of leadership. Hence, spirituality outside or beyond religion is more accessible, acceptable, and appropriate to tribal women. By acknowledging the important contribution to communitarian nature and the sharing mentality in tribal society nowhere there should there be gender biased participation if tribal heritage of community life is to survive. This challenges gender exclusive participation ant all levels of tribal life and in service to the wider circle of human community.

Positively saying, one may assume that all human beings like something good for human communities; but this may not be true in our dealings with others due to selfish desires and self-centred tendencies. Nevertheless, tribal tradition still supports and puts community welfare above individual benefit. To implement such traditions successful women are the motivators and facilitators to their men. Unless women are cooperative and supportive no men would work for the community welfare and benefit. Similarly, speaking kind or unkind words are often considered as coming from women because women are, to some extent, more communicative than men, and their voices are more sincere as determined by their accents. Thus, their words, whether kind or unkind, become very meaningful to the listener(s) either imperative or not for community living. Being the voices of women so sound and influential it is advantageous to use them for communicating the Good News of salvation for the whole life of human community members.

5. Tribal moral and Socio-ethical Values in Relation to attitude towards Senior Citizens

As mentioned before, tribal religion teaches respect and honour to elderly people. This ethical and etiquette protocol must be strictly followed not only for the orderliness and coherence of the family and community, but also for receiving blessings for the younger generation. For this reason, the Bru people show homage and reverence to their elderly citizens on their *Buisu* festival. They give them presents and appeal for their blessings. They retain and continue this practice even after they became Christians. The reason for this could be that their traditional teaching of respecting elders goes in line with Christian teaching - of respecting parents and elders - brought to them by Mizo missionaries whose tradition of respect for elders is strengthened by Christian teaching of the same. A Mizo poem teaching respect for elders goes as follow:[1]

Aia upa I biak dawnin,
Koh dan mawiin tawngkam hmang la.[2]

The poem teaches that when a Mizo needs to address anyone older than him/herself, he/she must use the appropriate etiquette and terms for addressing elders with polite and pleasing words. A typical Mizo would immediately admonish a person who addresses an elderly in disrespectful manner and speak to him or her unkind words. In addition, in Mizo culture, the younger one would help the older one by carrying the latter's load if they happened to be going together to same direction. A Mizo who does not know this protocol will not be spoken well of. In sum, in the area of according respect and honour to the elderly, Mizo culture, Bru culture and some other tribal cultures as well as Christian teaching and practices go hand in hand. This could be one of the reasons that Mizo and some other tribal groups would not regard Christianity as a strange religion and so embrace it happily.

The moral and socio-ethical values of tribal traditions towards the senior citizens is not covered much in the elements of tribal sacrificial ritual performances but is a lived and practiced principle of actions. The blessing words of grand-parents and parents to the youngsters (and also of senior citizens to strange youngsters) are believed to work really well for the welfare of recipients. Such being the case, tribal spirituality does not separate religion and secular spirituality because both consist of the said spirituality. Hence, the inclusive nature of tribal spirituality remains at every corner as human elderly people and younger generations live together in unity.

From a feminist viewpoint, the value of senior citizens' words for the youngsters does not make any gender discrimination on the part of the speakers and of the listeners. There is no difference in the weight of words whether it comes from the mouth of senior males or of females. Here, comes the question of gender equal opportunity, authenticity and authority in the preaching and other ways of communicating the Gospel which needs to be delivered for the benefit of all the believers. This really calls for further attention to women's participation in today's Christian ministry in and outside the institutionalized church.

6. Precious Tribal Concept of Ecological Worldview and Care

Tribal people understand the precariousness of the earth and its atmosphere. This is manifested in the way they treat and care for the land and its forests, vegetations, wildlife, birds and other living creatures. The main food of traditional tribal societies is rice and they, therefore, are peasant farmers depending on agricultural

1 This song, because of being contained in the text book, used to be memorized and sung by the author and her school mates during their education in Primary and Middle schools.

2 Translation of the quoted Mizo ethical song was done by the author.

products of rice and jungle herbs. But their farming systems are eco-friendly and harmonious with nature and the seasons. Even their shifting jhum cultivation would not cause deforestation, as they would not go back to the same tract before it completes a full cycle of reforestation (normally 7 - 10 years if the farming tract is a bamboo forests and 15 – 20 years if it is a wooded forest). The Tribal concept of an economy is not based on greed and maximum profit, but was a need-based economy.[1] Therefore, they do not have much interest in keeping surpluses. Bank savings for future financial security is foreign to them. For this reason, they would not kill animals and birds and catch fish for commercial purposes. They would hunt and fish only for family and community consumption. Of course, their hunting of wild animals, especially in Mizo society, has religious purpose affecting their them after physical death.[2] The system of community ownership of the land and villagers' farming according only to the need and size of their respective families is the epitome of the non-greedy and non-commercial culture of the tribal community. Even the village chief is bound by this community ownership of the land; he cannot permanently own the land as he wishes. Rather he would wish that his villagers become self-sufficient by farming the community land.

Tradition handed down through the centuries teaches the tribal people to be kind to trees, animals, birds and aquatic creatures. Those who torture these creatures unnecessarily would face misfortune. For this reason, hunting of animals and birds and fishing are prohibited during their breeding season. It is strictly prohibited to do mass fishing using any kind of poison including herbs even if consuming fish killed by such herbal "poison" would not affect human health. Hunting and catching animals and fish that are considered "unclean" or whose meats are considered not good for consumption as well as animals that are considered harmless (such as python) are discouraged.

On the whole, one can present a case for tribal religion as the best means for preservation of the earth and its atmosphere, along with all creatures living on it. For tribal religion, the earth and all living creatures of the earth are God's creaturely gift to humankind. For this reason, they would make sincere efforts not to spoil the land and its fertility for profit and self gratification.[3] They would exploit it only for sustenance and survival. In traditional Mizo society, the word

1 Samuel Longkumer, "An Enquiry into the Significance of Primal Religious Traditions in the Contemporary World" in *Tribal Voice*, 180.

2 In pre-Mizo or traditional religious belief there is a certain list of wild animals to be hunted for the fulfillment of *Ram lama Thangchhuah* requirement in order to let the hunter and his family go to *Pialral* and enjoy life there after physical death. It is also believed that all the animals which he hunted would follow him and the man in charge of the Gate of entry to *Pialral* and *Mitthi khua* would not dare to shoot at him whereas he would shoot everyone who did not perform the process of *Thangchhuah*.

3 Rosiamliana Tochhawng, "Humans and Nature in Mizo Tradition Towards Tribal Eco-Theology: Mizo Perspectives" in *Theologizing Tribal Heritage: A Critical Rellook*, ed. Hrangthan Chhungi, Delhi: CWM/ISET-ECC/PCI/ISPCK, 257.

"privatization" would be a foreign word. As the land is a community land, it goes without saying that all rivers and streams too collectively belong to the community. They would make every effort not to pollute village drinking water sources. To this, a Mizo ethical saying has this: *Tuikhur hnarah an e ngai love*, which means 'It is unethical to excrete the water source.' The society expects all its members to be conscious and responsible for maintaining the cleanliness and purity of the rivers and streams, especially drinking water sources.

Tribal religion grades all creatures as respectfully valuable and significant; this grading principle of belief contributes a lot to the maintenance of ecological balance and justice. Such being the case, religion and secular spirituality practically go side by side for environmental protection and ecological safeguarding and security. Hence, no demarcation between religion and secular, or, both are well taken care under tribal spirituality.

Furthermore, preservation of Sacred Grove in Khasi and Jaintia Hills in Meghalaya state is one of the most important heritage sites of the tribal in north East India due to the strong preservation of the forest and its products. This writer visited the thick forest called Sacred Grave twice; first, the Sacred Grove in the land which belonged to Mawngap town in 2006; second, the Sacred Grove in the land which belonged to Rymbhai town in 2012. It is about three hours' journey by car from Shillong city, situated to the east of it. When I visited those two Sacred Groves I saw that so many big trees, herbs, different kinds of wild plants and flowers growing there. The area covered by each of those forests, to my memory, seems to have been about ten acres. When I tried to pick up some orchids and other flowers from the covered area my hosting fathers and bachelors who had taken me there forbad me to do that because it was taboo to pluck any branches and leaves from off the trees in the area of Sacred Grove. Asking for the reason they told me that their ancestors' oral tradition was that the spirits who are guarding such thick forests and their products never allowed any item of the Sacred Grove area to be taken away. If this restriction is maintained and strictly kept there should always be sufficient forests for ecological and environmental balance as well as sufficient products of jungle food items for human beings, wild animals, reptiles and others.

In the traditional tribal ecological care and worldview women's careful economic management of water, firewood, and all food items including jungle food products may control the over-use of such things. If women are so greedy it may be that men cannot control them from over use of raw materials and natural products and cultivated crops. It is, therefore, women's cleanliness and awareness that keeps the water source clean and pure because women are responsible persons fetching water for domestic purposes; it is their ecological spirituality that controls their men from over-hunting wild animals in the jungle.

Whilst we are looking at the preservation of the Sacred Grove in different areas of Meghalaya state we can observe that women of Khasi and Jaintia Hills in

Meghalaya feel comfortable as their daily life and economy are related to the beauty of shadows of the forests, jungle herbs, plants and flowers. Their matrilineal family and society (although not a matriarchal society) does not seek the destruction of the forest, for the purpose of a huge income from their forest products. To this day, Meghalaya state remains naturally beautiful and attractive as women want to preserve their natural heritage of wild forests as the treasure of the community. Hence, they are the keepers of ecological balance.

There is a strong argument from a feminist perspective for the maintenance of Sacred Grove. In some of the religion-related performances women are forbidden to participate even if they are the ones who prepare all the elements of sacrifice and other rituals behind the screen. In the maintenance and ecological preservation of the Sacred Grove women and men are equally responsible as both sexes are forbidden to pluck the products of the Sacred Grove. This spiritual aspect of Khasi religion is so impressive and relevant in promoting secular spirituality in which women and men are equally responsible for caring for and maintaining the ecological balance through their constant safeguarding of the Sacred Grove.

7. Tribal Concept of Importance of Neighbourhood

Tribal people live a closely-knit community life. If human beings are social beings, tribal communities exhibit it more than other communities. Even wealthier families would prefer to live adjacent to their fellow tribes, people rather than living in isolation? Because of this, both good times and bad times are shared within the community. There is no such thing as "privacy" or "personal." What would others think about me is more important than whether I like it or not. The last thing an individual or a family would do is to displease their neighbours. A Mizo proverb says it all: *Thenawm do ai chuan khaw sarih do a thlanawm zawk*'[1] (Better fight against seven villages than fighting with one's neighbour').[2] The Mara people (one of the tribes living in southern part of Mizoram) have a similar saying: *Opa cha unawh lâhla liata a ypa hliâta a sôh via* (a neighbour is far more helpful than a brother who lives far away).[3] For this reason, one always needs to be on good terms with one's neighbours. So, we see that tribal communities protect each other with concern and care both in good times and bad. They also share whatever they have with their fellow villagers, especially with their neighbours. Tribal tradition has a rich heritage in the promotion of peace and harmony not only among neighbours but also among the different tribes and ethnic groups. Hence, respect and honour for the life of distant neighbours too would be upheld.

---

1 This wisdom saying was narrated often to the author by her parents and others during her childhood.

2 Translation of the quoted Mizo wisdom saying was done by the author.

3 This saying is told and translated on 28th January, 2013 by Rev. Dr. Laiu Fachai, Director of Serving In Mission (SIM) in North East India. He is also the lecturer in Old Testament Department in Aizawl Theological College, Aizawl, Mizoram.

This good neighbourliness is also true with other tribal communities in the NEI, be it traditional group or tribal Christians. For instance, if a Bru man in Mizoram is proven guilty of adultery with his neighbor's wife, the former is fined by the village traditional (*Chaudhury*) court, which impose upon him a heavy fine, normally a huge pig with or without a cash fine. The pig then would be slaughtered and both the culprits and victims would share the ceremonial feast after which they would peacefully live together as neighbours again. Good neighbourliness and peace in the neighbourhood counts above one's shame and one's anger against the neighbor concerned.

Living in a country where plurality of religions and cultures along with their respective practitioners are prevalent, tribal spirituality must be put into practice due to its care for life of the neighbours. If each and every member of our human community cares for his/her neighbour's life, then who would do harm to anyone and who would dare to kill his/her neighbour? Hence, caring for one's neighbour implies saving the life of each and every one of our human community because we are all neighbours. In a country like India where people fight on the basis of religion and their faith implies tensions and riots there is hardly a due care for the human life if the combatant belongs to another religious tradition. Hence, it is better to be humans than to be followers of a religion if one's affiliation to any of the religions results in one to hurt or kill on the basis of that religion. Here, saving human life and a caring faith needs not to be spoken badly of or held in low esteem by followers of any religion.

Further, it often happens that women are unreasonably condemned whenever and wherever there is misunderstanding between two families or among more families of a neighbourhood. On the other hand, when neighbourhood relationships are normal women are not praised at all. The fact is that women can be and always are peace makers among families of the neighbourhood or communities as well as between two angry men. Creation of good terms and relationships among families and communities is the task of women when a peaceful life is attacked. This has been shown by an incident which happened few years back when there was severe tension between Cachar Bengalis and Mizos of Vairengte village. The Bengali friends in Cachar-Mizoram boundary area tried to enter Mizoram in an angry mood looking for violent action against Mizo friends. It was then the Mizo women who went out to lay on the national highway in their desire for peace between the two communities. This resulted creating peace between both groups who hated enemies. Peace making is a great characteristic of women, and the avoidance of warfare and killing is a great source of happiness for them. The courage and commitment of the tribal women of Vairengte in performing such brave actions reveal the high quality of their life saving spiritual character. There are several other fine examples showing how much women love peace and harmony irrespective of difference in their religious affiliation. Secular spirituality in its true sense provides justice for members of humankind.

Conclusion

In general, tribal people in different parts of India and of the world have many similarities in their religious beliefs and practices. At the same time, there will be always some differences. In the same way, there will surely be differences among tribal groups in India and the NEI. Speaking from a feminist perspective on religion and secular spirituality in tribal tradition, one cannot avoid an appreciation of the tribal spirituality that pervades their religious beliefs implying their strongly held morality and actions. However, the richness of tribal spirituality warrants further researches in tribal religion and culture, not only for academic purposes, but more so for an understanding of the tribal people so that we all may live together with respect and dignity. Sacred focus in different ways, common concerns and explicit commitments in daytoday life are integrally and inherently related in a community life. With or without a particular religious commitment we experience in the secular arena so much goodness that finds expression in helping others, particularly in crisis. Then if it does not happen in some cases and if the opposite happens, how do we account for? This question may trigger further exploration!

8

Secular Spirituality of People's Movements in the Context of Religious Pluralism
A Feminist Perspective

Gabriele Dietrich

1. The Historical Background

Recently I attended an interesting seminar on "Implicit Religion." This was an attempt to draw on the writings of Prof. Edward Bailey,[1] a British author, who has tried to find religious contents in very ordinary secular settings like football fields or among people drinking beer in a pub (incidentally more male dominated surroundings, I would guess). I had been asked to present a paper on "implicit religion" in people's movements. I changed this into "Implicit Spirituality in People's Movements" because the term religion is alien to most of the activists in the secular world and many Hindu middle class people have a tendency to conflate it with "Theosophy," especially in a place like Chennai, which is home to the Theosophical Society. I tried to let the experiences in women's movements and working class organizations speak for themselves.

Since I have been involved in Women's Movements since the seventies and thus in discussions on Women's Movements and Religion since the mid-eighties, I have also been published on these experiences earlier, e.g., there was a major discussion in December 1986 at the autonomous Women's Conference in Bombay where there was a workshop on Women's Movement and Religion, coordinated by Miral Chatterjee of SEWA and myself. This was a rare occasion to reflect on the situation which we faced in our different organizations, where women belonging to different religious backgrounds came together for discussions on working class issues or against violence, while their family situation domesticated them into following traditional cultural roles. At the same time, women of the working

1 Edward Bailey, *Implicit Religion: An Introduction* (London Middlesex University, CSISRCS 1998).

classes also sometimes felt encouraged by their religious faith to rebel against injustice and oppression and to assert themselves, strengthened by their faith. This, sometimes confused middle class activists, because they had a tendency to take a more secular or agnostic attitude. The predicament created a debate which got into the EPW[1] immediately.

In addition, we were all part of the discussion on a uniform civil code, because we felt that a secular, gender-just family law would give women a better chance under the laws based on patriarchal religious traditions or the colonial Christian law. This somewhat naïve assumption had been complicated by the Shah Bano judgment of 1985, in which an elderly Muslim woman had gained the right to maintenance under Criminal Procedures Code 125 and 126 (Maintenance Laws), beyond the three months' rule under the Muslim family law. This led to an outcry by Muslim males, who saw their religious rights being violated. There had indeed been an anti-Muslim law polemic in the judgment of Justice Chandrachut. This led to the passing of the Muslim Women's protection Bill in May 1986, which directed Muslim women to the Waqf board for maintenance. This "pampering of minorities" brought the Hindutva forces on to the barricades and led to the disastrous decision of Prime Minister Rajiv Gandhi to order the opening of the locks of the Babri Masjid. This, in turn, led to rath yatras, shila nyas (transporting consecrated bricks) for a Ram temple at the "birthplace" of Ram and finally to the demolition of the masjid.

Later, after the destruction of the Babri Masjid on December 6th, 1992, I wrote an article assessing the impact of these momentous events on the religious identities of women in India.[2] The issue of the Uniform Civil Code was hijacked in this situation by communal forces, though it had appeared to be a very clear feminist demand earlier, promoted by pioneering human rights lawyers like Indira Jaisingh and Nandita Haskar.[3] Under the impact of this process, Shah Bano refrained from claiming her right to maintenance which she had won, because "she did not want to become the cause for a communal riot," as she said on TV. Ever since, there has been enormous work done by Flavia Agnes and her NGO Majlis to protect women from destitution and violence ever after.[4] Flavia, herself a victim of domestic violence, has later devoted her whole life to helping women to fight violence and gain economic independence. She has become one of the

---

1 *Women's Movement and Religion* in EPW, January 4, 1986.

2 Gabriele Dietrich, "Women and Religious Identities in India after Ayodhya" in Kamla Bhasin, Ritu Menon an Nighat Khan (Eds). *Essays on Women, Religion and Development from India and Pakistan* (New Delhi: Kali for Women, 1994).

3 Nandita Haksar: *Demystifying Law for Women* (New Delhi: Lancet Books, 1986).

4 Flavia Agnes: Give Us This Day Our Daily Bread. Procedures and Case Law for Maintenance (Majlis, Bombay 1992). See also the massive Omnibus edition, Women and Law in India, with her book Law and Gender Equality and her Introduction (Oxford University Press, 2004).

valiant and iconic women's lawyers who have the stamina to challenge patriarchy every day of her life.

I had all along taken a line that there was a need for "genuine religious reform" instead of an imposition of majority rule. This means each personal law needed reforming according to the values and traditions in a given settlement, but with the criterion of equality and gender justice, safeguarded by the Indian Constitution. As such reform was in many ways difficult to achieve, as it needed time. It was also possible to take recourse to a law which was designed to be used in inter-religious marriages, called the "Special Marriages Act," which was incidentally the most secular and gender just law available."[1]

2. The Present Situation

It is very sad that the communalization in our political life has once again polarized to new extremes after the BJP came into power after the 2014 elections under the leadership of Narendra Modi. The polarization and fragmentation goes on also in the name of caste and in the guise of cow protection, leading to the murder of one Mohammed Aqulak, hunted down on suspicion of storing or consuming beef, apart from the nearly "customary" murders of Dalits, which recently included setting fire to a house in which two small children died in the flames.[2]

We are now living in a situation where widespread protest is going on against the influence of the RSS and the attempts to make India a Hindu Rashtra. Many writers have given back their Sahitya Academy awards, scientists have come together in large numbers to stand up against the murders of rationalists and the obscurantist claims about "Vedic Science" and to affirm the freedom of debate and a cool scientific temper. The eminent historian Romilla Thapar has given lectures on "The Idea of the Secular" in Delhi and Mumbai, in October 2015, in which she also recaptured the idea of the Uniform Civil Code as a secular concept safeguarding gender justice and democracy within families, free from the tyranny of caste and religious exclusionism and fundamentalism. The country is in turmoil due to election campaigning in different states, which strongly reinforces the polarizations.

My attempt during the seminar on "Implicit Theology" was to give a glimpse of the history of the women's movement and the twists and turns which the debate took on under different historical circumstances. However, this attempt did not at all succeed in making visible the implicit qualities of subversion, transgressions and transcendence which were inherent in the history of such interactions. "Implicit Spirituality" was not conceded to women's movements in the first place, which

1 See my article: "The Secular State, Freedom of Religion and Women's Rights" in my book: *Reflection, on the Women's Movement in India: Religion, Ecology, Development* (New Delhi: Horizon India Books, 1992).

2 Ram Puniyani (Ed): *"Sacred Cow"* (New Delhi, 2015).
"*Two die as Dalit Family set afire in Haryana*, The Hindu, 21.10.2015.

irked me a lot. If it could be conceded in the pub or on the foot ball field, why was it not in the assemblies of movements concerned with the liberation of women? I was told by a dear (male) friend that perhaps we were only moving in our own "comfort zone." What is wrong with wanting a comfort zone, I wondered. To my consternation, the same person later apologized because, he said, there could be an association with "comfort women." (This was a reference to the use of Korean women as "comfort women" by Japanese soldiers in WW II). I was aghast. I had clearly not succeeded in making visible the spiritual dimension required to bridge the differences of culture, languages and religion in the effort to create gender-just family laws. Perhaps this was because the binding factor was the secular democratic constitution of the Indian republic. In the women's movement, we have always fought for freedom of religion, but also freedom from religion when necessary. We did not indulge in the theological arguments of our respective religions very much.

3. Religious Encounters in Secular Spaces

My point was that the women's movement itself was secular, but in order to come to terms with the situation, women had to transcend their fragmented identities and relate to each other in a given common space, reaching out to each other and understanding the common predicament. This required a certain spirituality and transcendence, e.g. When Flavia Agnes during a plenary at IAWS, the conference in Jadavpur University, took heart to point out that there was a majority communalist tendency in the Women's Movement which discriminated against minorities by viewing Hindu symbols as "part of our culture," while Muslim or Christian self expressions were perceived as "sectarian," this led to discussions and questions which were quite painful to face but which ultimately helped us to better understand each other and ourselves.

What I am trying to make visible is a history of inter-religious dialogue which happened in a secular space. Women encountered each other in solidarity, not necessarily as "representatives" of their religious community. This was quite far removed from identity politics. We reflected on patriarchies in different religious contexts, assertions of subversion, revolt, transgression and transcendence. We affirmed freedom of religion but also freedom from religion. These were the times when Uma Chakravarty, an agnostic historian in the History Department of Delhi University, wrote a book on the struggles of Pandita Ramabai and her conversion to Christianity.[1] Her focus was how Pandita Ramabai stood up against the patriarchal culture of her caste, religion and the colonial state, including the authorities of her newly acquired faith.

In the movement, we did not suffer from politics of representation. We encountered each other as unfettered human beings. Though some of this

---

1 Uma Chakravarti, *Rewriting History: The Life and Times of* Pandita Ramabai (New Delhi: Kali for Women, 1992).

happened in conferences, for example those of the autonomous movements on the IAWS, the exchanges were entirely informed by real life situations and nurtured by demonstrations and street actions. This kind of spirituality was not recognizable in the male dominated atmosphere of the conference on "Implicit Religion." It may therefore be necessary to raise the question of the role of women in inter-religious dialogue.

4. Alternatives to a Doctrinal Approach

There is, generally speaking, an under-representation of women in inter-religious dialogue for the simple reason that women are not considered to be "religious experts," whatever they may be. This has to do with the fact that religious training was mostly focused on men, as men were seen as the guardians of doctrine and ritual and thus needed to have a thorough understanding of the "basics" and of right and wrong. At the same time, it is a fact that the oral transmission of myths and rituals is often done by women. Even where women may have been quite prominent in the religious movement, as e.g., in the Jesus Movement, the Gospel of Mary of Magdala was excluded from the bible in the process of canonization and was only dug up by feminist theologians at the end of 20th century.[1] It is therefore crucial to widen the horizon and to shift the perspective from the expert sphere into the world of daily life.

Interestingly, such a shift was made in June 1983 at a women's conference in Harvard University, organized by Devaki Jain and Diana Eck,[2] where out of 26 women who made presentations 17 were from Asia, Africa and the Middle East and Latin America, while nine were from US and from Europe, one of them from Eastern Europe. They were scholars, activists and policy makers. The contributions from Latin America, South Africa and also India drew a lot from the lives of ordinary poor women, while other contributions highlighted the difficulties of feminists within the established structures of religion. Interestingly, this led to very diverse results, e.g., a participant from Thailand, Chaturman Kabil Singh, who had voiced her anguish about women not being able to be full members of the Buddhist Sangha, later became the first fully ordained Bhikkuni in Thailand, after many years of struggle, while Daphne Hampson decided to turn her back on the Anglican Church, which had caused her to lose her voice.

The second WRSCS conference of this kind took place in 2003, also in the US, but due to the events of 9/11, the conflict between Israel and Palestine and Islam and Judaism in West Asia, Feminist perspectives could not come to the fore. In the meantime, there was also the Asian Women's Resource Centre coming into being which started in Hong Kong by Sun Ai Park and was run

1 Karin King, *The Gospel of Mary of Magdala* (Polebridge Press, USA, 2003).

2 Diana Eck and Devaki Jain (Ed.), *Speaking of Faith: Cross Cultural Perspectives on Women, Religion and Social Change* (New Delhi: Kali for Women, 1986). See also my review in EPW September 19, 1987, 1597-1599.

from Kualalumpur for a long time. It has contributed a lot to Asian Feminist Theology through conferences and the Journal 'In God's Image,' but did not go into inter-religious dialogue very much, except when it moved to Indonesia from 2010-2014. It is now located in India, but the Centre cannot publish the journal from here and still has to find its feet.

5. A Dialogue "from the Margins"

An interesting study was published in 2006 by Helene Egnell, a Swedish researcher at Upsala University, who tried to trace Christian Feminist contributions in a situation of religious pluralism.[1] She has given a lot of attention to India. Her attempt is to change focus to religion "as practiced" and not as "as prescribed." She also puts emphasis on "the messiness of life." She has drawn strongly on Carol Gilligan's *In a Different Voice* (1982) which had to do with the abortion debate in the US in the early eighties. Gilligan saw women as primarily relational, while men appeared to be more focused on rules and rights. There is a danger in giving the impression of such roles being anchored in biological disposition, while the social formation of such attitudes needs to be scrutinized. The distinction between "Religion as Prescribed" and "Religion as Practiced" has replaced, in a way, the distinction between "great tradition" and "little tradition" which was criticized as being elitist. There is also a resonance with the distinction between "cosmic" and "meta-cosmic" religion, as developed by Aloysius Pieris, though these perspectives are not identical.

Egnell's approach is helpful in several ways: It highlights women's role as agents of peace keeping in conflict situations (e.g., in the Peace interventions attempted by Henry Martyn Institute), but also in the West Asian situation, where the Israel-Palestine conflict has pitted populations against each other in struggle over land, rooted in the history of colonial wars, anti-Semitism, the holocaust and neo-colonization especially towards the end of the 20th century. At the same time, she shows that these pre-occupations are not necessarily shared by women from South East Asia or Africa in whose identity formation the history of the two world wars was not a decisive factor.

It appears rather unavoidable in this day and age that this study takes off into a post-modern direction of identity politics, while the longstanding concern of Asian feminists with "the many poor," i.e., the emphasis on social justice and maintenance of God's good creation, is in a way pensioned off. Acknowledging difference is certainly important, but building alliances to overcome exploitation, destruction of nature and rising militarization, pre-supposes that a commonality of purpose is built up which strives for healing and wholeness in a world threatened by global warming, species loss and rising violence; such commonality has only been seen in ecological struggles of indigenous populations or in the struggles

1 Helene Egnell, *Other Voices: A Study of Christian Feminist Approaches to Religious Plurality East and West* (Upsala, 2006).

against nuclear energy. Such struggles have also been fought "from the margins", but their quest for life has not made sufficient impact to overcome the cultural fragmentation under neo-liberal globalization.

6. Overcoming the Ideological Vacuum

In the WRSC dialogue in Harvard in 1983 mentioned above, the dominant ideological trend was of Gandhism and non-violent struggle, while most leftist positions also were flowing in from Latin America, without being made more explicit.

It is quite strange that neo-liberal globalization has not been recognized in the fierceness of its onslaught on the resources base and resulting cultural fragmentation. This apparently has to do with "post-colonialism," which predominantly tries to reconstruct "culture," while the questions of undermining and breaking the neo-colonial onslaught which has overwhelmed the world in the last quarter of the last century and is still expanding, has not been of central interest.[1]

The debate on secularism and spirituality cannot be held in an ideological vacuum. The engagement for social justice and eco-justice can be nurtured by religious traditions which emphasize compassion, common humanity and responsibility to preserve nature for future generations. This requires curbs on the rule of money, critique of consumerism and building of democratic structures free from hierarchies, caste, sexism and religious discrimination. This sounds indeed rather utopian.

During the seventies, the dialogue section of the WCC had given attention to dialogue with faiths and ideologies. Organizations like Christian Peace Conference made attempts to promote Christian Marxist dialogue. This was however not sustainable due to the inability of socialism itself to reform. The struggles for Socialism in different Latin-American countries inspired movements of Christians for Socialism, which also worked for re-reading biblical texts in a radical political perspective.[2] The collapse of socialism under the impact of neo-liberal globalization has ended this trend, but it lives on as an important memory in the ecumenical movement. Under neo-liberal globalization post-modernism has taken over with emphasis on identity politics and culture.

I have recently been requested to contribute to the reflections which came up in the centenary year of Dr. M.M. Thomas, one of the most influential ecumenical theologians ever, and was impressed, when re-reading his ecumenical journey, in which Dr. Thomas had tried to contribute to the ideological formation of the WSCF, in the interest of anti-colonization and transformation of the mode of

---

1 See my article:"Why does Post-Colonial Feminist Theology need to relate to People's Movements." in *Asia Journal of Theology* Vol. 19, Number 1, April 2005.

2 See my article: "The Qest for Socialism in Times of Crisis" in Felix Wilfred's Book *Theology Going Public* (Delhi, ISPCK, 2013).

production towards social justice and democratic socialism, inspired by Marxism as well as the Sapta Kranti (seven steps revolution) of Ram Manohar Lohia.[1] At the same time, together with Paul Devanandan, he took a deep interest in inter-religious dialogue and opposed the Christian trend of conversion. He advocated "open secularism," i.e., secularism open to people of religious faiths who stand up for freedom of religion and a secular state. He also felt that conversions were unnecessary, but opposed anti-conversion laws. These conceptualizations are of great relevance in the present situation.

From the mid seventies, inter-religious dialogue became very important in the WCC, including the dialogue with secular ideologies as well. Stanley Samartha from India and Wesley Aryaraja (originally from Jaffna) carried this work forward. Wesley has worked on Theology of Religions and has contributed much to build mutual understanding and tone down missionary zeal as well as claims to the monopoly of salvation and truth.[2]

It is important to understand that secularism cannot be taken for granted in the Asian situation and needs to be defended all the time. While the Indian Constitution, thanks to the untiring work of Dr. Ambedkar, guarantees freedom of religion and a sovereign, secular, democratic, socialist republic, the present central government works hard to make India a Hindutva nation. Neighbouring countries are struggling with different degrees of religious fundamentalism, which polarise ethnic and religious minorities against each other. In some of our countries rationalists are murdered with impunity. Whilst writing this article, it so happened that the Bihar election results of Nov. 2015 were announced with a land slide victory of a two thirds majority for the secular alliance, a remarkable set-back for the central government and the forces of Hindutva. But what will the Janata Alliance stand up for? At present, it has saved secularism and a democratic socialist perspective and has resisted religious and caste polarizations. There is a clear emphasis on development with social justice and people's participation, a heritage of Jaya Prakash Narayan's "total revolution." Secularism is the binding force.

The ideological vacuum in inter-religious dialogue has to do with the absence of secularism in the political sphere and the totalitarian claims of religious nation states. We may feel good that the Panchshila Islam of Indonesia is better than what the Islamic State is trying to achieve in West Asia, but the anti-left pogroms under Suharto cannot be forgotten. The Buddhism to which Dr. Ambedkar converted in Nagpur to break the caste system, was very different from the Srilankan model, though he took his Deeksha from a Sri Lankan monk. Buddhism has produced different forms of state religion in Myanmar or Thailand for that matter, while

1 See my article "Political Aspects of the New Humanity in Christ" written for a Centenary Volume on M.M.Thomas to be published in the UK.

2 Wesley Aryaraja, *My God, Your God, Our God: Rethinking Christian Theology for Religious Plurality* (WCC Publications, 2012).

ethnic minorities have struggled to assert their own cultures. We can only hope that after the recent election in Myanmar the spiritual bond which tied Aung San Suu Kyi to the people will help to de-militarize and democratize the country and will help to evolve an economy which focuses on the poor and the preservation of natural resources. And of course, the Rohingyas need to be recognized as legitimate citizens. It would also be good if she studied Ambedkar and told the generals that Freedom, Equality and brother/sisterhood (solidarity) are primeval Buddhist values, together with Secularism and non-violence.

7. Responses to the Ecological Crisis and Global Warming

In India, people's movements which have addressed land struggles, working class issues, nuclear energy, big dams, caste atrocities, communalism and fundamentalism, find it difficult to come together and are often fragmented in single issue struggles. Ideological debates tend to be avoided and media as well as internet, facebook, whatsapp, sometimes substitute for direct involvement in local situations. Defending the constitution is crucial, as the right to life and livelihood gets violated with impunity and the gap between rich and poor is ever widening.

We know that we do not have much time left to come to terms with global warming, dwindling water resources, GM crops, rising levels of violence, intolerance and arms race. We need to pool our diversity of skills, resources and creativities, and have to overcome trauma and find life affirming solutions. But our political and economic life gravitates in the opposite direction.

It is extremely tiresome to deal again and again with the limits to growth debate which is quite old hat, having gone on since the early seventies in all earnest, the Club of Rome, the Brundtland Report and many follow-ups.[1] We have been involved in this for nearly half a century, but political parties and governments still win elections on the promise of unlimited growth. Just today my morning newspaper screamed with a full front page advertisement that 'free electricity is coming.' Why can such criminal lies not be stopped? Obviously, this is because energy companies are most powerful and the warfare about controlling the oil resources is going on unabated, while the same companies are now projecting themselves as ecologically friendly.

In the meantime, the fundamentalist religious forces who have been supported by the US and other Western powers have also spawned terrorism and the wars and attacks which are going on in West Asia and North Africa have been daily news for years. The recent terror attacks (October 2015) in Paris, significantly preceding the international climate summit in early December 2015, have aggravated racism, anti-Islamic resentment, hostility towards refugees and police state methods to curtail democracy, simultaneously with new military

1 See E.g., Donella Meadows, Jorgen Randers, Dennis Meadow, *Limits to Growth the 30 Year Update* (London: Earthscan, 2004).

interventions in Syria and other countries, which kill large numbers of the civil populations.

It is becoming more evident that global capitalism is destroying the earth in suicidal madness, still assuring us that the 'invisible hand' of the markets will look after us. This reminds of George Bush's advise to the American Public after 9/11 to 'go shopping' to boost the economy.

There have been many studies on global warming, one of the more influential and helpful ones by Naomi Klein, the Canadian researcher and activist who wrote earlier. on the cold war and has also been part of the 'Occupy Wall Street' campaign.[1] She is also part of the struggles of the indigenous populations in Canada to keep a hold on their lands, forests, fishing grounds, and culture, while energy companies have invested in fracking (for 'natural gas' as methane is nowadays called) and processing tar sands.

Whilst looking further in search of answers as to why we are not making more headway, I also returned to a book which examined the process of neo-liberal globalization in great detail and showed the disastrous effects of the making of global India.[2] The authors show with great clarity the ecological destruction achieved by the dismantling of environmental governance, crony capitalism, land wars and internal colonialism. They also outline an alternative value system and dismantle the illusion of technocratic solutions. They show a broad spectrum of different movements and local initiatives which try to recreate and revive nature in a decentralized democratic process of struggle and constructive work. The experiences are told as 'stories of tomorrow' which lead from developmentality' to 'ecologicality.' New forms of governance are developed and a new role of education and knowledge is envisaged. The examples given are very encouraging. How to achieve comprehensive policy changes is a big question.

While dwelling on Climate Change I also came across a new book by Tim Flannery, which gave me a different feel for the time perspective. After writing earlier on The Weather Makers, he has now come up with a new book *Here on Earth*.[3] The book raises the question as to whether we are heading for destruction or whether the Earth can be saved. He employs some Greek mythology to symbolize the tendency to murderous solutions (the Medea syndrome) -Vs- the life-giving principle of gaia (Earth).

Tim Flannery deals with the history of the cosmos and of the Earth, which then gets transformed by the history of humanity, a history of time spans which are quite beyond our imagination. He raises the question of whether 'survival

1 Naomi Klein, *This Changes Everything,* London: Allen Lane, 2014; Naomi Klein, *The Shock Doctrine: The Rise of Disaster Capitalism,* Toronto: Vintage Canada, 2008.

2 Asseem Shrivastava and Ashish Kothari, *Churning the Earth: The Making of Global India* (New Delhi: Viking, Penguin Books, 2012).

3 Tim Flannery, *Here on Earth: A Twin Biography of the Planet and the Human Race* (Penguin Books, 2012).

of the fittest' is the last word as a guiding principle as it is often assumed to be and whether the observations of Darwinism are then projected into the social Darwinism of a competitive market, where only profit rules. Flannery raises the question of whether a gigantic large-scale cooperation can be achieved. He uses the co-operation and co-ordination systems of ants as an example. He also raises the question of whether the earth has a system of self-healing or even inherent intelligence of her own, which he calls the gaya principle, a terminology from Greek philosophy, which was taken over by the New Age Movement, but he relates it to many concrete examples in the history of species loss, which has now taken on lethal proportions due to marketing, industrialism, colonial warfare and globalization. I started feeling that fifty years of limits to growth are, after all, not so long, though we are now compelled by global warming and the melting of the ice caps to create a great sense of urgency together with revolutionary patience.

People's movements have consistently worked for the survival of the under-privileged, Right to Life and Livelihood, preservation of soil, forest and water in people's hands as the Commons, not privatized in favour of ruthless companies. The women's movements have untiringly fought against structures of violence. Finding binding rules and mechanisms of governance to stop warfare, build sensible transport systems and renewable energy systems, get the CO2 back into the soil, preserve, forests and water, honor diversity and democracy, abolish totalitarianism of any kind, end poverty, healing the Earth, being healed by her - all this has to be our common effort.

8. Examples of Transformative Secular Spirituality

It may be helpful to conclude these deliberations with a brief list of examples of 'secular spirituality' in people's movements, which illustrate the forces of subversion, transgression and transcendence in different situations.

1. It so happens that we have reached a point where we can celebrate ten years of having gained and used the Right to Information, which on average is used by five million of people in India annually. This was the result of protracted struggles by people's movements, most of all the Mazdoor Kisan Shakti Sangatan and the National Campaign for Right to Information. This has given people courage to ask questions and concrete hope that corruption can be curtailed.[1]
2. The Women's Movements in India have consistently struggled against violence in the home, in public, in police stations or wherever it occurs. This has led to valuable legislation on domestic violence, sexual harassment in the workplace, significant changes in the rape law and also in the right to maintenance and livelihood. It is an enormous

1 See Aruna Roy and Nikhil Day, "Holding Power to Account," *The Hindu*, 20.11.2015, Madurai edition, 11.

struggle to achieve implementation of these laws. Very significantly, feminists have consistently refused to demand death penalty for rape, though rightist parties are propagating this. The feminist movement fully supports the struggle for the abolition of the death penalty. The State must not have the right to take life.

3. The campaign against sex-selective abortions has affirmed support for the girl child and mothers of girl children, whilst at the same time avoiding the trap of being drawn into general anti-abortion campaigns. It has now expanded the objectives to foster self-respect and capacity building instead of guilt feeling and self-hatred. Kudal Kitmatkar, a non-violent organization in memory of frontier Gandhi Ghafoor Abdul Khan, has campaigned for girl children and against alcoholism and family violence side by side. It has also built strong inter-religious co-operation.
4. Many women's organizations have worked for the reform of different Personal Laws, with varying success. One of the thorniest issues is the triple *talak* (divorce) among Muslims, as well as the question of maintenance. Organisations like Bharatiya Muslim Mahila Andolan (BMMA) have made very sensible proposals, but get stuck with the Muslim Law Board. In the meantime, others have worked in their own ways. The organization STEPS in Puthukottai (Tamilnadu) under the leadership of Ms. Sharifa has been working on building a Women's Mosque and has intervened very constructively in many family problems in the community. A group of young Muslim women at Mumra in Thane Dt. has built up a football club and is working on a calendar featuring Muslim women leaders.
5. The struggle of the LGTB community to break through sex and gender stereotypes and to attain recognition and dignity has made decisive contributions to overcome patriarchy and sexism in different religious communities and in society at large.
6. Participation of women in local bodies has helped to develop new styles of governance. In some situations, it has also helped to overcome the power of caste panchayats. Sanitation workers' unions have ceaselessly raised the issue of manual scavenging. Connections between un-touchability, patriarchy and waste management have been made visible. Many questions need to be raised and solved.
7. The un-tiring struggle of Narmada Bachao Andolan against big dams (now thirty years completed!) has raised the question of land rights for indigenous (*adivasis*) and local communities. It has also raised consciousness regarding the role of international finance institutions, the necessity to keep water as a common property resource and the need to protect forests. The presentday struggle to save Niyamgiri

in Odisha from bauxite mining can be seen in continuation of this perspective. This connects us with the struggles of local communities to protect land, water and forest from the companies which exploit and destroy.

8. The sharing of spaces and places of worship during struggles and participation in each other's festivals and meals has strengthened people's resolve towards solidarity. It has also led to family alliances across caste and religious boundaries, not necessarily without conflict, but with a lot of support from various movements.
9. The international campaign One Billion Rising has manifested itself in many protests against violence on women, across religious and national boundaries. In Asia, it has been promoted by Kamla Bhasin, a pioneer in gender training who has reached out to generations of young women through revolutionary songs and literature on patriarchy, gender, pluralism secularism, feminism, peace and more. Even before that, the struggles of countless movements for decades have led to the realization that women's rights are human rights and those wars must be ended.
10. Last but not least, the struggle of the women and local communities of Idinthakarai near Kudankulam against the VVER 1000 reactors from Russia, acquired through a contract only two years after the Chernobyl melt down, connects us with the international peace movement and also the struggle of the Bhopal gas victims for the liability of companies who sell us lethal technologies.

In all these cases, we have not asked the question as where the people in the forefront of struggles for justice, human rights and protection of life resources have received inspiration, motivation and courage. Perhaps, people's movements avoid asking the question openly fearing the exposure of religious identity and ideological obsession. At the same time, it is important that the study network of implicit religion and contemporary spirituality that has facilitated an exploration in the Indian context should think of providing tools for analysis for the secular movements not only in India but all over the world.

9

Understanding Religion and Spirituality in Current Debates on Secularism in India

Densingh Oliver

On the sixty sixth republic day 26th January 2015 the Indian government published an advertisement in which the words 'secular' and 'socialist' were missing from the preamble to the Indian constitution. One of the Shiv Sena party leaders Sanjay Raut said most Indians wanted to remove these words permanently from the constitution as India belongs to Hindus. The party said that the word 'secular' was not relevant for the country as India is a 'Hindu Rashtra' where people of other religions can live but that the Hindus will dominate. Ironically, the government defended itself and stated that these words were added only after 1976. In the same year on 28th September, a murderous mob came together to kill a Muslim man allegedly for having kept some beef in his refrigerator. This was part of the cow protection activities of the revivalist Hindus although there is evidence of beef eating of their parents in sacrifice-based religious practices. Earlier a 450 yrs old Babri Masjid was pulled down by a mob of Hindu extremists on 6th December 1992, which was followed by Godhra riots in 2002 and Kandamal riots in 2008 – in all these hundreds of innocent people lost their lives. Additional events of genocides in the name of religion and the continuous polarization of communities are the perilous ones. The informed community does not tolerate such acts of intolerance and show their opposition in various ways including returning their awards. It is in this context that we observe current debates on secularism. A note on religion and spirituality is in order. Both continued to be defined from different perspectives and, essentially, they seem to stand for non-material, transcendent and a sacred awareness of life.

Defining Secularism

The term 'secular' was derived from the Latin word *saeculum* which originally meant 'an age or generation, the times or the world' connected with the affairs of the world, not spiritual or sacred. The idea of secularism denotes that the social affairs of society must be solely guided by the present life itself. In the context of Western rationalism, secularism was defined as the attempt to establish an autonomous sphere of knowledge purged of supernatural presupposition.[1] According to Charles Taylor the word 'secular' itself is a Christian term and the word comes from the Latin word *Saeculum*, which means 'country or age, taking on a special meaning as applied to profane times, the time of ordinary historical succession, which the human race lives through between the Fall and the Parousia.'[2] Generally the meaning of secularism becomes clear if it is contrasted with its generally accepted view of being opposite to religion. In a general sense, secularism was a by-product of the experiment of humans in general for a better way of life. The notion of secularism is not a stable one or predetermined universal category but according to its historical and religious context it is changing. Thus, the Western secularism differs from the Indian secularism in nature and in meaning.[3]

The idea of secularism in the West emerged as an ethics of behavior and a prescription for political organization that promised to supersede the violence and irrationality that seemed inherent in collective forms of religious expression.[4] The principle of the separation of the State and Church received wide-spread acceptance during the latter part of the eighteenth century. The revolutions, rationalism and skepticism of the Enlightenment period worked together to reduce the dogmatism and fanaticism of religious groups and stressed the freedom of conscience which could only be guaranteed by Church-State separation. In the American context, James Madison and Thomas Jefferson were prominent leaders who advocated separation of State and Church.[5] However, the secular state was to some extent achieved with no hostility towards religion. The difference between Western and Indian forms of secularism is that while the former was born in the context of rationalism, intra-religious domination and anti-clericalism, the latter was stimulated in the context of modernizing colonial India.

Necessity and Development of Secularism in India

Secularism in India is a product of the imperial encounter, though there are pre-colonial traditions of anti-clericalism and anti-superstition in India.[6] The Indian

1 B. Satapathy and K. Panda, *Seculariam and Indian Perspective*, Ahmedabad: Karnavati Publications, 1998, 9.

2 Charles Taylor, "Models of Secularism," in *Secularism and its Critics*, ed. by Rajeev Bhargava, Delhi: Oxford University Press, 1998, 31-32.

3 O. Densingh, "Revisiting Post-Independent Debate on Secularism in Multi-faith India," in *Religion, Politics and Secularism in India: Essays in Honor of Asghar Ali Engineer*, ed. by P. Prayer Elmo Raj, New Delhi: Authorspress, 2016, 143.

4 Shabnum Tejani, *Indian Secularism: A Social and Intellectual History, 1890-1950*, Bloomington: Indiana University Press, 2008, 1.

5 Donald Eugene Smith, *India as a Secular State*, Princeton: Princeton University Press, 1963, 17.

6 Peter Van Der Veer, *The Modern Spirit of Asia: the Spiritual*, 163.

National Congress was founded in 1885 and became the first organised expression of Indian nationalism on an all India scale intent on leading India's nationalistic struggle for freedom from British colonial rule. Further, the idea of secularism was adopted voluntarily by the Indian National Congress, to cope up with the multi-religious situation. The slogan raised in the freedom struggle was '*hain sab bhai bhai*' which suggest, people of all these religions are brothers united in their struggle against foreign rule.[1] Thus, unlike Europe, secularism in India arose not so much in the context of conflict with organised religion, but as an attempt to unify the followers of different religious faiths in their struggle against the British by making it the premise of a united free India.[2] Therefore, during the freedom struggle, secularism grew out of the necessary pluralism of congress politics and was seen in the image of Nationalism and religious tolerance.

The notion of secularism was recognised as an essential platform for multi-religious and multi-caste India, as an instrument for unity of the people at large.[3] Diversity of traditions, heritage, religious practices, bigotry, fanaticism and mutual hatreds of Hindus-Muslims, Christians and Sikhs certainly did not help to smooth the the process of secularization. In the context of freedom and partition in 1947, the real challenge of the newly emerged nation was to create a proper scheme and structure for the smooth running of the government. After partition and Independence, a large proprtion of Muslims remained in India as they preferred this pluralistic India. At present, they form over 12% of the 1.3 billion population. Therefore, the leaders like M.K. Gandhi, regarded as the father of the nation and Jawaharlal Nehru, the first Prime Minister of India, preferred to keep India secular in the sense that the State would have no religion though the people of India would be free in both an individual and corporate sense to follow any religion of their birth or adoption. Under the leadership of Nehru India declared its policy of secularism, with the state aloof from taking sides in religious matters. To understand the real meaning of Indian secularism at the time of independence, one has to be aware of the discussions around the notion of secularism in India at Independence, especially the meaning, understanding or response derived from Gandhi, Nehru and from the Constitution of India.

---

1 Asghar Ali Engineer, "Secularism in India: A Minority Perspective," in *State and Secularism: Perspectives from Asia*, ed. by Michael Heng Siam-Heng and Ten Chin Liew, London: World Scientific Publishing Co. Pte. Ltd, 2010, 171.

2 Satish Chandra, *Historiography, Religion and State in Medieval India*, New Delhi: Har-Anand Publication, 1996, 96-97.

3 Ram Puniyani, *Communal Politics: Facts Versus Myths*, New Delhi: SAGE Publication, 2003, 191.

1. Gandhi and Nehru on Religion/Politics and Secularism

For Gandhi, morality (not theology) is the core of religion[1] and this religion is the basis of life which shapes one's activities. He was of the view that politics divorced from religions will be dragged to destruction. So, he advocated religion and morality as the basis of politics. Gandhi's approach to secularism was based on equal respect for all religions in the public sphere. Nehru, with his Western outlook advocated a liberal model of secularism and was very critical of the dogmas and superstitious beliefs present in religions. At the same time, he also believed that religion has tremendous power to generate peace and comfort to the deep inner cravings of human souls.[2] He advised people not to mix religion and politics in the governance of the state but encouraged respect for all religions.[3] He rejected the role of religion in the public realm because it checks the tendency to transform and progress inherent in human society which he believed secularism could achieve. He always uses the words 'secular democracy' together in his speeches, because he believed that one cannot exist without other.

Nehru's secularism had the following aspects: First, separation of religion from politics and other non-religious areas of life. Second, secularism must mean disassociation of the state from any kind of religion. Third, in a multi religious society all religions should have full freedom and people must extend tolerance to religions other than their own. Equal opportunities must be extended to all religions and there was to be no partiality on the grounds of religion. Finally, secularism means, above all, firm opposition to communalism.[4] He assumed that communalism would die its own natural death when scientific and technological education was imparted and a scientific temperament was cultivated in people.[5] It seems that, on the one hand, the Nehruvian understanding of state secularism as impartiality to religion is somehow similar to the Gandhian notion of *sarva dharma sambhava* (often understood as equal respect for all religions). On the other hand, although both upheld the ideas of secularism, their perspectives as to the place of religion were slightly but significantly different. Both Gandhi and Nehru understood the need of secularism for the modern democratic polity. Though Gandhi and Nehru had similarities and differences on secularism, the real test came with the Constituent Assembly and in the making of the Indian Constitution, particularly the clause on freedom of religion. However, the word

---

1 Bhikhu Parekh, *Gandhi: A Very Short Introduction*, New York: Oxford University Press, 1997, 44.

2 Jawharlal Nehru, *The Discovery of India*, London: Meridian Books Limited, 1951, 11.

3 Neera Chandhoke, *Beyond Secularism: The Rights of Religious Minorities,* New Delhi: Oxford University Press, 1999, 47-48.

4 B. Satapathy and K. Panda, *Secularism an Indian Perspective*, 15. Also see, Kiran Angra and Karamjeet Kaur, eds., *Relevance of Nehru's Thoughts in Present Scenario* (New Delhi: Pragatisheel Prakashan, 2012), 182-183.

5 Asghar Ali Engineer, "Secularism in India- A Minority...," 173.

'secular' was inserted only in 1974 during an amendment. But as we stated at the beginning Hindutva is the greatest challenge for safeguarding the constitutional secularism and its appropriate expression in a multi-faith India. Violations have caused public ridicule of religion by many thinking minds.

2. Current Debates on Secularism

The contemporary discussions on secularism raise important questions like, what is secularism and what does it mean in India today? Is secularism fragile or strong? And so on. Various secular theories are proposed, alternatives are suggested and new interpretations put forward to understand and to push secularism forward. Some critics reject the notion of secularism because of its western origin, arguing that it is a product of western modernity which can only produce undesirable results in an unsuitable context like India. Some others defend secularism with a disguised criticism of its evolution in India. But others argue for the re-conceptualization of secularism to suit the Indian context.

Ashis Nandy (b. 1937), a well known political psychologist and social theorist, argues for the rejection of secularism in India. He sees secularism as an 'imported idea from Europe into South Asia' which is 'increasingly incompatible' to South Asian culture. He sees the cultural inappropriateness and the ineffectiveness of existing secularism in India and feels that the ideology and politics of secularism has exhausted its potential and that 'we may have to work with a different conceptual frame which is already vaguely visible at the borders of Indian political culture.'[1] For him secularism was a product of enlightenment and modernity and this modernization causes religion-as-ideology and then makes secularism meet its challenges to the ideology of 'modern statecraft' (scientific management of secular institution).[2] For Nandy this modern scientific nationalistic secularism is in crisis. Modernization first produced religion-as-ideology and then generates secularism to meet its challenge to the ideology of modern statecraft. Secularism has become a handy attachment and helps the elites or counter-elites to legitimize themselves as the soul arbiters among traditional communities, to claim for themselves a monopoly on religious and ethnic tolerance of political rationality. So, he strongly rejects the notion of secularism by saying, 'To accept the idea of secularism is to accept the ideologies of progress of modernity as the new justification of domination, and the use of violence to sustain these ideologies as the new opiates of the masses.'[3]

Nandy is of the opinion, that instead of trying to build religious tolerance on the good faith or conscience of a small group of de-ethicized, middle-class

1 Ashis Nandy, "The Politics of Secularism and the Recovery of Religious Tolerance," in *Secularism and its Critics,* edited by Rajeev Bhargava (Delhi: Oxford University Press, 1998), 326.

2 Ibid., 324.

3 Ibid., 343.

politicians, bureaucrats and intellectuals a far better and serious venture would be to explore the philosophy, the symbolism and the theology of tolerance in the faith of the citizens. So, he holds that the state system in south Asia must learn something about religious tolerance from every day Hinduism, Islam, Buddhism, and Sikhism rather than wishing that ordinary believers of faiths will learn tolerance from the various fashionable secular theories of statecraft.[1] He draws inspiration from Gandhi's idea of religious tolerance and says, 'Gandhi's religious tolerance came from his anti-secularism, which in turn came from his unconditional rejection of modernity.'[2] But for the following it is an outcome of dialectic between Protestantism and science.

T. N. Madan (b. 1933) is a sociologist and anthropologist of religion and secularity in India, and he does not go for an outright rejection of secularism, rather, he wants it to be 'put in its place,' because it was never indigenous to India. He feels that, secularism in India is impossible as a shared vision, impracticable as a basis for state action and impotent as a blueprint for the future, because by its nature it is incapable of countering religious fundamentalism and fanaticism.[3] He categorically denies the existing notion of secularism saying, 'secularism is the dream of a minority that wishes to shape the majority in its own image, that wishes to impose its will upon history but lacks the power to do so under a democratically organized polity.' Therefore, for him, 'secularism is a myth that draws a cover over the failure of this minority to separate politics from religion in the society in which its members live.'[4]

Further, Madan believes that, we should look towards spreading the ideas of tolerance among the different religious communities rather than saying that all religions are essentially mutually hostile. So, the remedy lies in, among other strategies, educational programmes that include the history of secularism and as well as comparative religion.[5] He strongly believes that a lot could be achieved by spreading knowledge about religious tolerance among the masses. Hence, civil society is more responsible for the harmony, because the state has its limitations. He is of the opinion, that we talk more about minority rights and less about human rights which is perhaps wrong but the truth is that, whether I am Christian, Hindu or Muslim, I have certain human rights. This realization and its implementation are needed for making the society more pluralistic, just and humane.[6] Finally he

---

1 Ibid., 338.

2 Ibid., 344.

3 T.N. Madan, "Secularism and its Place" in *Secularism and its Critics*, ed. by Rajeev Bhargava, Delhi: Oxford University Press, 1998, 298.

4 Ibid., 298.

5 T.N. Madan, "Critiquing Secularism" in *India Revisited: Conversation on Contemporary India*, New York: Oxford University Press, 2008, 76.

6 Ibid., 80-81.

comes to the conclusion that, the only successful way for secularism in south Asia would be with the interreligious understanding.

For Amartya Sen (b. 1933), an educationist, economist and philosopher, secularism does not mean that the 'state must steer clear of any association with any religious matters whatsoever.' But what is needed is a 'symmetric treatment'[1] of all religious communities by the state as the preservation of religious freedom which does not in any way violate the principles of secularism. Therefore, to be secular in the political sense, the state does not have to withdraw from dealing with religions and religious communities altogether. Dealing with several questions levelled against secularism in India, Sen makes it clear that Indian secularism is valid and India can be a secular state in its true sense and even if there are some dissatisfactions, they do little to undermine the basic case for secularism in this country.[2] He offers an unambiguous defense of Nehruvian secularism. He is of the opinion, that abandonment of secularism would make things far more bitter than they currently are.[3] Sen in his book *Argumentative Indian* elaborates his belief that India has a great tradition of living with plurality, the ability to live with difference which is not opposed to secularism.

Rajeev Bhargava (b. 1954), a noted Indian political theorist and exponent, thinks that the secular constitution of India is not a case of total failure; areas of concern should be looked in to. He disagrees with Madan, Nandy and others on the understanding of Indian secularism as a modernist project and its crisis. He argues that these critics fail to see that India developed a distinctively Indian version of secularism.[4] Every context produces its secularism and Indian secularism includes both the traditional and modern principal values of liberty, equality and fraternity/tolerance. He explains two principal form, political secularism and ethical secularism. Political secularism has two versions, one that excludes religion from politics and the other which advocates a principle of political neutrality. Ethical secularism, he believes, under conditions of diversity, remains a defensible ideal.[5] Whilst ethical secularism requires that the believers give up everything of significance, political secularism demands only that every one (believer, non-believer) gives up a little bit of what is of exclusive importance, in order to sustain that which is generally valuable. If everyone is assured that politics will not be invaded by any one ultimate ideal, then all are likely to restrict the scope of their respective ideals.[6] The political secularism requires the exclusion of ultimate ideals

1 Amartya Sen, "Secularism and its Discontents," in *Secularism and its Critics,* ed. by Rajeev Bhargava, Delhi: Oxford University Press, 1998, 456.

2 Ibid., 484.

3 Ibid., 485.

4 Rajeev Bhargava, *The Promise of India's Secular Democracy*, New Delhi: Oxford University Press, 2010, 63-64.

5 Rajeev Bhargava, "What is Secularism For," in *Secularism and its Critics,* 488.

6 Ibid., 495-496.

for the protection of ordinary life, for our need to live, eat, speak and relate to one another.[1] At the same time he also says that, political secularism cannot, in the long run, hold a viable community. It merely provides a way of living together, not a way of living together well. He goes on to say that, although political secularism has a better chance of acceptance, we now find that political secularism has no place of the idea of living together well.[2] Ethical secularism justifies the separation of religion from politics by appealing to ultimate ideals. Here, believers and secularists could hardly ever live together. He believes that in sub-continental culture, it is impossible to separate religious from non-religious practices. He argues that, 'rather than espouse the untenable thesis of the separation of all religious and non-religious practices, it is possible to argue instead for the separation of some religious and non-religious institutions.'[3]

Further, he believes that the primary characteristic of Indian Constitutional secularism is 'principled distance.' In this interpretation, a secular state neither mindlessly excludes all religions nor is it merely neutral towards them.[4] The Indian Constitution departs from the conventional Western model. It allows the state to interfere in religions and opposes domination within and between religions. It is democratic because it fosters equality of status and political equality. It necessitates a departure from strict neutrality to equidistance. This version of secularism opposes domination within religions and between religions as it fosters equality of status and political equality. It will reduce the oppressive practices (like the caste system and patriarchy) within religion if it means intra-religious domination.[5] He also believe that India is a secular state which aspires to the suspension of intra-religious domination which is why the lives of religious minorities in India are comparatively better than the lives of minorities in many other countries.[6] So in India, secularism is not anti-religious but at the same time it is not *sarva dharma sambhava*, equality of all religion. Indian secularism embodies critical respect. This critical respect for all religion is completely consistent with the identification of local faults within them.[7]

This, he calls contextual secularism with a policy of 'principled distance.' It seeks the separation of religion and politics but from a non-absolutist standpoint. It rejects absolutism. Contextual secularism allows politics to keep a principled distance from religious institutions. He says, the relation between religion and politics requires neither fusion nor complete disengagement, but a principled distance with two forms. First, it requires a commitment to some version of

---

1 Ibid., 498-499.

2 Ibid., 498-509.

3 Ibid., 488.

4 Ibid., 87-93.

5 Ibid., 84-85.

6 Ibid., 187.

7 Ibid., 91.

political neutrality. Only when religion has been distanced from politics can the state do its best to help or to hinder different sorts of believers and unbelievers to an equal degree. The second form requires that the boundaries between religion and politics be respected. Each is valuable in its own right and respects their own limits. The world of worship and congregation, prayer and conscience must not be intruded upon by politicians and bureaucrats.[1]

In this context, what kind of secularism is best? It should be based on '(1) a strong defense of minority rights, to be supplemented on the one hand by, (2) deploying the resources of religious tolerance to isolate bigotry and encourage internal reform and on the other hand by, (3) consolidating whatever common good already exists.'[2] So he views that, the desire behind contextual secularism is to secure a dignified life for all, eliminate? discrimination on grounds of religion, check religious bigotry, and manage frantic destructive conflicts that plunge societies into barbarism, violence and cruelty.[3]

Neera Chandoke (b. 1947), a socio-political scientist, subscribes to Bhargava's view of principled distance as the defining characteristic of secularism in India. She says, 'Secularism, we can say, outstripping provisions for freedom and equality, stipulates that the state will maintain an attitude of principled distance from all religious groups.'[4] Further she says that Indian secularism was 'designed to allow people to live together in civility. This is what contemporary critiques of secularism seem to forget.'[5]

However, there are some questions and clarification that need to be addressed in the ongoing discussion on secularism. Nandy has prescribed a renewed religious tolerance which he claims is inherent in every day Hinduism, Islam, Buddhism, etc. Hence, the problem with Indian polity is that the bad side of religion is generalized about religion today. The recovery of religious tolerance is desirable but the nature of tolerance or the level of tolerance differs from religion to religion and emerges from personal convictions, as religion becomes a more personal affair in pluralistic approaches. But the growth of intolerance between religions urges us to use the symbols and theology of various faiths in our interreligious relations. This is possible only when there is openness to others and a willingness to listen without prejudice. To oppose religious fundamentalism, Madan offers two recommendations. One is to keep religion in public life and use its resources of tolerance to prevent fanaticism and interreligious conflicts and the other is to deconstruct the existing idea of secularism and admit the need for some form of secularism reconstruction in the Indian cultural context. In this process, education

1 Ibid., 493-494.

2 Ibid., 542.

3 Ibid., 516.

4 Neera Chandoke, *Beyond Secularism: The Rights of Religious Minorities,* New Delhi: Oxford University Press, 1999, 48.

5 Ibid., 50.

which includes a history of secularism and interreligious programmes largely helps to bring about a relevant understanding. Value based education must take inter religious relationships seriously and inculcate fraternity even from childhood.

At independence, India adopted secularism as its political mantra. However, in the recent past the politicization of religions threatens the secular character of the state, hinders the process of national integration, and gives rise to fear, tension, intolerance and conflicts in society. Therefore, the contemporary discussions on secularism question the genuine values of religions and the credibility of secularism. So, it becomes imperative that the notion of secularism ought to be an ongoing debate in this changing context. Though these debates are sometimes heavily polarized, one thing to be noticed is that the opponents as well as the supporters of secularism in India are equally concerned about the rise of religious fundamentalism and fanaticism.

Understanding Religion and Spirituality through Interreligious Dialogue and Cooperation

In the name of common humanity and fraternity there is a flurry of slogans in the Indian media and the public arena. Still lacking are interfaith dialogues with commitment and openness, promotion of understanding and good will, and collective social engagement in acts of regeneration and reconstruction. When politicians speak about religion they use religion as ideology. Religion as ideology breeds suspicion, prejudice and hatred. But religion as faith is committed to creating a community of believers practising the ethical imperatives of their faith in solidarity with other communities irrespective of their faith and creed. Religion as faith strives for the betterment of others, and contributes towards the welfare of the entire creation. Therefore, the need of the hour is to project religion as faith, using the language of love and faith. This will help us to classify what is religious fundamentalism and fundamentals of the religious scriptures. Israel Selvanayagam distinguishes between fundamentalism and the fundamentals of the Scriptures.[1] He views that religious fundamentalism is one of the greatest threats in the world today. 'Fundamentalism breeds fanaticism and fanaticism breeds bigotry.' 'One of the basic characteristics of all forms of fundamentalism is a lack of humility and openness, which militates against the sharing of faith in a spirit of dialogue.'[2] But those who hold the fundamentals of the scriptures never allow their faith, love and hope to be overcome by fundamentalist trends.[3] In this context, interfaith relations will be of great help in promoting religious tolerance for a peaceful co-existence as it makes reference to the fundamentals of their scriptures. So, tolerance of religions and tolerance within religion are important in all our discussions. The

1 Israel Selvanayagam, *Being Evangelical and Dialogical: Healthy Balance in a Multifaith Context*, Delhi: ISPCK, 2012, 187-194.

2 Ibid., 193-194.

3 Ibid., 194.

religious tolerance that exists in all religions or faiths should be rediscovered not only on an intellectual level but also in day to day living experience with the help of a dialogue of life. At the same time an interfaith approach to national issues may prove to be creative and problem solving.

For example, currently a burning issue relates to the Uniform Civil Code and civil laws to ensure that they conform to equal rights for all citizens with no exceptions. Resolving the differences between the civil laws and the laws of each religion and caste will have to be discussed with the communities concerned and not only with those currently controlling religious and caste codes. According to Romila Thapar a uniform civil code does not mean just doing away with the laws of one religious code[1] but reconsidering jointly the social laws of all religious codes and arriving at a 'common secular civil code.' In this process, injustice and discrimination against minorities and against the underprivileged will need to be negated. She asks, 'Is it not time now to start work on this?'[2] Liberty, equality and fraternity are the democratic principles that promote and give us a vision of a better society.

Public Secular Spirituality: A Way forward

The use of public theology is more than speaking and keeping the 'faith' in the public sphere. Public theology as a form of applied theology is not a direct expression of faith and witness. It is thinking critically, at this time and in this place, about the meaning and truth of claims expressed and implied by religious faith and witness. It focuses in particular on the ethical and political implications of religious self-understanding and life praxis. So, it is a critical thinking along with others concerning religious faith and public life.[3] David Tacey in his book *The Spirituality Revolution: The Emergence of Contemporary Spirituality* recognizes that we have outgrown the ideals and values of previous times and reveals an image of the spiritual situation of our era. Recent discoveries in physics, biology, psychology and ecology have begun to restore status to previously discredited spiritual visions of reality. He believes that we are in the midst of a genuine spiritual revival. I assume that the future of religion depends on having a vision of the genuine spirituality that transcends the political enslavement and uncovers the universal spiritual wisdom that could transform our fractured world in the name of religious fundamentalism and bigotry.

1 For example, widow remarriage is easier in Islam than Hinduism. But this fact is not publicly acknowledged.

2 Romila Thapar "Indian Society and the Secular," *(Jamia Millia Islamia: Asghar Ali Engineer Memorial Lecture,* August 19, 2015*),* http://thewire.in/2015/10/18/what-secularism-is-and-where it needs-to-be-headed-12539 (30 April 2016).

3 David Bromell, "What is public Theology?," (University of Otago: Centre for Theology and Public Issues, May 2011), http://www.otago.ac.nz/ctpi/otago032508.pdf (25 April 2016).

Though India is not part of post secular age, derivative discourse on post secular spirituality is on the way to realisation. Many times modern western understanding of secularism considers religion to be an embarrassment to the core idea of the secular state; progress and human autonomy. But in this post secular age religion in the form of post secular spirituality is returning to the stage. This contemporary phenomenon of secular spirituality, seeks to integrate the natural and supernatural dimensions of human life meaningfully rather than searching for the proofs of God's existence or claiming monopoly over truth. In this context, the term 'spirituality' does not discriminate between religion and denomination, or between believers and unbelievers. This brings us to post-secular holism.[1] Secular spirituality is crucial because it goes beyond the religiosity or piety and pre-fabricated notions. Jesus never discarded his adherence to his religious tradition, but was critical of its deviation. He went beyond by questioning the religious dogmas and customs and focused on promoting fullness of life to all. He never separated people on the basic of religion. In secular spirituality, there may be openness, mutual trust and accommodation and it may have a space for the convergence of all religious faith communities, humanistic values and secular ideas.[2]

Many believe that the concept of secularism in India privatized religion in to the private sphere that created the resurgence within religions and religious fundamentalism. But the freedom of religion in the Indian constitution to preach, practice and propagate, and official recognition of religious communities to maintain their own educational institutions clearly shows that the privatization of religion has not taken place in Indian society,[3] rather it affirms the public presence of religions. The critiques of secularism like Nandy and Madan also believe in the positive presence of religion in public. Interreligious co-operation will help people to be religiously more tolerant towards other faiths and unite them in positive nation-building. This requires every religion to rediscover its theology of religious harmony contextually.

---

1 Cornel W du Toit, "Secular spirituality versus secular dualism: Towards post secular holism as model for a natural theology," http://hts.org.za/index.php/HTS/article/viewFile/416/316 (30 April 2016).

2 Indukuri John Mohan Razu, *Secular Spirituality: Contesting the Aberrations of Religiosity* (Bangalore: Candid Publication, 2014), 76-77.

3 Rajeev Bhargava, *The Promise of India's Secular.,* 104.

10

Freedom of Religion in Secular India From a Legal Perspective

Faizan Mustafa

1. An Alarming Situation

Indian civilization displays a 'manifest tendency towards an outlook that is predominantly religious.' The effect that religion has had on the progress of Indian history is tremendous. It is therefore quite remarkable that the emergence of India as a secular state in the mid-twentieth century is a remarkable social, political and religious phenomenon. Freedom of religion is the topic of contemporary relevance due to the recent release of a report of the United States Commission on International Religious Freedom in which India has been criticized for restrictions placed on free exercise of freedom of religion. Frequent utterances by the RSS and BJP leaders and failure of the Prime Minister in taking any concrete action against these leaders has created a kind of fear in the minds of religious minorities. Even Julio Ribeiro, former Director General of Police had to admit that after the 2014 general elections he lives in fear of his small and peaceful community (Christian) is being targeted. Incidents of violence against Churches have become routine and the so called *GharVapsi* (reconversion to Hinduism) is basically aimed against Christians and Muslims. I will try here to examine constitutional guarantee of freedom of religion in India. How the Indian judiciary has restricted this guarantee through what may be called an 'essentiality test.' How this test has been used by the courts to decide purely religious questions? Finally, I would like to examine the debate on religious conversions and the issue of the constitutionality of anti-conversion laws.

As a starting point, let me state that Islam gives freedom of conscience to all human beings. Muslims can invite non-Muslims to Islam, but they cannot compel them to embrace Islam. They cannot persuade anyone to accept Islam by moral, social or political pressure. Islam not only forbids coercion in the matter of faith but also prohibits the use of abusive language against the deities of other religions.

'Do not abuse those whom they appeal to instead of God.' No Islamic government can ban propagation of other religions in its territory. The followers of other religions are also entitled to construct their places of worship and Muslims cannot interfere with them. This has been from the time of the Prophet (PBUH). The Charter of Madina which lays down the rules to govern relationship of Muslims with non-Muslims was a perfect document of tolerance and human rights and is far superior to British Magna Carta of 1215 which merely talked about few procedural rights. It clearly laid down that Jews will not be injured, nor any enemy aided against them. The Jews were in fact one community with the believers by the orders of the Prophet (PBUH). They were even included in the defense of Madina. The rights which an Islamic State gives to its non-Muslim citizens should not be confused with the rights given to minorities in modern States. An Islamic State is an ideological State. People are divided into two groups: Muslims (who believe in the ideology of the State) and non-Muslims (who do not believe in that ideology). Since the Islamic State is an ideological State it is to be run primarily by those who believe in its ideology. Non-Muslims cannot take up the positions from which they can influence the ideological basis of the State. Otherwise they have full freedom to live according to the precepts of their religion. Any deviation from this position needs to be studied in particular contexts.

2. The Distinctive Nature of Indian Secularism

Secularism in India evolved in a context markedly different from that in the West. While secularism in the west was conceptualized as a response to a history of religious absolutism, in the Indian context it came as a response to the imminent threat posed by communal politics of the freedom struggle. Further, the role that religion played in the struggle for independence and the fact that religion was in fact a way of life for people in India was not lost on the makers of the Indian Constitution.

When faced with the daunting task of drafting the constitutional provisions on the issue of religion and the role of the State in dealing with religious issues in a multi-cultural and a plural society as India, the framers of the Constitution adopted a secular state based on three principles of equality, liberty and neutrality. 'According to the principle of equality, the state was to give no preference to one religion over another. The principle of neutrality demanded that the State did not interfere in religious affairs or organizations of religious communities' and according to the principle of liberty, 'the state was to permit the practice of any religion, within the limits set by certain other basic rights, which the state is also required to protect.' The State does not endorse any particular religion and all the religions enjoy complete protection under the Constitution. Since, India is a pluralistic society and religion, especially has been a very volatile subject in India before independence, the makers of the Constitution thought that in order to maintain stability, it was desirable to have a State which does not adopt any particular religion. Thus, what was contemplated by the framers, was to have a State where secularism is 'not merely a passive attitude of religious tolerance but, a positive concept of equal treatment of all religions.'

It is necessary to examine the constituent assembly debates on the inclusion of secularism in the text of the Constitution. One of the first efforts to include the word 'secular' in the text of the Preamble was made by Shri Brajeshwar Prasad. He advocated that the word 'secular' be incorporated in the text of the Preamble because that would boost the 'morale of the minorities.' Also, such an inclusion would help keep in check the '*loaferism*' that is prevalent in politics. However, the motion was not voted upon. Shri Brajeshwar Prasad's amendment was ridiculed more for the reason that it attempted to make the nation a socialist country rather than a liberal democracy, the agenda with which the Constituent Assembly had set out. The discussion on the concept of secularism took upon itself its final mantle in the dying days of the Constituent Assembly where almost all the members of the Assembly had come to form a common understanding that the establishment of a secular state was inevitable for the foundation of a liberal democracy. It was understood that the movement for the separation of religion from state formed the foundation for the democratization of the latter. Therefore, for India to be recognized as a democracy, secularism was a necessity. Despite this clarity in thought, the most troubling issue was that of the kind of secularism sought to be included. Would secularism mean a complete separation of the state from religion with no overlaps at all? Or, given the Indian context, would fostering equal respect for all religions suit the Indian situation?

One of the first discussions held with respect to secularism was on the wording of the Preamble. Amongst the many motions moved by Assembly members, one of them was to begin the Preamble with the words 'In the name of god.' This was objected to on the basis that the rationale behind adopting a new Constitution was to encourage a scientific temperament amongst the citizens of the country and not stick to arcane and narrow minded models of oath-taking. It was said that by invoking god's name, a 'narrow or sectarian approach' was being adopted. However, the counter-argument to that was that in invoking the name of god, it was not a particular religion which was being appealed to. The opponents to the inclusion of the term God in the Preamble can be informally categorized into two categories – the first type of opposition came from the quarter which insisted that since religion is a matter of personal choice, the will of the collective must not be imposed. Another category of opposition was from a voice which called for separation of religion from the purview of state not because of individual freedom but because the sacred could not be left to the whim of changing majorities. The sacred should not be dependent on the vagaries of democratic voting. Nevertheless, the proposal to include the reference to god was not pursued and therefore not incorporated into the final version of the Constitution.

After having looked at the discussion on the preamble, there are three major positions which can be observed. First, an understanding can be identified as 'no concern theory' which saw a strict line of separation between state and religion. Since democracy was the desired result, individual liberty and freedom were essentials which necessarily meant that the choice of an individual was not to be meddled with when it comes to questions of his or her faith or his or her choice of a religion or the denial of it. This understanding of secularism necessitated that God may not be referred to in any way in the text of the Preamble because that would necessarily leave out those citizens who do not belong to any faith. A strong opposition to the state's involvement in religious affairs was that, given recent independence, the need of the hour was to strengthen the Indian identity, i.e., the identity of being Indian, of being citizens of the Indian state and not belonging to one or the other religious group or community. The goal which was therefore sought was to recognize individuals as citizens of the State and not belonging to any particular community.

It was clear that the Constituent Assembly had finally resolved to not take into consideration matters of religion when it came to dealing with individuals as citizens of the State. Moreover, such an understanding of secularism promoted the impression that religion, in the newly independent nation was a divisive force and therefore had no place in the constitution.

The second understanding of secularism which was also popular among the members of the then Assembly was that the state should maintain its distance from religion not because such a relationship would weaken the State but because it would demean religion. To allow the state to meddle in religious affairs would be make the sacred dependent on the whims of changing majorities, because the components of the state are never stable, whereas religion, in contrast, is. Religion, in this scenario was understood to be a system of absolute truth over which none but the Supreme Being had control.

The third understanding which emerged from the discussions on the concept of secularism was that of 'equal respect.' This understanding, much like the first, called for religious liberty and the individual being free to decide upon his or her religious affiliations. However, taking a more practical understanding of the ground realities, it called for the State to play a role in religious affairs, although limiting it to respect all religions alike, and not favoring one community over another. In a deeply religious society such as India, according to this theory, it was imperative that the State respect all religions alike.

Having observed the discussions with respect to the drafting of the Preamble, it became quite clear that there was a constant clash between the no-concern and equal respect theory of secularism. However, such a clash was not limited to the discussion on the Preamble alone but pushed such considerations into other provisions as well even where there was a hint of religious involvement. Such provisions included provisions with respect to parliamentary procedure and the linguistic reorganization of states.

3. The Core Issue of the Freedom of Religion

There were discussions as to the very name of this freedom. It was described as the right to worship or practice. It was also proposed to be named as the right to freedom of conscience, to freedom of religious worship and to freedom to profess religion. However, later the Constituent Assembly's Minorities' Sub-Committee decided to rephrase that same right as the right to freedom of conscience and the right freely to profess, practice and propagate religion.

The argument against freedom of religion to be restricted to merely that of worship was that by doing so, religion was being narrowed to only a set of rituals meant to be performed only in a circumscribed place of worship such as a temple or a mosque. Such an understanding truly ignored the real meaning of religion, which was understood as a way of life. Another factor that attributed merit to the argument of the proponents of 'practice' was that India being a multi-religious society, the Constitution could not be expected to lay down the essentials for all religions and hence to broadly define right to freedom of religion in terms of 'practice' would be a more tenable option.

The proponents of 'worship' understood that to interpret freedom of religion only in terms of 'practice' would be to exonerate all those practices which were by nature anti-social such as the practice of dowry or *sati* (widow-burning) or even the purdah (veil) system. All these practices would from thence take on the garb of sanctity of practice as they would be protected for reasons of freedom of practice of religion, although in themselves being against the freedom of an individual. Another contentious issue with respect to freedom of religion was the right to propagate the faith. This entailed discussions on the conversion of minors and the role of consent. Finally, when the draft Constitution's articles relating to religion were being discussed, it was recommended that a separate provision be included expressly to declare that the State had no role to play in the sphere of religion. Despite such deliberation and discussion, the phraseology of the kind of freedom of religion envisaged in the Constitution remained ambiguous till the very last days of the Constituent Assembly.

After the discussions on the two extreme positions with respect to secularism, there did emerge a third 'middle path' which sought to merge the two extremes. To provide an illustration, this theory would seek to combine the right of religious worship and uniform civil code with the political reservation for minorities. However, this position didn't gain much popularity and failed to make its way into the final text of the Constitution. The position that finally found its way into the Constitution defined the right to freedom of religion as the one to 'practice' and not 'worship.'

The drafting committee of the constitution was in two minds as to the extent of the right to freedom of religion. While K.M. Munshi proposed that the right to religion should include the right to freely practice and profess the religion, without any aid from the State, Ambedkar, the Chairman of the Constituent Assembly, proposed that no person could deny their civil obligation to meet the demands of their religion. However, K.M. Panikkar objected to Ambedkar's proposal saying that there might be some exceptions where one might have to give up their civil obligations to meet the demands of their religion. A consensus was finally reached on practice of religion but subjected to certain limitations, like that of public order, health and morality. The debate was not yet over. There were also debates over whether to include the 'right to propagate.' There was also a demand for an explicit article preventing any ties between State and the religion. Thus, the position as it stands today is that the State has to maintain a neutral position reasonably distant from all religions equally. Article 25 of the Indian Constitution ultimately gives the right to all citizens freely *profess, practice and propagate* their respective religion; subject to certain limitations such as those pertaining to *public order, morality and health.*

In order to maintain the neutrality of the State towards all religions, members of the Constituent Assembly suggested keeping religious instruction out of State funded institutions, to prevent the intermingling of the State and Religion. The argument forwarded by Mahmood Ali Baig was very interesting and has mirrored the argument of many a multi-culturist who has advocated personal laws' continuation as they are linked to the right to religious freedom. And since, for the pro-personal law group, religion is more a 'way of life' and less of a spiritual phenomenon, for a free *practice* of religion, it would be of paramount importance that the communities follow their own means of civil/social regulation. Hence, the arguments, particularly in favour of the personal laws, were subsumed by the idea that religious freedom and religious laws were interconnected, and the former was almost meaningless when the latter was being interfered with.

The original men of the 'no-concern camp,' Munshi and Ambedkar finally found some middle ground. It was decided that the Uniform Civil Code (UCC) would not be immediately enforced (or be justifiable); however, there could be gradual implementation when there was representation from communities seeking to accept a common civil code. Hence, if there was no acceptance of such a code, and if the communities were not yet ready to give up their personal laws, there could be no UCC. From the Constituent Assembly Debates on the Uniform Civil Code and Personal Laws, we could conclude that the complexity of the issue essentially lies in the question of whether we treat the idea of a UCC as a factor that could unite diverse groups with various cultural backgrounds or as a question of religious freedom. In addition, whether personal laws are in harmony with constitutional safeguards enshrined by the Indian constitution or not.

Firstly, there is a presupposition that a 'uniform civil code' means a 'common civil code' without making any enquiry into alternative interpretations. In other words, 'uniformity' does not necessarily mean that India must give up on its twin principles of pluralism and equality. It means that they must have been seen as harmoniously entwined and sufficiently balanced. There is no basis for us to interpret a 'uniform civil code' to mean a 'common civil code.' Instead, the difference allows us to treat these 'common base values' as those of equality, gender and social justice. However, the reform must be organic – as has been the case with the recent introduction of the model nikah-nama. The Indian constitution is quite detailed in the manner of which it organizes itself in relation to religion. The right to religious freedom is detailed in Articles 25-28 of the constitution. The Indian Constitution combines freedom of religion clauses with a mandate to the state to intervene in religious affairs. Article 25 allows the state to regulate or restrict any 'economic, financial, political or other secular activity which may be associated with religious practice.' Article 25 (1) of the Constitution guarantees to every person the freedom of religion in India. However, Article 25(2) gives the 'State the power to make any law regulating or restricting any economic, financial, political or other secular activity which may be associated with the religious practice.' The State can also intervene and make legislation providing for any social welfare or reform or to throw open Hindu religious institutions of public character to all classes and sections of the society. Thus, the State has the power to regulate secular activities associated with religious practice but not the regulation of religious practices as such. The activities which the State seeks to regulate must be of an 'economic, commercial or political character though these may be associated with religious practice.' The question which now arises is how to decide whether certain activity is religious or secular. This distinction becomes important because if it is religious, it cannot be regulated. This brings forth a further question - as to what is 'religion' and which practices are 'religious.' The Supreme Court answered this question in the *Sri Lakshmana* case in 1996: 'religion is the belief which binds the spiritual nature of men to a super-natural being. It includes worship, belief, faith, devotion, etc., and extends to rituals. Religious right is the right of a person believing in a particular faith to practice it, preach it and profess it.' What religious practice has to be decided by the court with reference to the doctrines of particular religions or practices regarded as tenets of religion. In order that a practice be treated as a part of the religion, it must be regarded by the religion as an 'essential' part of that religion. This, it is said, is necessary otherwise even purely secular practices, not essential to that religion, will be clothed with religious sanction and may claim to be treated as religious practices within the meaning of Article 25.

The right to freedom is further clarified in Article 26 which provides for corporate freedom to all religious denominations, permitting them to maintain their affairs in matters of religion, to own and acquire property and to administer property in accordance with law. Then Article 27 lays down that taxes could be levied for religious purposes as long as it is not specifically appropriated for the payment of the expenses of any particular religion. It is argued that Article 27 seeks to prohibit any spending of a public nature on religious activities. There are two problems with this view. First, the framing of Article 27 is such that it does not seem to proscribe the enactment of a law to incur expenses for the promotion or maintenance of any particular religion. It merely protects a citizen from being compelled to pay such a tax. The other view is that Article 27 only prohibits the compulsion of a citizen to pay taxes to be *appropriated specifically* in favour of a particular religion and that the levy of a general tax for the benefit of all religions would be perfectly constitutional. This view finds support even in the opinion of D.D. Basu who argues that Article 27 would not render unconstitutional any appropriation or levy of taxes that either benefits religious institutions along with secular ones without any discrimination, or by which all religious institutions benefit equally. Thus, Article 27 does not cover the issues of government spending on religion entirely or, as Smith puts it, it 'may reinforce the armour of individual rights, but it sidesteps the basic question of public policy.'

The question, then, that begs to be answered is, considering that Article 27 does not explicitly prohibit state spending on religion but merely proscribes the compulsion of an individual to contribute to such spending, does this imply that the Constitution permits the state to expend public funds on religion? If such an inference is readily drawn, it would lead to an apparent inconsistency in the constitutional scheme of Articles 27 and 28 of the Indian Constitution. While the former seemingly suggests that the state can expend public funds on religion so long as it does so equally for all religions, Article 28 seems to prohibit state funding or the giving of aid for religious instruction in educational institutions. One might object that Article 28 allows partial funding of institutions imparting religious instruction and does not forbid state funding of religious instruction in toto, but this deliberate exclusion can be rationalized on account of the social justice role that the welfare state in India plays by recognizing that while religious minorities have been given the right to establish educational institutions of their choice, they may in fact be unable to do so and may require some financial assistance from the state. By preventing institutions that receive such assistance from providing religious instruction, the state will in fact detract from the promise of secularism made to the religious minorities in India. Finally, Article 28 provides that religious instruction could be provided even in educational institutions partly funded by the state provided that the institution had been established under an endowment or trust which required that religious education is imparted.

In 1976, the word 'Secular' was added to the Preamble of the Constitution by the 42nd Amendment, thereby making the concept of secularism explicit in the constitution. Later, in the landmark judgment of *His Holiness Keshavananda*

Bharti v. State of Kerala,[1] the Supreme Court held 'secularism' to be a part of the basic structure of the Constitution. The Nine-judge bench of the Supreme Court went on to discuss the concept of secularism in India and noted that '...while the citizens of this country are free to profess, practice and propagate such religion, faith or belief as they choose, so far as the State is concerned, i.e., from the point of view of the State, the religion, faith or belief of a person is immaterial. To the state all are equal and all are entitled to be treated equally.' Similarly, there have been several cases of different kinds recorded in the judicial history of India. We will point out some of them in due course.

4. Indian Secularism and Essential Practice Test

In the absence of a definition of secularism in the Indian Constitution, the Supreme Court's reading of it is noteworthy. Judicial interpretations, for the most part, have declared secularism as the fundamental law of the land and sought to delineate the boundaries of the sacred and the secular.[2] Secularism is part of the preamble to the Indian Constitution and has been defended by the Supreme Court as part of the un-amendable basic structure of the constitution.[3] The courts first declared secularism to be part of the un-amendable basic structure of the Indian Constitution in the *Keshavananda Bharathi*[4] case but it was the *Bommai*[5] case where the Supreme Court comprehensively held that secularism is central to the Indian Constitution. Though, the Indian idea of Secularism is different from the western one, it still adheres to equal treatment of all religions. The Supreme Court's idea of secularism as developed in the *Bommai* case is three pronged. First, the court held that secularism was necessary to ensure the right to freedom of religion and thus, the right to equal treatment by the state irrespective of religious affiliation.[6] Second, the court asserted that secularism (the constitutional frame in relation to religion) derives from the Indian civilizational or cultural ethos of tolerance and communal harmony.[7] Third, based on the belief that Secularism comes from Indian civilizational ethos, the court pronounced in the words of Justice Jeevan Reddy, 'a positive secularism, asserting for itself a revolutionary and civilizational role to decisively intervene in situations where

1 AIR 1973 SC 1461.

2 Sanghamita Padhy, *Secularism and Justice: A Review of Indian Supreme Court Judgments*, EPW Vol. 39, No. 46/47, Nov. 20-26, 2004, 5027-5032.

3 42nd amendment to the Indian Constitution.

4 (1973) 2 SCC 255.

5 (1994) 3 SCC 1.

6 Justice Ramaswamy observed: '*the state guarantees individual and corporate religious freedom and deals with an individual as citizen irrespective of his faith and religious belief and does not promote any particular religion nor prefer one against another. The concept of the secular State is, therefore, essential for successful working of the democratic form of Government.*'

7 (1994) 3 SCC 1.

such secular civilizational values are under threat.' Therefore, in addition to freedom of religion, the Indian secularism has also been interpreted by courts to have an interventionist reformist side.[1] This stems from the inclusion of anti untouchability type provisions in the constitution.

The essential practices test strikes the conception of secularism at two levels. The first limb of Indian secularism is freedom of religion. The essential practices test takes away this freedom of religion as the practitioners of the religion are not allowed to decide what constitutes part of their religion and what does not. This becomes ever more problematic as secularism mandates that the organs of state, including judiciary, treat all religions equally. The application of essential practices test by the Supreme Court doesn't seem to be in line with the principle of secularism. The Court has interpreted and disapproved practices of both Hinduism and Islam for not being essential enough to be offered an Article 26 protection.

The Supreme Court while applying the essential practices test to Islam seems to be influenced by majority Hindu conceptions. This is a very dangerous trend of freedom of religion of the minority community being denied through the application of essential practices test which can be illustrated by the following three examples. (i) In *Hanif Qureshi v. State of Bihar*[2] case the Supreme Court's judgment on Cow Slaughter, was very much influenced by the majority community's beliefs regarding cows being revered by the Hindu community and their aversion to cow slaughter. The issue was complex because the Quran and the tradition allow cow slaughter and eating of beef; the Mughal Emperors banned it out of respect for Hindu sentiments although beef eating was in practice in ancient times; in any case the right of a butcher cannot be taken away. (ii) In the *Ismail Faruqui v. Union of India*[3] case while dealing with the issue of the acquisition of Babri Masjid land, the court held that while offering of prayers is an essential practice, the offering of such prayers in the mosque is not, unless the place has a particular religious significance in itself. The Court relied on the decisions of the Lahore High Court which allowed for the acquisition of mosques to answer the question of the religious significance of praying in the mosque. The most obvious authority, the Quran, was not referred to by the Court. The Quran and Hadith prescribe congregational prayer and mosques provide the means to achieve this objective. The land under dispute here was the Babri masjid and it was acquired by the Indian state after the majority Hindu community staked a claim to it. This example again shows how the court's decisions can be influenced

1 Mathew John, "Indian Exceptionalism? A discussion on India's experiment with constitutionalism secularism," Asia Research Center Working Paper - 17.LSE - 2006.

2 AIR 1958 SC 731.

3 AIR 1995 SC 605.

by pressure from the majority community.[1] (iii) The case of *Fasi v. S.P of Police,*[2] and in this case, the petitioner, a police officer, challenged a regulation which did not permit him to grow a beard as violation of his freedom to practice his religion. The petitioner placed reliance on the Hadith number 780.781 given in Sahih-Al-Bukhari. Before discussing the Court's ruling, it is essential to understand the position occupied by the Hadith and the authenticity of the authority cited by the petitioner. After the Quran, it is the teachings and practices of Prophet Muhammad that are sources of Islamic life and law.[3] Additionally, Sahih Bukhari is considered to be the most authentic of the collections of prophetic teachings. The Court rejected the petitioner's argument by relying on the fact that certain dignitaries do not wear a beard and that the petitioner did not have a beard in his previous years of practice. Therefore, the Court here chose to rely on the fact that certain members of the community did not follow the practice without even dealing with the authentic sources cited by the petitioners and their importance in Islam. The Supreme Court's repeated rejection of practices central to Islam show a scant disregard of secularism by the same institution which declared it to be part of the basic structure of Indian Constitution.

The second problem is the reformist agenda followed by successive Supreme Court judges through the essential practices doctrine. The most striking aspect of the essential practices doctrine is the attempt by the Court to fashion religion in the way a modern state would like it to be rather than accept religion as represented by its practitioners. The Court's use of the essential practices doctrine has served as a vehicle for legitimating a rationalized form of high Hinduism and delegitimizing usages of popular Hinduism as superstition.[4]

Nearly all the cases where the Supreme Court applied the essential practices test to Hinduism, display the judges' inherent desire to reform and modernize the majority religion. In *Shirur Mutt*[5] the Supreme Court started with its mission to reform temple entry for untouchables. This was continued in the *Devaru*[6] case. The court targeted temple intermediaries like priests and attendants (in cases like *ERJ Swami v. State of TN*[7]) by declaring them to be a non-essential part of the religion. This trend was given a boost by Justice Ramaswamy in 1990s when he allowed for state regulation of all major Hindu shrines like Tirupathi, Jagganath,

1 Mathew John, Op.cit., 8.

2 (1985) I LLJ 463 Ker.

3 Aisha Musa, "Hadith as scripture: Discussion on the Authority of Prophetic Traditions in Islam," Published by Palgrave Macmillan (2008).

4 Mathew John, op.cit., 3.

5 AIR 1954 SC 282.

6 AIR 1958 SC 255.

7 AIR 1972 SC 1586.

Kashi Vishwanath and Vaishno Devi.[1] Therefore, it is quite evident that judges like Justice Gajendergadkar and Ramaswamy pursued their own agendas of reforming and modernizing Hinduism under cover of the essential practices test.

These reformist tendencies have continued through numerous future cases like the *Tandav dance* case[2] and others. These reformists of the Supreme Court making judgements through the essential practices doctrine are clearly against the idea of secularism as it takes away the freedom of religion of some groups by not allowing them to decide their own practices. Therefore, it can be stated without any doubt that the essential practices test is opposed to the idea of Secularism as it has taken away the freedom of religion from all communities and has especifically failed Islam.

The whole concept of providing constitutional protection only to those elements of religion which the court considers 'essential' is very problematic. First, it assumes that there can be objective criteria to decide what is essential and what is not. This is a false assumption as the idea of religion is a very subjective concept. As observed by the Australian High Court in the case of *Jehovah's Witness v. Commonwealth,*[3] 'What is religion to one is superstition to another?' Second, such an approach assumes that one element or practice of religion is independent of the others. This approach assumes that some things are central to religion and others are incidental. This is not the correct understanding of religion as all elements and practices together constitute a religion. Third, this approach assumes that religions are static and what was central a few centuries ago should still be central today. This is wrong as like everything else, religions also change and evolve with time. Therefore, a practice which may not have been central two centuries ago and thus be absent from the scriptures, may have become central today.

The essential practices test has proved to be the biggest deterrent to freedom of religion in India. It was created by the Supreme Court out of thin air and without any constitutional basis. The constitution of India provides protection to religion and not only to 'essential' or 'central' elements of a religion. The doctrine has been propounded by judges who considered themselves to be social reformers and not just the adjudicators of disputes. The reformist judges misused the doctrine to throw out practices which they considered superstitious and backward.

Until 2004, the stand taken on the basis of the utility of cattle in the Hanif Qureshi judgement was followed while dealing with cases concerning

---

1 Ronojoy Sen, *Legalizing Religion: The Indian Supreme Court and Secularism*, Policy Study - 30, East West Centre Washington - 2007. Available at www.eastwestcenterwashington.org/publications, 13.

2 Commissioner of Police v. Acharya Jagdishwarananda (2004) 12 SCC 770.

3 (1943) 67 CLR 116.

cow slaughter.[1] In 2004, in the case of *Om Prakash v. State of Uttar Pradesh,*[2] the prohibition of the sale of eggs in the municipal region of Rishikesh (a Hindu pilgrim city) was upheld by the Supreme Court on the grounds of culture and religious values of the dominant narrative of the religion. It was the opinion of the court that the inhabitants and pilgrims would prefer a *clean* vegetarian environment in the city. This approach has taken away the very basic freedom of a community to decide what is part of their religion and what is not. Thus, the Supreme Court must reconsider its reliance on the 'essential practices' test. Likewise, there are many challenges to freedom of religion granted in the Constitution.

5. Politicization of Religion

The General Elections of 2014 were eye opener for all of us on how sometimes the vote block politics becomes fatal for the Secular nature of the country. The General Elections of 2014 saw the re-emergence of Bharitya Janta Party (BJP) into power after the 1999 elections and thus claiming a heavy majority in the Parliament.[3] BJP as a party has always been accused/suspected of its pro-hindutva character and its ties with organisations such as RSS (Rashtriya Swayamsevak Sangh),[4] which is known for its strong beliefs in establishing India as *Hindu Rajya* (nation for the Hindus).[5] The 2014 elections saw some explicit examples of religious fanaticism and vote block politics. The BJP worked on an agenda of luring votes from the Hindu community, which is a clear numerical majority in India. Inclusion of the Babri Masjid dispute in the BJP election manifesto,[6] appealing to Hindu population by use of religious symbols, addressing the crowd with continuous reference to Hindu Gods and Goddesses - all part of religion based politics in India.

While, there is a sufficient evidence now to debase the legitimacy of the present Government on pretext of it being a threat to Secularism, what has happened since the General Elections has only made matters worse. There are several current incidents, conceptions and statements that have been made since the elections that have made situation no better. The case against BJP has only gone worse. Hate speech specifically targeting the Muslims have made it into the

1 Abdul Hakim Quraishi v. State of Bihar, AIR 1961 SC 448; Hashmatullahv. State of Madhya Pradesh, (1996) 4 SCC 391.

2 AIR 2004 SC 1896.

3 Refer: http://zeenews.india.com/news/general-elections-2014/results

4 Christian Jaffrelot, "Myth of Moderation," May 12, 2014; Available at: http://indianexpress.com/article/opinion/columns/myth-of-moderation/

5 Sunny Hundal, "Does Narendra Modi threaten secular and liberal India?," May 16, 2014; Available at: http://edition.cnn.com/2014/05/16/opinion/india-election-modi-hindu-nationalism/

6 Arshad Afzal Khan, "Come polls! Modi vows to build grand 'Ram Temple,' July 7th, 2013; Available at: http://timesofindia.indiatimes.com/india/Come-polls-Modi-aide-vows-to-build-grand-Ram-temple/articleshow/20951406.cms

news over and over again. There are prominent figures who have made statements that completely wipe out the meaning and importance assigned to secularism by the Constitution of India. Particular deities have been roped into election campaigns. There are accusations and counter-accusations that arouse communal passions. In a secular country there should be neutral fact finding committees as the official Election Commission also is suspected of indirectly siding with a particular religious or caste community. The accusation against Muslims for conducting '*Love Jihad*'[1] on Hindu Girls has flared up a new wave of agony; and the members of RSS have been attacking Muslim boys and couples on the pretext of *Love Jihad*.[2] In the other news, there are statements also being made by influential persons, stating that all Indians are scientifically and culturally Hindus, thereby completely ignoring the presence of all other religious communities in India.[3] Besides, saffronization of school education with text-books of a distorted history of India, particularly stressing that the Vedic Aryans were indigenous people and allowing Hindu symbols in government spaces create feelings of insecurity among the religious minorities.

6. Anti-conversion Laws as a Violation of Freedom of Religion

There are two arguments which can be made to further the argument that anti-conversion laws as they exist today violate the freedom of religion as guaranteed under Article 25 of the Indian Constitution. The first argument hinges on an argument which was not considered by the Supreme Court in the *Stanislaus* case. The Court, while articulating the right to convert, understood it to be a part of the right of propagation alone and hence held that such a right does not exist. However, the court did not adjudge and decide whether conversion was an essential practice under Christianity which deserves constitutional protection and sidestepped the whole issue while determining the meanings of the word propagation. *Arguendo*, it can also be argued that the original intent of the concept of propagation under Article 25 included the right to convert also. The Constitutional Assembly Debates gives a clear idea of the burning debate which took place during the inclusion of Draft Article 19 (which later became Article 25) from December 3-6, 1948.[4] The presentday concerns of forced conversions were raised then also and a comprehensive answer was received from the floor of the house. K.M. Munshi categorically noted that the Christian community

1 Term coined to define a situation when a Muslim boy marries a Hindu Girl.

2 Farzana Versey, "Colonising India's Muslims: Love, Jihad and Political Lusts"; October 17- 19, 2014; Counterpunch; Available at: http://www.counterpunch.org/2014/10/17/love-jihad-and-political-lust/

3 "All Indians are Hindus-Culturally and Scientifically"; October 17, 2014; *Times of India*; Available at: http://timesofindia.indiatimes.com/city/lucknow/All-Indians-are-Hindus-culturally-and-scientifically-says-Swamy/articleshow/44843049.cms

4 H.M. Seervai, *Constitutional Law of India: A Critical Commentary* (4th edition), Vol. 2, Universal Law Publishing Co., 1287.

demanded a right to propagation not with the intention of converting the masses but because propagation was a fundamental part of practising and professing their faith.[1] It was also noted in those debates that the right to propagation should not be seen as a right given to the minority community but as a general right available to all communities so that all people are made increasingly aware about other religions. S.V. Santahanam was of the opinion that the right to conversion was introduced with due care as it was not an absolute right but subject to the state regulation when force or undue influence is being exerted.

Moreover, if a reductionist understanding of propagation is taken seriously, the inclusion of such a term in the Constitution would be rendered meaningless. This is so because the mere right to propagate for the enlightenment of others would already be covered under the Right to free speech and expression under Article 19 (1) (a) of the Constitution.[2] Thus, the right to convert was actually included in Article 25 and sufficient safeguards have been provided for that right also. It has been demonstrated above that anti conversion laws are less related to maintenance of public order but more to do with controlling religion and religious freedom. It goes against the idea of religious equality as the courts have failed to recognize an important tenet of non-Hindu religions like Christianity and Islam. Therefore, the only unfortunate conclusion which can be derived is that these legislations are motivated by religious ideology more than anything else.

Thus, the anti conversion laws must be to be understood in a context where the commitment of the legislative of the state to the cause of secularism is questionable. In such circumstances, it is the duty of the legal system to be the gatekeeper and not allow religious intolerance to have the upper hand. The major consequence of the current state of anti conversion legislation is that it makes the convert not the subject of the conversion but the object of the conversion by taking him/her out of the analysis.[3] It recreates and reinforces social hierarchies by portraying certain sections of the society as inherently unable to take decisions on their own and therefore weak. The ultimate result of such legislation is that individuals find it harder to change their own identity without the close scrutiny of the state. It seems as if the right to convert others is constricted; however, the right to convert oneself is at best a matter of indifference.

---

1 *Constituent Assembly of India* (Vol. VII), December 6, 1948, available at: http://parliamentofindia.nic.in/ls/debates/vol7p2oa.

2 "Anti-Conversion Laws: Challenges to Secularism and Fundamental Rights," South Asia Human Rights Documentation Centre, *Economic and Political Weekly*, 2008, 70.

3 Laura Dudley Jenkins, *Legal Limits on Religious Conversion in India, 71 Law and Contemporary Problems* (2008), 109; available at http://scholarship.law.duke.edu/cgi/viewcontent.cgi?article=1469&context=lcp [accessed 14 October 2012].

Concluding Remarks

In my opinion, the state has to take a middle path between the assurance of complete religious freedom and stringent restrictions on this freedom by regulating it. Communities are a unifying force between human beings and they are formed for the successful pursuit of each individual's objectives.[1] When community interests and individual self-interests come in conflict, these have to be reconciled. For this to be achieved, there must be an authority which carries out the duty of reconciliation by enabling freedoms.[2] It is extremely important to have an authority to do this as reconciliation will not happen if structural inequalities exist between groups pursuing different interests in a society. The authority should then assume the role of a neutral arbiter and not favour one group over the other. By enabling freedoms, this authority, in fact, facilitates the realisation of true freedom, which if left to be reconciled and realised by individuals in the groups themselves would not be possible.

This forms the theoretical basis for endorsing intervention by the state to impose regulations to curb the excesses of the freedom of religion. In this context, it is imperative for the state to enable religious freedoms to all religions. What freedom of religion means to one group might not mean the same to another. Hence, enabling freedom of religion to all religious groups must be achieved in a substantive manner, and not a formal manner. This means that structural inequalities and power imbalances in a plural society need to be taken into consideration by the State whilst imposing restrictions on a particular religious group. For instance, the Indian society has undergone the trauma of partition,[3] and in this framework, it is important for consideration to be given to what it means for a minority community[4] to practice their religion without fear of being discriminated against, and also to consider the degree to which the right to dignity may enable an individual or a group of persons to enjoy the right to freedom of religion without the expectation and fear of either implicit or visible manifestations of hate and incitement to religious hatred.

On the whole, in multi-religious Indian secularism and freedom of religion may seem to reflect a noble ideal that can lead to respect for religion and spirituality. But, as this paper has shown, in light of the the legal implications around issues pertaining to different religious communities, even genuine commitment and serious practice are subjected to ridicule and distortion in the frenzy of majority politics and half-baked secular thinking. Is a fresh exploration with an open mind

1 John Finnis, "Community, Communities, and Common Good" in *Natural Law and Natural Rights* 134, 136 (2nd ed., 2011).

2 Arthur Ripstein, *Authority and Coercion*, 32 Philosophy and Public Affairs 7 (2004).

3 The aftermath of the partition of the country witnessed many instances of communal riots between Hindus and Muslims.

4 In this context, the minorities being discussed are Muslims.

possible? The Indian Constitution assumes the role of 'a secular scripture' which needs to be interpreted justly without prejudice; otherwise, governments and judiciaries also may move close to the religious fundamentalists!

11

Human Sex, Sacred or Profane? Hindu-Christian Perceptions

Israel Selvanayagam

An Observation

It is little wonder that the groundbreaking book *Sex in the World's Religions* by the well-known writer of comparative religion, Geoffrey Parrinder, starts with the following words: 'Sex and religion are two of the commonest concerns of mankind. Often opposed to physical and spiritual, temporal and eternal, they seem to occupy different and clearly defined territories yet they are always crossing the frontiers. For man cannot live by bread alone and even his sexual intercourse is shot through with fantasy, while religion takes and turns its eyes upon the slightest manifestation of sex, as the history of the great world religions demonstrates.'[1]

First, Parrinder deals with "Sacred Sex in India" and the penultimate chapter is entitled "Christian Diversity." He rightly observes that 'Nowhere have the close relationships of religion and sex been displayed more clearly than in India and, with divine and human models of sexual activity, sacramental views of sex were abundantly illustrated.'[2] He points out that the sacred-profane polarity has been maintained, overcome and balanced. Sexuality reached its height with divine symbols such as phallus and yoni, divine couples engaged in romantic plays, getting married, copulating and so on. The cultural norm of the female being malevolent before marriage and benevolent after along with moments of tension is noted. Even the obscenity of young women being made to walk naked before a god is not concealed and often such acts are spiritualized while eroticism and asceticism are kept at opposite poles with tension; the stress of excess and extremity is kept in check. Sex and divinity have inspired much Indian painting, art, literature and architecture. In Christianity, sex is dealt with less explicitly with

1 G. Parrinder, *Sex in World's Religions*, London: Sheldon Press, 1980, 1.

2 Ibid., 5.

an emphasis on faithfulness in a wedded relationship. The matter is complicated because of the convergence of the views and practices of Judaism, Greek traditions, the customs of ancient Rome and the challenges of modern thought. In this paper, we will present both the Hindu and Christian traditions as both distinctive and interactive from a dialogical perspective.

Cotton and Fire

There is a saying in southern India that 'do not put cotton and fire close to each other' signifying the closeness of persons of the opposite sex. Obviously, there is a warning against attraction, romantic aberration and addiction, obsession and obscenity in matters of sex. It is hardly surprising that for a long time, study and scholarly scrutiny of human sex was regarded a taboo. As observed:

> Until comparatively recently it was thought improper to devote any study of the sexual characteristics of human beings; puritanism went as far as to set the phenomena of sex outside the scope of legitimate investigation, and men who have thought of and studied this subject were looked on askance and with suspicion, and their work was often submitted to ignorant and prejudiced moral sensors, who, by their unfair actions, added to the obloquy under which this subject remained.[1]

This is in spite of the fact that the problem of sexual activity or non-activity (or impotence) is the cause of number of breakdowns in families, relationships and prejudiced assessments from the perspective of cultural norms.

While many want to celebrate sex as the greatest divine gift, what makes it ambivalent? Basically, it has two sides. On the one hand, it is seen as the expression of love, satisfaction of fulfilling an innate, inherent and inner urge, and the means of producing a family. On the other hand, it often generates irresponsible behaviour even with violence and falls victim to commercialization. In India, particularly among the non-westernized, even if the sexual urge is burning like a fire inside, outwardly there are expressions of artificial shyness and rebuking smiles. Even with the sexual proximity of western cultures, sex is treated with some sort of concealment if not reverence. For example, no one would normally ask his/her friend 'how was the sex last night?' It seems there is a hesitancy about feeling, understanding and expressing sex.

More than any other religious traditions the Christian and Hindu traditions in various measures affirm sex and attach to it some sort of sacramental significance and divine involvement. In this essay, we will explore the original significance of sex in these two traditions, discuss issues of chastity and its power which can turn violent, the projection of the tension between extremes, counter-cultural notions to the customary norms of purity and pollution with reference to Hindu and Christian stories.

1 O.A. Wall, *Sex and Sex Worship in the World*, Delhi: Inter-India Publications, 1979, 38.

Sex in Judeo-Christian Tradition

In both the Hindu and Judeo-Christian traditions, sex is seen as appropriate for stories of creation. Thus, in the creation story of the Bible God created humans as man and woman for companionship and enjoyment of close intimacy. Adam declared that Eve was the bone of his bones and flesh of his flesh. Leaving his parents, Adam was united with his wife and they became one flesh. 'The man and his wife were both naked, and they felt no shame' (Gen. 2: 25). After the transgression, part of God's punishment for Eve was 'Your desire will be for your husband, and he will rule over you' (3: 16). What is missing in the whole of the Bible is the new condition in the redeemed life! However, one insight is that sexual intercourse was seen as the mark of deep intimacy and profound knowing, e.g., 'Adam knew his wife' (4: 1). But later in the Bible there are excesses, extremes with cruel acts (e.g. David and Solomon) of violence in relation to sex. There are allegories of sexual acts to signify God's loving yet agonizing love with his people and their drift towards prostitution.

The Bible is full of admonitions against adultery, fornication, etc. However, we do not have any clues about the sexuality of Jesus and his apostles. In a dialogue with his disciples Jesus said that some were eunuchs by birth and others made by men and still others renounced marriage because of the kingdom of heaven (Mt. 19: 12). Elsewhere he said that the cost of discipleship was to renounce one's wife and family (Lk. 14: 26). Paul had a veiled jealousy against some other apostles being accompanied by wives (1 Cori. 9: 5). In the context of expecting the imminent return of Jesus there was controversy over marrying. Paul's advice was that the unmarried should remain so. But, he adds, 'if they cannot control themselves, they should marry, for it is better to marry than to burn with passion' which would also reduce immorality (1 Cor. 7: 1, 8-9).

Nevertheless, the positive, even sacramental side of sex has been maintained in Judeo-Christian literature. For example, in a famous Jewish Kabbalistic or mystical text from the end of the thirteenth century, following an esoteric reflection on God's partnership with humans both within and alongside Him in creation, we find the following lines:

> And you who have power to see and understand, is it possible there is something unseemly in that of which God is a partner? If so, the union of a man with his wife, when it is proper, proves to be the mystery of the foundation of the world and its civilization…, and through the act they become partners with the Holy One Blessed be He in the act of creation. This is the mystery of what the sage said, 'when a man unites with his wife in holiness, the Shekhinah (God's presence) is between them in the mystery of man and woman.[1]

---

1 Quoted, Charlotte Elisheva Fonrobert, "Taming the Powers of Desire: Love and Sex in Jewish Culture," in *Love, Sex and Gender in the World Religions*, ed. Joseph Runzo and Nancy Martin, Oxford: One World, 2000, 113.

The beautiful love poem *Song of Songs* also has been interpreted in the allegorical sense of love between God and God's people or Christ and the Church. But in the Rabbinic traditions it was declared to be the 'holy of holies of the scripture' both in an esoteric sense and that of public delight.[1] Such profound reflections do not find expression in Christian teaching, matrimonial liturgies[2] and in counseling couples who still are unsure of the best expression of their sexual love without any shyness and guilt.

Positive Affirmation and Certain Aberrations in Brahmanic Literature

The Sanskrit word *kama* is ubiquitous and popular in Hindu scriptures. It is not easy to illustrate a single definition of this term. In common parlance, it means desire or longing. But in its special sense it means love, sensual instinct, sexual pleasure, aesthetic sensation, romantic feeling and lust. *Kama* is a personified Vedic god, although he is better known from the prominent stories of the Puranas (ancient stories). At least in one Vedic text *kama* denotes the primal germ of mind and the original creative impulse (Rig Veda X.129). In other Vedic texts, he/it is described as the desire of a thirsty steer for water, the longing for the pleasure of conjugal love, and erotic power.[3] In Hindu mythology *kama* is presented as youthful, filling minds with sexual pleasure but at the same time distracting yogis from their spiritual pursuits. For this reason, Buddha considered it the fundamental cause for all suffering. But the Hindu tradition chose to retain the tension between the positive experience of sexual desire and the temptation to be obsessed.

Kama for prosperity and progeny was the principal motive in Vedic sacrifice. The renouncers criticized it as demeaning and enslaving. The Jains went to the extreme of suppressing it by severe austere practices, even to the extent of some ascetics resorting to self-annihilation! Immolation! Suicide! The lay Buddhist were instructed to enjoy sex with a pure mind whilst maintaining the order of monks

---

1 See Ibid., 120.

2 It would be fruitful to study the matrimonial liturgies with particular reference to sex. For example, *The Church of South India Book of Common Worship* (Revised Edition 2006) in the 'Exhortation' part of the Marriage Service has the following passage. It is ordained: That marriage gives full expression to the love between man and woman that in marriage husband and wife belong to each other, and with affection and tenderness freely give themselves to each other. That in marriage husband and wife may give to each other life-long companionship, help, and comfort, both in prosperity and adversity; That marriage is the foundation of true family life where God may hallow and direct the natural instincts and affections created by God and redeemed in Christ; That marriage is God's appointed way for the continuance of the human race, that children may be born and brought up in families in the knowledge of our Lord Jesus Christ to the glory of God in an atmosphere of security and trust; That, marriage being thus held in honour, human society may stand upon firm foundations (p. 128).

3 Rigveda V.36.1; IX.113.11; Atharvaveda XIX.52.1; see Margaret and James Stutley, *A Dictionary of Hinduism: Its Mythology, Folklore and Development, 1500 B.C. – A.D. 1500*, New Delhi: Heritage, 1986, 139.

and their monasteries. When these and other movements were overcome by the revival of Vedic religion with political patronage around the dawn of the first millennium CE there were drastic new developments of affirmation, assimilation and amalgamation in various fronts.

An *ashrama dharma* was worked out marking four stages of an individual's life. The first was the student stage (*brahmacarya*). A student was dedicated to live with a guru in his hermitage in the forest for several years and be instructed to maintain a discipline and pure mind. However, temptations could not be fully avoided. One warning with harsh punishment was for sleeping with his guru's wife as noted in the literatures of the codes of conduct produced around this time. The second stage was that of the householder (*grihastha*) with years of enjoying sex with one's wife and engaging in procreation. During the third stage (*vanaprastha*), one retired into the forest with or without a wife and returning home occasionally. The fourth and final stage would be that of complete renunciation (*sannyasa*). Thus, this new scheme of life was most comprehensive.

Likewise, the Hindu tradition stipulates four goals of life (*purushartha*): wealth (*artha*), desire or longing (*kama*), duty to maintain order (*dharma*), and final release from worldly life (*moksha*). However, there were different opinions about the order of importance and the place of *kama* was hotly debated.[1] It was little wonder that there were some popular texts in the name of *kama*, i.e., *kamasashtra* and *kamasutra.* The most popular of these was the third century CE Vatsyayana's *Kamasutra* to which, exceptionally, the women have access inside the tradition and everyone outside. Sexual enjoyment is celebrated in this text as the foremost of pleasures. The king had the special privilege of experiencing *kama* with courtesans who were trained in the arts of love. At the same time, a brahmin's sexuality emphasizes rational control which orders his world according to the principles of maintaining ritual purity and of controlling elements within it which threaten to disrupt that purity, particularly his own desire and its focus, namely of his wife and other women of his household.'[2] Thus, sex is positive and legitimate but within the controls of caste order and the restrictions of purity-pollution. Women have equal enjoyment as sex was their right and duty. Vatsyayana offers advice to anyone, male or female, on the uses of drugs to put lovers in one's power.[3] There is advice for good conversation between a husband and wife with relaxing acts like enjoying a paan in order to create the mood for making love. Other texts such as *Manudharmsastra* and Kautilya's *Arthasastra* also talk about sexual behaviour within the prescribed rules on social order and gender. However, they are much more conservative than the *Kamasutra.*

1 See I. Selvanayagam, *Vedic Sacrifice: Challenge and Response*, Delhi: Manohar, 1996, 181ff.

2 Gavin Flood, *An Introduction to Hinduism*, Cambridge: Cambridge University Press, 1996, 65.

3 Wendy Doniger and Sudhir Kakar (tr.), *The Kamasutra of Vatsyayana*, London World Classics, 2002, 7. 1-2

Later Developments in the Christian Tradition

We have already referred to a Jewish reflection on sexual intercourse, to be enjoyed in the presence of God. But this beautiful idea seems to have been forgotten when the Christian movement spread in the Hellenistic and Roman world. Biblically speaking, a genealogy has been maintained, but Jesus' conception is noted as of the Holy Spirit in the uterus of a virgin (young woman, Is. 7: 14) without the participation of a male partner. The assumption here is that human coitus is profane and a divine child cannot go through that process. Furthermore, John the Baptist, born of an old couple, was vowed to be an ascetic living in the wilderness. Compared to him Jesus was liberal, eating and drinking with ordinary people. Jesus had women friends and disciples but no questions have been raised about his sexuality. And Jesus' approach to a woman caught in adultery and destined for stoning to death (Jn. 8) showed how all-inclusive he was in pointing out the initiating and integral role of men in adultery, and how compassionate he was in forgiving the woman and sending her away with a note of warning. Jesus' close relationship with Mary, Martha and Mary Magdalene is read with extra-biblical conjectures that he had a love affair with them. But confining ourselves to the Gospel evidence all one can say is that Jesus had compassion towards female victims caught up in the cross currents of unjust traditions and exploition by men. Also, some women friends and disciples who played an important part in his ministry were seriously committed to his ministry. In the first church council in Jerusalem, of the three shortlisted ethical rules one was to abstain from sexual immorality (Acts 15: 20). They were left with a plethora of definitions of immorality.

Taking Jesus' teaching literally, church fathers such as Jerome (and Cyril) of the 4th century advocated celibacy, promoted celibate orders, and established monasteries and nunneries.

> There was strong advice to subdue sexual desire by fasting, self-castigation and self-denials of all kinds. Some became insane and fanatic. They suppressed the voices of the critics or violently reacted to them. Later, some tried to stem this tendency. St. Augustine and Chrysostom taught the sanctity of the Christian family life, but multitudes preferred celibacy and chastity. The Council of Gangra in 363 anathematized those who asserted that marriage was a sin; trying to stem this unnatural asceticism of the early church. In some sects, mutilation of the sex organs was practiced.[1]

The underlying assumption was that sex was profane and a hindrance to sacred vocation. And also,

> The early church fathers considered coition to be a sin and a fall from grace, and they taught that the unmarried would attain greater glories in heaven, some of them saying that those of either sex who had indulged in coition,

1 O.A. Wall, *op.cit.*, 209ff, 402.

> even though in wedlock, could not enter into heaven at all. This led to the establishment of religious celibate orders; to triumph over one's sexual desires was the greatest merit to be achieved, and some church fathers and female saints went so far, to gain complete triumph, that they had beautiful companions of the opposite sex live with them and even sleep with them because complete self-control under such circumstances was supposed to deserve greater reward hereafter than if it had been maintained under less tempting conditions.[1]

It is observed that 'by the medieval period one in twelve to fifteen persons in Europe was a monk or nun vowed to celibacy,' recognized as the superior vocation for Christians. A combination of circumstances and developments surrounding the monastic movement over its first eight centuries helped to create a sexual ethic within Christianity that distrusted human sexuality, encouraged abstinence, and also blamed women for the human temptation to sexual pleasure, which was understood as the centre of sexual sin.'[2] Holiness was regarded as identical with celibacy. Procreation was the only justification for sexual activity although St. Augustine argued that such activity was venially sinful since pleasure was unavoidable in sex. It was normal for the monks to retreat and join communities in the wilderness. The uncertainty and confusion of many lay people pushed the unwed mothers to take their children to orphanages. There were homes for prostitutes too.

The Reformation did not see celibacy as a necessary corollary to a spiritual life, indeed it saw the possibility of spiritual progress in married life. Since that time, it has been argued that sexual activity is not only for procreation but also for sharing love and joy. Also, there is encouragement for enjoyment of sex between a husband and wife who can control their family by contraceptive methods. Presently in the Protestant Church, celibacy is rare although few individuals who have consciously committed to it are respected for witnessing to a dimension of Christian life which tells that meaning and enjoyment of life is not limited to sexual activity. In some societies, sexual intercourse outside wedlock is tolerated. Among scholarly circles sexuality including sexual ethics is socially constructed and left open to change.

Christians on the whole, continue to be reluctant to talk about sex publicly and especially in connection with the life of dedication and devotion to God. They have struggled with connecting sex as a positive instinct, and even a great gift of God, with devotion. Anders Nygren (1890-1977), a Swedish Lutheran theologian, published his best-known classic, *Agape and Eros* (1932-39). For him the first one is unmotivated and self-giving love and the other, love that

1 Ibid., 172.

2 C.E. Guddore, "Sexual Ethics" in *Christianity: The Complete Guide*, ed. by J. Bowden, London: Continuum, 2005, 115f.

desires to attain a higher good.[1] It appeared to be clarifying the clear distinction between supernatural love and natural or erotic love. But no one can argue that this clarification has settled the issue. If sexuality is part of the original blessing in creation, how can it be secondary or in opposition to God's love? With sexual activity as an expression of pure love, and deep intimacy between two persons, not only can couples experience intimacy with God but also understand that aspect of God's love.

In an ascetic and celibate condition, not many acknowledge openly the struggle and tension they go through between discipline and temptation. Because of this there is no helpful model in the sacred space. The puranic image of Siva appears to fill the gap. Wendy Doniger's groundbreaking study entitled *Siva: The Erotic Ascetic* details with many stories of Siva being pulled between two extremes. Her conclusion gives us a glimpse into this fascinating figure.

> In many myths Siva is merely erotic or merely ascetic, as a momentary view of one phase or another. But in the great myths, transcending the limits of mundane causality, he participates in cycles of cosmic dimensions which melt into single image as they become ever more frequent, making an almost subliminal impression in their brief symbolic appearances, creating an infinite complex mosaic. The conflict is resolved not into a static icon but rather into the constant motion of the pendulum, whose animating force is the eternal paradox of the myths.[2]

It stands to reason that Siva's constant struggle between the extremes epitomizes the struggle of conscious humans although the language is different.

Violation of Gender Balance and Violent Reaction

Both in Sanskrit and vernacular traditions the idea of the virgin power of an innocent woman is 'violently' made subservient to the interest of the male through the institution of marriage. We will point out few examples. The Tamil word *ananku* is associated with the Goddess in the Tamil Saiva devotional literature. In the ancient Tamil society, it was regarded as a terrifying power residing in puberty in a girl's breasts, waist, etc. For instance, a hero says to his beloved: 'You think that there are spots (a sign of puberty) on your afflicting (*ananku*) breasts, but my heart thinks they contain a god (*ananku*).'[3] This feminine sacred power is malevolent outside of wedlock but once married becomes benevolent to her husband. In other words, 'The sacred power that a woman possesses can work in two ways. If she is married and in an auspicious condition, it protects her

1 A. Nygren, *Agape and Eros*, London: ET, 2 vols., 1932-1939.

2 W.D. O'Flaherty, *Siva: The Erotic Ascetic*, Oxford: Oxfor University Press, 1973, 318.

3 George L Hart III, *The Poems of Ancient Tamil: Their Milieu and their Sanskrit Counterparts*, Berkeley, University of California Press, 1975, 21.

husband; if she is not, it can bring destruction.'[1] Manikkavacakar, the foremost of the Tamil Saiva poet-saints and teachers, portrays Siva as the bridegroom of *ananku* and her dance partner.[2] 'Clearly *ananku* is held in check and rendered beneficent by the marital bond requiring wifely submission.'[3] This goes well with the other roles she is given: dependent maid, goddess (very few times), fearful wife, part of Siva, a position which was achieved with great spiritual effort and so on. Most important is for a devotee to see the goddess as the paradigmatic image for a devotee and servant of the Lord.

There are several myths to the effect of debating who is supreme, Siva or Shakti and the compromise is that 'neither can exist without the other.' Again, the compromise is the wedding and in great Siva temples there is both wedding hall and sleeping room for the couple. At the same time, there are some striking myths about the reaction of the female power in relation to marriage and sex. The most remarkable figure in this regard is Kali who has maintained a difficult relationship with her husband or consort Siva. On the one hand, she is a godly mother and on the other, a ferocious avenger. Her very appearance suggests a counter-cultural movement within the sex-related episodes in Hindu traditions. The following description is most representative:

> She is dark as a great cloud, clad in dark cloths. Her tongue is poised as if to lick. She has fearful teeth, sunken eyes, and is smiling. She wears a necklace of snakes, the half-moon rests on her forehead, she has matted hair, and is engaged in licking a corpse. Her sacred thread is a snake, and she lies on a bed of snakes. She holds a garland of fifty heads. She has a large belly, and on her head, is Ananta with a thousand heads. On all sides, she is surrounded by snakes...She has a snake-girdle and an anklet of jewels. On her left is to be imagined Siva in the form of a boy. She has two hands and has corpses for ear ornaments. Her face, decked with bright, new jewels, shows she is pleased and calm.[4]

---

1 Ibid., 99.

2 G.U. Pope, *Tiruvacakam of Manikkavacakar*, Madras: University of Madras, 1979, hymn: line: 20: 22; 13: 27.

3 Glenn Yocum, "The Goddess in a Tamil Saiva Devotional Text, Manikkavacakar's Tiruvacakam", *Journal of the American Academy of Religion*, XLV/1 supplement, March 1977, 373.

4 Quoted, D. Kinsley, *The Sword and the Flute: Kali & Krishna, Dark Visions of the Terrible and Sublime in Hindu Mythology*, Delhi: Motilal Banarsidass, 1995, 81. Further, in Kinsley's own words, '...when she is rarely associated with the battlefield, has a warm, voluptuous appearance. She is naked, full breasted, and heavy hipped. She is said to enjoy sexual intercourse with Siva, taking the "reverse" position in her aggressiveness. She subsists on the hot, rushing blood of all creatures and is frequently shown drinking fresh steaming blood from a skull bowl. Despite her destructive features, she is the Mother of all, and as such she reveals a sexually creative presence that is hot and thirst.' 155.

In the Tamil version of the myth of Kali slaying the buffalo-demon she is presented as a 'murderous bride.'[1] The first night turned out to be disastrous as the bride Kali resumed her dance on the body of Siva. The latter, without fleeing, sought a 'death in love' at her hands. His survival did not guarantee any tension-free conjugal relationship between the two.

Kali is often associated with *tantra* which, apart from other peculiarities, celebrates sex in the form of cults and reverses the values of the brahmanic framework of purity and pollution. We will be content here with few examples. First, an observation of a basic element:

> Tantric ritual coition is surrounded by all kinds of esoteric notions that are fundamental to Tantra and without which the particular practice makes little or no sense....one of the conceptual pivots of the Tantric spirituality is the notion of *rasa*...It denotes essential life-sustaining fluid, and as such has been known since Vedic times. The bodily fluids – notably semen and virginal secretion – early on came to be viewed as power-charged substances that the aspirant on the path to freedom and immortality needs to harness carefully.[2]

Rasa is connected with the divine draft *soma*, *amrita*, the nectar of immortality and *reta*, the divine seed. According to certain Tantric texts, during intercourse there should be mind control, drawing back of semen before it falls into the woman's vagina and preserving it and the yogi can look at it in his palm and even smell it.[3] The so-called transgressive rites of Tantra involve sexual union and the oral consumption of sexual fluids, above all menstrual blood, as a sacramental meal. This is one element of the Kamakhya cult in Assam in which the goddess's menstrual period is believed to be creative and cosmically significant. Sexual intercourse of her devotees is allowed in front of her.[4] In the sex-based, matriarchal Tantra, to counter the *linga* (phallic symbol)-puja (Siva) there is yoni (vagina) puja (Goddess) as well.

There is another story of protest against a husband doubting his wife's chastity. Sita, a goddess and heroine of the epic Ramayana, who was abducted by the demon (*a title for anyone against the brahmanic system*) - king Ravana of Sri Lanka and redeemed by her husband Rama, was put to the test of fire. In actual fact Ravana appeared to be so mature and self-restrained that he never touched, let alone forced Sita to have sex with him. Sita was intent on being loyal to her otherwise trustworthy husband. But the 'lustful Rama' accused

---

1 David Shulman, "The Murderous Bride: Tamil Version of the Myth of Devi and the Buffalo-Demon," *History of Religions*, 16/2, 1976, 120-146.

2 George Feurstein, *Tantra: The Path of Ecstasy*, Boston: Shambhala, 1998, 232.

3 See Ibid., 233f.

4 Hugh Urban's detailed study of the Kamakhya cult revealing though many will find the facts quite uncomfortable. Ref. Urban, *The Power of Tantra: Religion, Sexuality and the Politics of South Asian Studies*, London: I.B. Tauris, 2010.

her of unfaithfulness and thought she was polluted in Ravana's place. A similar doubt occurred once while Sita was pregnant with her two sons and staying in the hermitage of guru Valmiki, the author of the Ramayana. Sita pleaded her innocence yet did not doubt Rama's chastity. In fact, she cooperated with him for his sexual pleasure even just before her banishment. Rama's behaviour is justified by the natural tendency of a man but also for the public witness that 'Rama's wife is above suspicion.' Finally, after proving her innocence by fire three times, though Rama acknowledged that Sita was chaste and innocent, she swore her faithfulness to Rama. This was attested by her wish of being received by the goddess earth with the witness of gods who tried earlier to persuade and correct Rama. Also, she showed that that the world in which she ruled was not heaven where Rama and other dominant male gods reside but in mother earth.[1]

A similar test is noted in the Bible – Numbers 5:11-29 - for an unfaithful wife. If she sleeps with someone and if her unfaithfulness is undetected, the jealous and suspecting husband can take her to the priest. The priest would prepare a bitter drink with the mixture of the dust of the tabernacle and give her. The oath is that if she is innocent nothing would happen, but if guilty a divine curse causes her thigh to waste away and her abdomen to swell. Some rituals are attached to it. Interestingly, in both the stories the husbands go free!

Beyond Violence and Doubt: Krishna's Love Game with the Milkmaids

As a dark-skinned deity, Krishna shares with Kali's colour, vigour and, occasionally, voluptuous qualities. They are sexually hot. But Kali is terrifying with a blood-tipped sword, while Krishna is attractive with a smile and flute. It was this flute that aroused kama in the teenage-but married- yet chaste milkmaids of Vraja who enjoyed a love game with their lover in an autumn moonlight in a forest near the river Yamuna. It is described in the Rasalila section of the 9th century Bhagavata Purana in which Krishna is not one of ten avataras of Vishnu but identical with the supreme God Vishnu himself.[2] The call was from the weary world of routines and duties to a romantic world of excitement and joy. After a moment of love-talk with casual intimacy and mutual chiding the ladies were led to a new surrounding with natural beauty and laughter.

In the whole episode of this encounter there was laughter, amorous pleasures from compassion, even though Krishna's satisfaction is self-contained. There were singing, frolicking, jokes, smiles and glances with Krishna playfully scratching their breasts, girdles, thighs, hair and hands with his nails, and embracing them

1 For details with revealing reflection, see Wendy Doniger, *The Hindus: An Alternative History*, New Delhi: Penguins, 2009, 224-239.

2 Chapters 29-33; the following translation is consulted: Edwin F Bryant, *Krishna: The Beautiful Legend of God, Śrīmad Bhāgavata Purāṇa, Book X – With Chapters 1, 6 and 29-31 from Book XI*, London: Penguin Books, 2003.

with outstretched arms; he aroused the kama in the women and gave them pleasure' (29: 43-46).

When they swelled in pride Krishna disappeared and a period of separation made the gopis mad with pain (*viraha*), and guesses with bitter weeping. When he reappeared each one of them responded differently: one ecstatic woman caught hold of Krishna's hand in her folded hands, placed his arm on her shoulder, accepted his chewed betel nut with folded hands, placed his feet on her breast, bit her lips with her teeth and with her brows knitted in a frown, she glared at him 'as if she could strike him with a look of rebuke'; another dwelt on his lotus face with unblinking eyes, as though drunk but not satisfied, drew him in her heart, through the apertures of her eyes then sealing them shut 'like a *yogi* immersed in bliss.' (32: 4-9). The women worshipped that inciter of *kama* by massaging his hands and feet, which they had placed on their laps. They praised him with their eyebrows quivering, with playful looks and laughter. Then they spoke somewhat angrily' (32: 10-15). Krishna explained that the purpose of his disappearance was to intensify their love for him and to have obsessive concentration on him.

The culmination of the encounter was a circle dance. It was vigorous dancing, with braids and belts secured fast, faces sweating and smiling, garments on their breasts slipping, waists bent, shining like a lightning in the clouds (33: 7). 'They were intent on amorous pleasure and overjoyed by Krishna's touch. Their throats decorated with dye, they sang loudly as they danced, and the world reverberated with their songs' (33: 8). One *gopi* sang a duet in harmony and he praised her. Another was tired and her jasmine flowers and bracelets became loose. Kṛṣṇa was standing by her side. He put his arm around one woman and smelt her blue lotus and sandal fragrance. Krishna gave his chewed betel nut to another who kissed him next to his cheek. Another, fatigued, placed his hand on her breast (33: 9-13). 'Thus Krishna, the Lord of Lakshmi, sported with the beautiful girls of Vraj with freely playful smiles, amorous glances and with caresses and embraces. He was like a child enraptured by his own reflections' (33: 16). The women found pleasure by touching his limbs and they could not keep their garments in place (covering breasts) and hair intact. Content with himself the Lord became manifest as many forms as the milkmaids and enjoyed his pastime with them (33: 17-19). 'With great compassion, Krishna lovingly caressed with his very soothing hands the faces of those *gopis* who were exhausted from the pleasures of love' (33: 20).

Thrilled by the touch of his finger nails the gopis sang of his auspicious deeds. Just like the chief elephant Kṛṣṇa went with them to the water followed by bees etc and enjoyed without any inhibition (33: 21-22). Seen from the various manifestations of *kama,* what we see here is pure and selfless manifestation. Within the text, itself there are questions about the sexual behaviour of Krishna the divine. The answer is that he is beyond the customary norms. However, it is interesting and significant that the game does not go to the climax of conjugal love and coitus. Perhaps the author wants to indicate the elements of a pure sharing of sexual love. Also, the sacred meaning of life is mingled with the narrative and that is the main reason that the game is taken as an allegory of the fascinating divine love and the response of devotional love of the devotees.

The final sentence of the text is also interesting and significant. 'Achieving supreme devotion to the Lord, one quickly frees oneself from lust, the disease of the heart' (33: 39). This implies that lust is an enemy of devotional love, which is pure, mutually giving and receiving. Jesus told that 'anyone who looks at a woman lustfully has already committed adultery with her in his heart' (Mt. 5: 28). Paul writes: 'Those who belong to Christ Jesus have crucified the sinful nature with its passions and desires' (Gal. 5: 24). Some internationally known honest men with 'born again experience' (e.g. Jimmy Carter[1]) have admitted occasions of looking at certain women lustfully. One may argue that it is natural for men and women, married or unmarried, young or old, to be attracted by certain charms. When an incidental look become intentional and to what intensity, may be a question for Hindu-Christian dialogue with openness.

Continuing Controversy and Concluding Remarks

In both Hindu and Christian traditions sex is a primordial instinct and a creative impulse, the greatest gift for sharing love, pleasure and procreation. But it is evident in the literature and human experience of both the traditions that it is a great treasure to be handled with the greatest of care. Excesses, extreme positions and emotional manipulation are possible. The primary emotion to handle is honesty, openness and love; or else the sex scandals of the religious will continue to rock the world. Admitting the struggles of celibacy, the costly balance should be maintained between erotic excess and ascetic extreme. Moreover, sexual instinct or desire is not a biological necessity as social institutions and cultural norms intervene and complicate the matter. Marriage as an institution often serves men to convert the malevolent virgin power of their brides to be benevolent and submissive. The violent reaction to such cultural norm can create a nasty and inauspicious scene. It seems the alternative is to bring in the divine love which teaches a couple mutual arousal, mutual participation and shared orgasm. There is mutual commitment and responsibility as an outcome of love making, e.g. progeny, for the love to continue. But such an ideal is threatened by many inhuman forces. Being trivial, insecure, momentarily excited and mere gratification is not only superficial but also dehumanizing. 'Beastly rape' on the bed of wedlock and outside is anathema and it is openly pointed out in India; so also, the savage practice of what is known as 'honour killing.'

There have been famous sex gurus in the Hindu tradition with various degrees of good standing. Though their perversion is easily detectible, their positive affirmation of sex, connecting it with spirituality or enlightenment, and challenging the hypocrisy on the matter, have not gone without a positive

1 Several years ago he told a journalist in response to a question.

response of the masses. For example, guru Osho Rajneesh (1931-1990) claimed to have enlightenment when he had intercourse with a young girl in America. After experiments and teaching in Bombay and Pune he moved to the USA in 1981 for silence and communication in silence. He was able to acquire 64000 acres of land in the middle of Oregon state and created Rajneeshpuram, the largest spiritual centre in US history with 5700 residents in 1984. Being charged with misleading people he was sent back to India. He was liberal in his teaching sex and connected it with fun, sport, exercise, health and super consciousness.[1] For him having sex was relaxing and transforming, but keeping it in mind and repressing it was unhealthy. He questioned the sexuality of great figures such as Jesus and the pope. His and many other gurus' influence in America is seen in the relentless and insatiate pursuit of the knowledge and practice of sex in an exceptional extent.

We have no space here to discuss the controversies of the stranger ethics of the 'Christian west' and persistent, yet outlawed practices such as temple prostitution and impregnation of a childless wife by a strange man (with supposed mind control) in a sacred spot in 'Hindu India.' However, in conclusion, we return to the metaphor of cotton and fire. Truly it is dangerous to keep them close to each other. But there is a location where they become one and serve devotees in a ceremonial and auspicious way. On the bowl of the Indian brass lamp the cotton wicks with the moisture of oil burn giving a beautiful array of light. The open secret is that the wick is soaked in oil. To say that the oil symbolizes love, both human and divine, is not unreasonable in the light of the contents of this essay!

1 Ref. Osho, *From Sex to Superconsciousness*, Pune: Osho Media International, 2011; first edition (1973).

12

Environmental Spirituality

W. S. Annie

A Personal Story

When I was about ten years old, my father hired an elderly person to clean our garden and the surrounding area. I too joined him in the cleaning job; plucking grass, cleaning up the garbage and removing the shrubs to look clean. Our house stood two feet higher than the road level. A slope was laid from the compound wall of the house, to the road, so that the compound wall was intact. Lush green grass grew on the slope. I wanted the grass on the slope, to be plucked off. The elderly person told me, that the grass should not be plucked off. The grass roots bind the top soil and stop soil erosion. If the slope were to get eroded during the rains, the compound wall would get weak and would eventually collapse. Today, as I recollect the elderly person's words, I thankfully remember and salute the older generations who had much knowledge of their surroundings, their ecosystem and knew how to conserve it and use it prudently.

This paper has four sections. The first section deals with environmentalism and tries to show the differences between environmentalism in the West and the East. The second section narrates the life and work of five Indian environmentalists. The third section culls the spiritual aspects we find in the environmentalists' arguments and their movements. Finally, the paper ends with a discussion on the unfinished agenda of the environmentalists, which highlights the urgency of this issue.

1. What is Environmentalism?

World renowned author of the environmentalist manifesto, Professor de Mattei wrote:

> On earth, [there is] a prodigious hierarchy of created beings of inorganic material culminating in human ... Environmentalism is presented as a vision of the world which turns this hierarchy upside down, by eliminating God and

> dethroning human. Human beings are placed on a level of absolute equality with nature in a relationship of interdependence, not only with the animals but also with the inanimate components of the environment which surround them ... The Earth with its biosphere forms a sort of unitary, cosmic-geo-environmental entity. It becomes something more than 'a common home': it represents a divinity.[1]

Mattei's definition would consider human beings and nature as equals, bestowed with divinity that is different from Christian theology. Nevertheless, Christian theology would also like to be in line with the environmentalist, even though, human beings are considered superior to nature, but, the fact remains that both human beings and nature were created by God, and humans can never survive without nature though nature can survive without human beings. However, for life in its balance and fullness nature and humans need each other.

2. How is Environmentalism in the West: An Observation

Environmentalism in the developed countries is different from environmentalism in the developing countries. Rachael Carson who was a Marine Biologist took note of the absence of the singing Robin in the spring season. This inspired her to write her book, *Silent Spring* in the year 1962. It was a spring without the sweet singing of the 'singing birds.' On the mornings that had once throbbed with the dawn chorus of robins, catbirds, doves, jays, wrens, and scores of other bird voices - there was now no sound; only silence over the fields and woods and marshes She was able to trace the absence of the 'Singing bird,' to the excessive usage of Dichlorodiphenyltrichloroethane (DDT).

Due to the excessive use of the pesticide DDT, the earth worms in the fields carried large amount of DDT in their internal organs. The singing birds that consumed such earthworms were poisoned with DDT which in turn affected the shell formation in the birds. Birds laid eggs without shells. Such eggs failed to hatch. Over the years as no little ones were hatched the numbers of birds that sang in the spring declined. Now, there was silence in the spring season which used to have the birds singing. Rachel Carson's studies, the actions and publication paved way for environmental consciousness in the West. As Carson recorded the absence of the birds in the spring, many such studies that recorded the disappearance of different species, environmental pollution, climate change and so on, have appeared. In the West, modern environmentalism was begun by scientists. Many movements like Green Peace, political parties like the 'Green Party,' in England and others have arisen. In the West environmental concerns are the concerns of the urbane and the educated. They are post-materialist.[2]

---

1 akacatholic.com.Blog Post the-environmentalist-paradox. Accessed on 01.03.16.

2 Vasanth Srinivasan, "Green Shoots of a Possibility," *The Hindu*, 28th December 2015, 13.

3. Environmentalism in the East

The Environmental crisis, in India, is well captured by Madhav Gadgil and Ramachandra Guha when they write,

> while bureaucrats in Delhi watch American soap operas on their Japanese television sets, the vast majority of women in villages of Bihar and Rajasthan can neither read, nor even listen to a cheap transistor radio. While citizens of Bombay get drinking water brought to their taps from rivers dammed tens of kilometers away, women in villages of Saurashtra must trudge long distances to bring home a pitcher of water. While obesity clinics sprout up in Madras and Bangalore, fully one-third of the Indian people cannot afford to buy enough food to keep their body and soul together.[1]

In the developing countries environmentalism originated for different reasons, particularly very much to do with the livelihood and survival issues of the poor. Not by scientists as in the west but in India the concern was brought to the fore by the protests of rural communities. In India, environmental concerns revolve around necessities. They are the concerns of the rural poor, the Adivasis, the fishermen, the tribal people, even the urban castaways.[2]

A CSE pamphlet co-authored by Agarwal and Sunita Narain highlighted a distinction between the 'survival emissions' of the poor, as for instance the methane released by paddy cultivation, and the 'luxury emissions' of the rich, such as the noxious gases released into the atmosphere by automobiles and industry. The conventional wisdom out of Washington sought to suggest that the poor were as responsible for global warming: thus, countries such as India and China needed to be as quick and ready in their remedial measures as, say, the US and Germany. World Resources Institute (WRI) reports, in sum, sought to blame the victims and reward the polluters. This is a unique illustration of the 'environmental colonialism' that rules international negotiations on climate change and the protection of biodiversity. Today, the reality is that northern governments and institutions can, using their economic and political power[3] to intervene in Bangladesh's development. But no Bangladeshi can intervene in the development processes of northern economies even if global warming caused largely by northern emissions could submerge half their country. Agarwal always sought to approach environmental problems from the perspective of the poor. His oeuvre provided an intellectual and moral challenge to the belief that the poor were too poor to be green. He demonstrated that in the biomass economies of the rural third world, the poor had a vital interest in the careful management of forests, soil, pasture, and water. (The rich could more easily shift to alternative

---

1 Madhav Gadgil and Ramachandra Guha, *Ecology and Equity: The use and Abuse of Nature in Contemporary India* (New Delhi: Penguin Books, 1995), 3.

2 Vasanth Srinivasan, "Green Shoots of a Possibility," *The Hindu*, 28th December 2015, 13.

3 *Economic and Political Weekly*, January 19, 2002, 206.

fuels and building materials.) In his later work, he showed likewise that the more prosperous the country or community, the more likely it was to insulate itself from the harmful effects of pollution, while passing on the burden to the disadvantaged.

Agarwal's conclusions were crisp and unambiguous. The 'first lesson' is that 'the main source of environmental destruction in the world is the demand for natural resources generated by the consumption of the rich (whether they are rich nations or rich individuals and groups within nations).' The 'second lesson' is that 'it is the poor who are affected most by environmental destruction'; thus, 'eradication of poverty in a country like India is simply not possible without the rational management of our environment and that, conversely, environmental destruction will only intensify poverty.'[1]

In India, environmental movements began as resistance movements against displacement, exploitation, alienation of the earth people or the women, tribals, Adivasis from their resources, natural habitat and environment. Such movements have been organized and led by some extraordinary individuals who epiomise an integrated spirituality the basic components of which are vision, imagination and commitment to sustained struggle. We illustrate with the life and work of five environmentalists, who worked, struggled, protested, fought for the environmental resources that would sustain the life of people, for whom they worked or the people group to whom they belonged. When Medha Patkar, Baba Amte and Binayak Sen relocated themselves into a different group to work for them, Mylamma and C. K. Janu, who were tribal women, worked for the well being of their own tribal community. Mylamma's land was polluted and made sterile by the Coco Cola company. C. K. Janu belonged to the tribal group that was alienated from their own ancestral land or forest. Their struggles and protests are against the genocide of their own tribal communities.

The main concern of this paper being, 'environmental spirituality,' very important questions that rise pertaining to spirituality, will have to be answered. The questions include: what inspired these individuals to commit themselves to such causes, that are spiritual? What sustains them in their day to day struggle? From where do they get the energy, the strength to go on, to survive, such torture and harassment? (Binayak Sen - two years of imprisonment, C. K. Janu – lathi charged in police custody, Medha Patkar – frequent imprisonment, hartals, dharnas, and Mylamma – intimidation by the Coco Cola hired Mafia).

Over the years, people in religious circles are understood as religious, that is, spiritual. People who claim to be secular are understood as non-spiritual, people who claim to be atheist or agnostics, are understood as having nothing to do with God. But, close observation reveals that there are many similarities between people who claim to believe in God and people in the environmental movements

1 Ramachandra Guha, "Environmentalist of the Poor," *Economic and Political Weekly*, Jan 19, 2002, 204-207.

and elsewhere. This leads us to revisit our definitions, our understanding of the concepts, 'religion,' 'spiritual,' etc. The life and work of these environmentalists helps us to realise the fluidity of such concepts. It helps us to realise how dangerous it is to ignore/reject people on the basis of such a narrow understanding, when in reality we (so-called religious people, Christians) need to join hands, cooperate with such environmentally committed people and work together for the 'Common Good.' Environmental spirituality also helps us to revisit the dualism of matter/spirit that we have inherited from western Christianity and have loved to hold on to, dearly, for centuries. Are only human beings spiritual and does all matter (universe) have no value or less value or is divine? The life and work of those we describe[1] briefly may eventually answer, many of the above questions.

4. Life and Work of Five Indian Environmentalists

(i) *Medha Patkar* was born in Mumbai, Maharashtra, to Indu and Vasant Khanolkar on 1 December 1954. Patkar earned an MA in Social Work from Tata Institute of Social Sciences, after which she worked with voluntary organisations in Mumbai's slums for five years and in tribal districts of North-East Gujarat for 2 years. Medha Patkar became an environmentalist when she witnessed the suffering of the people of the Narmada Valley which she wanted to study as a Research Student. She left her position on the faculty of the Tata Institute of Social Sciences as well as her unfinished PhD when she became immersed in the tribal and peasant communities in Maharashtra, Madhya Pradesh and Gujarat.

Talking about a life of struggles, constant confrontation and dharnas, hartals, she responded 'that her parents were activists and it was natural for her to follow in the footsteps of her parents.' She does not overtly believe in God nor is she part of any institutional religion as she considers that all organised, formal religions have let down and betrayed, poor people. She bitterly accuses all religions, saying, 'No religion wants poor people.'

Medha Patkar initiated and is still working with Narmada Bachao Andolan (Save the Narmada Movement) with a mass base in tribal and peasant communities in Maharashtra, Madhya Pradesh and Gujarat and support groups with more than 30 centres all over India and the supporting coalition of NGOs in more than ten countries, called Narmada Action Committee.

Medha Patkar founded the National Alliance of People's Movements (NAPM) with the objective of 'facilitating unity and providing strength to peoples' movements in India, fighting against oppression, further questioning the

1 We have taken only five for study. India has produced many more committed environmentalists like Sunderlal Bahuguna of the Chipko movement, Chandi Pradad Bhatt, S. P. Udaya Kumar of the anti nuclear plant agitation at Kudankulam in Tamil Nadu, Vandana Shiva, an anti globalization activist and environmentalist, Mercy Matthew who turned into Daya Bhai and lives among the tribals fighting for the rights of the bonded labourers and the displaced tribals, adivasis and many more.

current development model so as to work towards a just alternative.' She is the national convener of the NAPM.

Patkar served as a Commissioner to the World Commission on Dams, the first independent global multi-stakeholder Commission constituted to enquire on water, power and alternative issues, related to dams, across the world. She provided a detailed analysis of large dams and in-depth recommendations on the planning of large dams or any development project. The final report was signed unanimously, with an additional comment from Patkar.

Tata Motors started constructing a factory to manufacture their $2,500 car, the Tata Nano at Singur, West Bengal. She protested against this operation. Patkar's convoy was assaulted, allegedly by CPI(M) activists, at Kapaseberia in East Midnapore district while on her way to strife-torn Nandigram. In October 2008, Tata announced that the factory would not be completed and that the production of the Nano will be set up in Sanand, Gujarat.

Lavasa is a project by Hindustan Construction Corporation, in Maharashtra. It is a yet-to be completed city. Lavasa Project is criticised by P. Sainath for unjust use of water in a state known for the worst rate of farmer suicides. Medha Patkar with villagers of Lavasa protested against the environmental damage in Nagpur. She also filed a PIL-Public Interest Litigation in Supreme Court against the Lavasa project.

Medha Patkar openly supported the anti-corruption campaign of Anna Hazare. In support of Anna Hazare campaign, she said, 'Our goal is not Jan Lokpal alone. There has to be a Jan Andolan, a mass movement. We will try and bring together many people's movements.'

A demolition took place on 2 and 3 April 2013 in the Golibar area, Mumbai, Maharashtra evicting people from 43 houses and displacing more than 200 residents. Medha Patkar with more than 500 slum dwellers went on an indefinite fast to protest against any further demolition until the inquiry into the matter was completed. Patkar has alleged corruption and 'atrocities' by builders in the city's slum rehabilitation scheme, and called for the halting of six projects by the Slum Rehabilitation Authority, until a proper inquiry is conducted.

To save the Sugar-Cooperative sector in Maharashtra from falling into the hands of politicians, Medha Patkar organised protests. She explained that 'the politicians are interested in the prime plots of land, old equipment and machinery,' of sugar co-operatives and accused the state of selling assets of industry at give-away prices.

Medha Patkar along with other activists registered PIL in the High Court, alleging violations by property tycoon Niranjan Hiranandani by building luxury flats instead of affordable houses. Hiranandani had signed a lease for the 230 acres of land in 1986 at rate of Re 1 per hectare in a tripartite agreement with the state and Mumbai Metropolitan Region Development Authority. Responding to PIL, Maharashtra High Court judges have said that 'we appreciate the elegance of the construction with the intent of creating an architectural marvel for the city of Mumbai, we see the specific intent of wholly ignoring the most vital, and perhaps the only, condition in the tripartite agreement (to create affordable houses of 40 and 80 sq m).' If calculated according to the current market price, the extent of the scam would be around Rs. 450 billion. Patkar expressed strong opposition to the land acquisition in Kovvada of Ranasthalammandal in Srikakulam district, Andhra Pradesh saying that the nuclear plant would be a disaster for the ecology as well as the people of the region.[1] Patkar continues to work for the tribal people and works in solidarity with many movements.

(ii) ***Mylamma*** was directly affected by Coca-Cola's operations in Plachimada, in Kerala's Palakkad district. The water in her well (in Vijaynagar colony in Plachimada) had been so heavily polluted by Coca-Cola's operations that it was deemed unfit for human consumption. Mylamma was a central figure in the campaign to hold Coca-Cola accountable for water shortages and pollution in the area, and it was under her leadership that the community forced the Coca-Cola bottling plant to shut down in March 2004. The plant has remained shut down ever since. Mylamma, a member of the Eravalar tribe, was the founder of the Coca-Cola Virudha Samara Samiti (Anti Coca-Cola Struggle Committee) in Plachimada which has spearheaded the campaign against Coca-Cola.

The fundamental question raised in the struggle was about 'right to water' manifested mainly in three forms such as the interpretation of 'right to water' as an indispensible part of the right to life, declaration of water as the common property of all and finally rejection of the notion that water is a commodity.[2] It seems that the people of Plachimada and nearby villages had perceived the concept that free access to clean water is an inalienable right. It was because of this perception that they could not accept the alternative for a Jalanidhi Project in Plachimada, a water supply scheme sponsored by the Japanese Government based on the neo liberal principle, 'pay and use.' For them, water constitutes the basis of life. They even treated it as an object for worship. There is a god of water by the name Varunan. In short, the village community in Plachimada considered water as a spiritual entity with a pivotal role in human life. To quote Veloor Viswanathan, 'Water is a gift from God. The God of water is Varunan and it is the medicine for all sorts of diseases. It is the basis of our life.'[3] As the operations of the factory resulted in a water crisis with a double jeopardy of scarcity and contamination, people felt humiliated and were made to feel restless.

In the words of Mylamma, 'suddenly we felt terribly helpless, facing the fact that we were robbed. Our precious water resource had been stolen... lakhs of liters every day... Where would I get fresh and pure drinking water anymore?

1 Readanddigest.com/a-short-biography-of-medha-patkar. Accessed on 04.02.16

2 K.V.K. Iyyer, "Plachimada Oru Pratheekam" in Vasudevan, P.A. (ed.), *Plachimadayile Jala Chuzhanavum Janakeeya Prathirodavum*, Calicut: Mathrubhumi, 2005, 38.

3 J.B. Pariyadath, *Mylamma Oru Jeevitham*, Calicut: Mathrubhumi, 2006, 20-32.

How many kilometers should we have to walk to fetch a drop of water?'[1] This sense of helplessness, backed by her primal tribal religious understanding of water, that, 'water belongs to all. It is a common property' inspired her to spearhead the agitation against the Coca-Cola Company, that was looting their precious resource and depriving the tribals of their livelihood.

It should be mentioned that the right to water is not a new idea advanced by the people of Plachimada. On the contrary, it was a matter of concern, which was inherent in every stage of human culture. Hence, this should be analyzed in the light of an innumerable number of struggles for the right to water across the world. The World Water Conference held in 2003 in Plachimada in connection with the anti-Coca-Cola agitation emphasizes the universal character of the right to water. Delegates from around 30 nations participated in this international conference, which finally approved a declaration popularly known as Plachimada Declaration. The first four statements in the declaration directly refer to right to water.[2] They are as follows: (a) Water is the basis of life; it is a gift of nature; it belongs to all living beings on earth. (b) Water is not private property. It is a common resource for the sustenance of all. (c) Water is the fundamental right of all people. It has to be conserved, protected and managed. It is our fundamental obligation to prevent water scarcity and pollution and to preserve it for generations. (d) Water is not a commodity. We should resist all criminal attempts to market, privatize and corporatize water. Only through these means can we ensure the fundamental and inalienable right to water for the people all over the world. The Anti-Coca-Cola Struggle Committee has held a continuous vigil directly outside Coca-Cola's factory gates since April 22, 2002, demanding its permanent closure.

Mylamma lived with her extended family in Vijaynagar Colony in Plachimada, and is survived by three sons and a daughter. Mylamma was the recipient of the prestigious 'Speak Out award,' by the Outlook magazine and the Sthree Shakthi Award. Mylamma passed away on Jan 6, 2007.[3]

(iii) ***C. K. Janu*** was born in Thrissileri Chekot colony, near Vellamunda, a tribal village, in Wayanad district, Kerala, to poor adivasi parents who were from Ravula community, called Adiya due to their historical background, one of the several adivasi groups in Kerala who used to be indentured labourers. Adiya literally means slave and they are mostly landless agricultural labourers. She did not have any formal education but learned to read and write through a literacy campaign which was conducted in Wayanad, an area in the north of Kerala, bordering Karnataka and Tamil Nadu.

Janu started her career as a domestic servant at a local school teacher's house, at the age of seven where she spent 5 years. By the age of 13, she had tarted working as a labourer for a daily wage of rupees 2. Later, she learned tailoring and

1 *Coca Cola: Quit Plachimada; Quit India*, Mumbai: Vikas Adhyana Kendra, 2008, 1-18.

2 P.A. Vasudevan, "Plachimada Oru Sthalamalla" in P.A. Vasudevan, (ed.) op.cit., 2005.

3 https://plachimada.wordpress.com/tag/mylamma. Accessed on 14.02.16.

started a small shop which, subsequently, had to be closed down due to financial constraints.

Janu, in her early years, was influenced by Comrade Varghese who led a tribal uprising in Tirunelli forests of Wyanad and started her social career by speaking out from personal experience. Soon she became identified as the voice of Adivasis. Janu began her activism as a member of the Kerala State Karshaka Thozhilali Union (KSKTU), a union of agricultural labourers affiliated to the Communist Party of India (Marxist) and continued to be involved at the party's invitation. She worked as a campaigner for the Union till 1987 when she quit the party after becoming disillusioned with them as she felt the party was less interested in the cause of the tribals. She then embarked on a tribal tour to understand their problems and to mobilise them for struggle.

Her stint with the Communist Party of India (Marxist) helped her to gain experience in party politics. In 2001, Janu led a protest march through the state and held a long sit-in strike in front of the Secretariat in Thiruvananthapuram to demand land for landless adivasis which lasted 48 days and resulted in convincing Kerala Government to distribute land to the adivasis. In 2003, she also led the occupation of land at Muthanga. The occupation ended with massive police violence in which a policeman and an adivasi were killed. It came to be known as the Muthanga incident and Janu had to undergo imprisonment and face 75 charges filed against her. After the Muthanga agitation, Janu shifted her concentration on to occupying land at Aralam farm, a huge cooperative farm that the government had promised to distribute amongst landless adivasis.

Janu is sometimes described as the first 'organic' leader of adivasis in Kerala. She has often cooperated with national and international indigenous people's organisations but was always very wary of being funded by any organisation. Most of the activities of the Adivasi Gothra Maha Sabha are funded entirely through the solidarity of poor adivasis and dalits.

Her autobiography, a small book consisting of only 56 pages, *Janu: The Life Story of C K Janu*, was published in Malayalam by DC Books in 2003. The book was later translated into English by N. Ravi Shankar entitled *Mother Forest: The Unfinished Story of C.K. Janu.*

The Muthanga Incident refers to an incident of police firing on the Adivasis (tribal clans) in the Muthanga village of Wayanad district, Kerala. On 19 February 2003, the Adivasis had gathered under Adivasi Gothra Maha Sabha (AGMS) to protest the Kerala Government's delay in allocating them land, which had been contracted in October 2001. During the protest, Kerala Police fired 18 rounds resulting in two immediate fatalities (one of which was a police officer). In a subsequent statement, the Government placed the official death toll at five. A video of the firing was aired on several news programmes and prompted noted author Arundhati Roy into writing an open letter to the then, Chief Minister of Kerala, saying "You have blood on your hands."

The agitation was deemed a success as, according to Janu, nearly 10,000 Adivasi families have received land following the 2001 agreement and over 4,000 hectares of land including the Aralam Farm land in Kannur district has been assigned to the landless Adivasis. The forest is a microcosmos for the adivasis. They believe that their dead ancestors live in the trees, streams, birds and animals of the forest. To alienate them from the forest is to alienate them from their meaning, essence of life.

In January 1994, the Kerala government presented her with the award for the best Scheduled Tribe Social Worker; however, she declined the award because the government had thus far not acceded to the thirteen demands of Kerala tribals.

Janu represented India at a UN Conference of the tribal leaders from all over the world. She also toured Europe in 1999 on behalf of the Peoples' Global Action Group and gave speeches at more than 120 locations in eight countries. In 2000, Janu participated in the second International Conference of the People's Global Action Group in Bangalore.[1]

(iv) ***Baba Amte*** was born to Devidas and Laxmibai Amte in the city of Hinganghat in Wardha District of Maharashtra on 26 December 1914. His was a wealthy family. His father was a British government officer with responsibilities for district administration and revenue collection. As the eldest son of a wealthy landowner, Murlidhar (original name) had an idyllic childhood. When he was fourteen, he owned his own gun and hunted boar and deer. When he was old enough to drive, he was given a Singer Sports car with cushions covered with panther skin. He never appreciated the restrictions that prevented him from playing with the 'low-caste' servants' children. 'There is a certain callousness in families like my family' he used to say. 'They put up strong barriers so as not to see the misery in the world outside and I rebelled against it.'

Trained in law, he developed a successful legal practice at Wardha. He soon became involved in the Indian struggle for freedom from the British Raj, and started acting as a defence lawyer for leaders of the Indian freedom campaign for those whom the British authorities had imprisoned in the 1942 Quit India movement. He spent some time at Sevagram ashram of Mahatma Gandhi and became a follower of Gandhism for the rest of his life. He followed Gandhism, including yarn spinning using a charkha and wearing khadi. When Gandhi came to know that he has saved a girl from British soldiers who were lewdly taunting her, Gandhi gave him the name – Abhay Sadhak (Fearless Seeker of Truth).

One evening, Baba Amte was servicing latrines in the posh localities of Vadodara. It was getting dark. He thought he saw a corpse in a gutter. Close examination established the fact that it was a leprosy patient Tulsiram, still breathing. He had no toes or fingers left. Moggots were crawling all over his body. He had only two holes on his face in place of his nose. It was a horrifying sight. Baba Amte went home later having covered him with a bamboo mattress. This

1 www.sacw.net/Nation/gatade18032005.html. Accessed on 21.02.16.

incident triggered restlessness in him. Later, Baba relinquished his position as a lawyer and went to Kolkata to find out more about leprosy. Baba gave up a decent and comfortable life in order to work for the well being of leprosy patients.

In those days, leprosy was associated with social stigma and society disowned people suffering from leprosy. There was also a widespread misbelief that leprosy was highly contagious. Amte strove to dispel the misbelief and once allowed bacilli from a leprosy patient to be injected into him while participating in an experimental test aimed at proving that leprosy was indeed not highly contagious. In fact, leprosy is believed to be spread through contact with cough droplets or fluid from the nose of an infected person.

Amte founded three ashrams for treatment and rehabilitation of leprosy patients, disabled people, and people from marginalised sections of the society in Maharashtra, India. On 15 August 1949, he started a hospital in Anandvan under a tree; in 1973 founded the Lok Biradari Prakalp to work for the Madia Gond tribal people of Gadchiroli District. Amte seems to have had a Christian influence too. His Ashram hospital, had a picture of someone walking under a shadowy cross, with the caption, 'I cannot carry the cross and try to walk under its shadow.'

Amte devoted his life to many other social causes, most notable among which were generating public awareness towards the importance of ecological balance, wildlife preservation, and the Narmada Bachao Andolan. He was awarded the Padma Shri in 1971. Mandakini Amte (Baba's daughter-in-law) left her governmental medical job and moved eventually to Hemalkasa to start a hospital, a school, and an orphanage for injured wild animals, including leopards and lions.

Following Gandhi's Amte led a spartan life. He wore khadi (hand spurn) clothes made from the looms at Anandwan. He believed in Gandhi's concept of a self-sufficient village industry that can empower seemingly helpless people, and successfully brought his ideas into practice at Anandwan.

Amte also used Gandhian principles to fight against corruption, mismanagement, and poor, shortsighted planning in the government. Thus, he used non-violent means to fight the Indian government in the fight for independence. In spite of his emulation of social and political work, unlike Gandhi, Amte was a humanist (agnostic too!).

Baba was at the forefront of two movements; "Barth Jodo March" promoting national integration and 'Narmada Bachao Andolan,' fighting against consumerism. In 1990, Amte left Anandwan for a while to live along the Narmada River and join Medha Patkar's Narmada Bachao Andolan, which fought against both unjust displacement of local inhabitants and damage to the environment on account of the construction of the Sardar Sarovar dam on the Narmada river.[1]

1 www.thefamouspeople.com.Activists. Accessed on 20.02.16.

(v) *Binayak Sen*, is no ordinary medical doctor. Few doctors, after all, spend three decades working in a region threatened by what former Prime Minister Manmohan Singh called the 'single biggest internal security challenge ever faced' by the country. And that was before Dr. Sen was jailed on charges of 'waging a war against the state,' which prompted a group of Nobel laureates to petition for his release. Sen was released in 2009, after spending two years in jail, but still faces charges of supporting the Maoists, also referred to as Naxalites, which he denies.

The Maoists had been leading an armed movement to capture political power in 13 states in India over four decades, and claimed to be fighting for the poor, dispossessed and marginalized. Sen ran mobile clinics in the interior of Chhattisgarh, one of the states most affected by the Maoist insurgency. In 2005, he led a 15-member team that published a report criticizing the Salwa Judum, which Human Rights Watch calls 'a state-supported vigilante group aimed at eliminating Naxalites.'

The Chhattisgarh state government alleged that Sen's work, and in particular his association with the Maoist leader Narayan Sanyal, amounted to helping wage 'a war against the state.' Although, that charge was dismissed, he was found guilty of sedition and conspiracy, and sentenced to life imprisonment by a lower court in Chhattisgarh in 2010. He was granted bail by the Supreme Court in 2011 and an appeal against the conviction is pending in the Chhattisgarh High Court. A group of 40 Nobel laureates described him as 'an exceptional, courageous, and selfless colleague, dedicated to helping those in India who are least able to help themselves,' in a 2011 letter appealing for his life sentence to be overturned.

Sen studied medicine in Christian Medical College (CMC) Vellore and the ethos of this famous institution founded by Ida Shudder (e.g. dedication to service) should have influenced Sen. His work in Chhattisgarh was with village communities, some of the poorest in India, and training health workers to look after their needs. As a medical doctor, Sen, was able to analyse the reasons for malnutrition and tribal land alienation. As the tribals were alienated from the ancestral forest, land they were deprived of the food resources, which resulted in the malnutrition of the tribal population in Chhattisgarh. Earlier, he had helped establish a hospital for mine workers in the area. As a logical outcome of his work, he was involved with human rights work, and was the general secretary of the state unit of the Peoples' Union for Civil Liberties.

In this capacity, he was instrumental in documenting and exposing deaths due to hunger and malnutrition and to the displacement of over 600 tribal villages by the state-sponsored militia called Salwa Judum (S.J.) in southern Chhattisgarh. In 2006, the S.J. was banned by the Supreme Court of India. But it was in 2007 that he was labelled a Maoist supporter, for reasons best known to the Chhattisgarh state government. He was arrested in 2007 and charged with sedition, as well as under internal security acts, spent two years in jail during the trial, was released on bail by the Supreme Court, convicted and sent to jail again, and again was released on bail in 2011. His appeal against the conviction is still pending in the state high court.

He was approached by Narayan Sanyal's family to help him with his legal cases and his health needs. In his capacity as a P.U.C.L. activist, he visited him in jail several times in the presence of senior jail officials, as they testified at his trial. His time in prison was a time of deep despair, as he was unable to figure out the logic of the juridical action against him. At the same time, it gave him an opportunity to know the stories of many fellow prisoners who were undergoing the same trauma as himself. He came across many such instances where people had spent substantial amounts of time and were later let go. In some instances, the judges have indicted the police for fabrication of evidence and illegal detention, but, about those indictments, nothing has happened.

Reflecting on his situation he said, 'I did not do anything that was, to the best of my knowledge, wrong or illegal. I didn't expect anything like this happen to me; I had in fact worked with the government to provide essential services in these areas. After coming out of jail, I have been part of a nationwide process for the repeal of unjust and oppressive laws. There was no physical intimidation that I faced in jail. However, I was kept in solitary confinement. Life in jail is itself a form of mental intimidation.'

Sen faced a virulent media trial in Chhattisgarh in the printed and electronic media, as well as on the Internet. The ordinary journalist in Chhattisgarh relies to a large extent on government (including police) hand-outs. It was the contribution of dedicated national journalists who turned their spotlight on the real story. It was only over a period of time that a campaign against the patent injustice in his case built up, and many prominent citizens at national and international levels besides sections of the national media took a positive view about him.

Sen poignantly points out the state of national discourse in India, as he says, 'It is surprising that so much of the public discourse is about the issue of violence. Large sections of the population in the "affected areas" are living in a state of perpetual hunger, to the point of famine, and lack appropriate and basic health care. Their access to common property resources, essential for their survival, is denied to them as a result of state action, to a point where the very survival of entire communities is called into question – but this does not become the centre of the discourse.' He has clarified on many occasions that he does not condone the violence either of the agencies of the state or of those who oppose the state. First of all, he wants to clarify that he has always engaged with the state to help it function better. He was part of the steering committee for health in the 12th five-year plan, and earlier part of the advisory group on structural reforms in health care for government of Chhattisgarh.[1]

However, recent developments make it plain that the planning commission is unlikely to carry out its stated commitments to the universalization of health care.

1 https://india.blogs.nytimes.com/20/12/10/a-conversation-with... Accessed on 10.03.2016.

'The alternative strategies that most public health workers are advocating, is the universalization of health care and for increased resource allocation in the health and nutrition sector. The distress due to chronic hunger, lack of health care and widespread displacement of the people, who constitute one sixth of humankind, cannot be constrained only by questions of national identity. These are matters of concern for the entire world community.' In fact, the current, Narendra Modi Government has cut expenditure for all public services, including health.

Five environmentalists have been introduced above. None of them are scientists. All of them became involved in their respective movements in response to the survival, livelihood issues of the people. None of them are ultra-religious. They are 'secular,' in the very Indian understanding of the term. All of them, did have some triggering or inspiring factor that got them into their work and it is the unfinished task of 'human survival with dignity' that seems to propel on continuing the struggle. Some positive results and the support they receive from the people who believe in 'The Common Good,' is the encouragement and hope that helps them to survive different setbacks and assaults.

5. Redefining Spirituality

Religion is the root of any culture, and environmentalism has become a fully-fledged religion in its own right (in the west). It is the most comprehensive, in the world today, so far as world view, theology, ethics, politics, economics, and science are concerned. Many of us may not easily be able to accept Edward Bailey's observation, that, 'there is spirituality in the pub.' Normally, for religious people anything connected with God or divine is spiritual and without it is unspiritual, material or worldly. This may reflect very narrow understanding of spirituality. As the Spirit hovers everywhere, so, does spirituality, and it has a very much wider meaning. The individuals studied above are from different religions and also from no religious persuasion. But, the following aspects of spirituality are common in all of them.

Human beings are spiritual (religious) people. Institutionalised religions would always wish to highlight their religious symbols (Krishna, Rama, Jesus Christ, Buddha, etc.). The Indian environmentalists like Baba Amte and Medha Patkar may not openly confess their allegiance to such institutionalised religious symbols. However, they would sense and acknowledge the presence of the Sacred or God, who is not the private property of any religion. God belongs to everybody. They would also strongly critique and protest against the religious institutions for partying with the oppressive forces, structures that keep people in perpetual hunger, which leads to the death of millions. But, the Indian environmentalists are spiritual as they feel related and value the relationship. They believe in the wellbeing and flourishing of all life. They detach themselves from pomp, luxury and prestige. They 'protest' against all that crushes life and they work to preserve life. They have shown tremendous strength, in facing persecution by the powers and principalities of evil forces. The above study helps us to refine spirituality in the following terms.

(i) *Spirituality is to do with relationships*

Baba Amte was not able to dissuade himself or cut himself off from the predicament of the leprosy patient Tulsiram. Tulsiram's memory haunted him. He did not want anybody to suffer like Tulsiram. Baba Amte was not able to shed, shake off his attachment to another human being. Although, Baba claimed to be atheist or agnostic, he was deeplyspiritual.

Western scientific technological modernity has promoted the idea that human beings can do without 'nature.' But, on the contrary, the different environmental movements, peoples' movements, bring to our attention, interdependence humanity and nature and their survival, which depends very much on nature.

(ii) *Spirituality is well-being, the flourishing of life*

Almost all human beings are involved in activities that help life to flourish. Men and women bear and rear children, work hard for the well-being of their families. But, something unique-about these individuals is, that they are able to extend their being, their self, to others and towards 'nature.' Medha was unable to tolerate seeing the Narmada rising, during the rains, submerging the fertile fields, houses, forests of the politically powerless, the innocent tribal population who lived in the banks of Narmada. She would not tolerate the loss of their livelihood, displacement from their ancestral lands and the pauperisation of the entire tribal, adivasis communities. This compelled Medha to discontinue her job at the Tata Institute of Social Science and also leave her Ph. D programme incomplete to join with the tribes in their struggle to obtain justice (if the dam's height were to be raised, that would prevent the tribal lands from being submerged). The tribes of Placimada would not accept that water has to be purchased. The poor would go without water, if they had no money with which to buy it. Baba Amte had zero tolerance for such obscene poverty.

(iii) *Spirituality is detachment from pomp, luxury, prestige*

Any sincere historian and social scientist would humbly acknowledge the Christian contribution to the field of education and health in India. Countless young doctors, nurses, teachers went to remote villages to work for the poor and the down-troddeny. However, this situation has changed. Christians now prefer going abroad to make money, rather than going to remote villages to serve the poor. Binayak Sen, educated at CMC, Vellore, who worked in poor, remote villages, in backward Chhattisgarh for more than three decades, refused to indulge in pomp, luxury and prestige. Baba Amte relinquished his Mayor job in Nagpur to serve the leprosy patients, who were usually treated as untouchables in Indian society.

(iv) *Spirituality is to 'protest against' all that crushes life and fails to preserve life*

Medha Patkar, Mylamma, Janu, Amte and Sen - all involved themselves in some kind of public protest. Protests are not easy. Medha was imprisoned many times. Janu was beaten up very badly. Sen was imprisoned for nearly two years without reason. In fact, it has to be said that their, very being, self and soul, is of a different kind that negates the powers, the mega materialistic, consumerist attitudes that crush and destroy life. Sen's very work as a doctor to the tribes and his association with Narayan Sanyal - the Naxal - was a protest, against the mining lobbies that who apparently wished for the genocide of the tribes. M.M. Thomas, one of India's foremost theologians, coined and propagated the words 'spirituality of combat,' which have fired many people including some environmental activists. Though Patkar, Amte and Sen happen to be Hindus, Janu and Mylamma belonged to tribal communities who would not attribute their work to any religious symbol like 'God.' They worked for the good of common humanity.

(v) *Spirituality is powered by a Moral Agency that helps endures suffering*

As George Zachariah, a green theologian of India, affirms,

> Globalization as the colonization of the life world is a fundamental ethical issue because it not only robs the moral agency of the community, but it also assumes moral agency through its claims of universality and the propaganda slogan of 'There is no Alternative' (TINA). Thus, the ethical imperative in the contemporary world is to reclaim the moral agency of the dispossessed. Moral agency empowers the community with the discernment of its historical responsibility to be sensitive, critical, morally indignant, compassionate and creative - to understand what the reality is, and to strive collectively to transform it radically back to what *ought to be*. Put differently, moral agency is the political and spiritual power *to interpret* and *to change* the world. A people with moral agency are, therefore, the architects of a different world because they believe that "another world is possible."[1]

The struggle of our environmentalists is directly and indirectly against the agents of globalisation. The environmentalists are leaders empowered by moral agency who give leadership to their respective movements, who dream of a different, better life.

6. The Unfinished Agenda of the Environmental Spiritualist

The Chennai deluge (2015) is said to have been caused by global warming, El Nino and unplanned constructions in the city. The earth's temperature has

1 George Zachariah, *Alternatives Unincorporated: Earth Ethics from the Grassroots*, London: Equinox Publishing Ltd., 2011, 36.

been increasing to dangerous levels. The preservation of the environment, that is, environmentalism can never be at the cost of poor nations and poor people. The poor have never contributed to global warming for the sake of luxury. It is the developed nations and their consumerist life style which has caused global warming. They are challenged by environmentalists with their factual analysis, life style and mobilization of awareness at great risks as we have illustrated aove. If green politics does not restrict itself to urban environmental activism (as in the west) but emerges as a binding agent of all groups and concerns, it definitely has a future in India.[1] The Paris Climate Agreement reflects pressure from environmental movements.[2] The hope is that finally common humanity will win overcoming all narrow religious and communal interests.

1 Vasanth Srinivasan, "Green Shoots of a Possibility," *The Hindu*, 28th December 2015, 13.

2 Joshau H. Koritz, "Environment," *The Hindu*, Dec 17, 2015.

Appendix

A. Highlights of the Women Panel of the Conference (Hyderabad)

As none of the presentations defines the word 'secular spirituality' we also avoid its definition while talking about it from socio-feminist perspective in a tribal context. Tribal community life cannot have any boundary between religion and secularity because tribal society is a closed-knitted society. In tribal people's life and society their spirituality is expressed in religio-social activities and celebrations.

1. ***Spirituality of obedience, of resistance, and of rejection*:** a) Women of every society, as required and demanded by patriarchal mindset and dominion, are expected to be obedient to men so long as there are good relationships and care. This 'spirituality of obedience' is more relevant to home and family life. b) When a man is taking too much advantage of women's obedience and loses respect and care for women, women's spirituality then turns to that of resistance and rejection. Having no regard for the suffering of women, men and ignorant people lament breaking of family, togetherness and peace. Instead of silent suffering at the hands of unkind men women of tribal societies often take the challenge of single parenting in order to take responsibility for their children's nurturing and care.
2. ***Spirituality of Co-operation and support for good***: Women have great talents of co-operation and support for men as well as their fellow women for maintaining a healthy life. Forget about the desire for popularity and fame in society, they constantly maintain their commitment and readiness to serve for the welfare of society due to their vision and longing for gender justice in society. If the people upon whom they put trust and confidence fail to live up to that trust, their spirituality of co-operation and support will be diverted to another way, and the further course and final result may not be desirable.
3. ***Spirituality of practicality and praxis***: Generally women are very practical whereas men are better with theoretical presentation and expression. Women want to put theory into practice and action. When they grieve or sorrow they shed tears and cry; when they are joyous and happy they laugh, shout and scream. They do not hide their feeling in order to cheat others through their looks and facial appearance.

4. ***Women's spirituality of practical involvement and participation***: Women's spirituality in public is visible through practical involvement and participation as manifested in their constant performance of singing, dancing and generous living through giving and sharing. Women are those who (if not hindered at all) through their practical involvement or participation in common issues cause houses warming, programmes warming, society warming and and lives warming and brightening.
5. ***Secular spirituality is closely attached to Women's daily life and activities***: Women's constant commitment to serving others makes society and public life lively. Their attachment to water and washing, fire and cooking, regularly visiting the jungle and forests with trees and herbs, manifest their inherent spirituality in all their occupations and activities.
6. ***Secular spirituality in Partnership***: We see this not only in living together but also in eating together, and working in fellowhip and and family bond. Our social and religious programmes with a sense of sacrament and reverence become moments of celebration and sharing. Women long for secular spirituality in partnership with men at all levels of life, activity and Christian ministry of worship and service.

B. Implicit Religion: Bibliography of writings by Edward Bailey

(i) Volumes

Belief, [including: Appendix of 2 individual interviews of Implicit Religion]
London and Sydney: Batsford, 1974
Hb. ISBN 0 7134 1579 7, and Pb. ISBN 0 7134 2938 0

Implicit Religion in Contemporary Society,
Kampen, Netherlands: Kok Pharos, 1997
(Re-printed by Peeters, Leuven, 2001, 2006 etc.)
Pb ISBN 3 89271 694 3 90-390-0581-8 and 9 789039 005811

Implicit Religion: An Introduction,
London: Middlesex University Press, 1998 & 2006
Pb. ISBN 1-898253-24-2 and 9 781898 253242, £9.50

The Secular Faith Controversy: Religion in Three Dimensions,
London: Continuum, 2001
Hb. ISBN 0-8264-4924-7, and Pb. ISBN 0-8264-4925-5

The Secular Quest for Meaning in Life: Denton Papers in Implicit Religion
Intro and ed Edward Bailey
Lampeter: Edwin Mellen, 2002 (reprinted 2004, 2006 etc.)
Hb. ISBN 0-7734-6999-0

(ii) Essays

"Implicit Religion and the Definition of Religion," in *Defining Religion: Investigating Boundaries between the Sacred and the Secular*, (ed.) Larry Greil, New York: JAI, 2003, 55-66.
Hb. ISBN 0 7623 0976 8, 9 780762 309764, ISSN 1061 5210

"Implicit Religion," in *The Oxford Handbook of the Sociology of Religion*, (ed.) Peter Clarke, Oxford: Oxford University Press, 2008, 801-816
Hb. ISBN 978 0 19 927979 1, 9 780199 2797

"The Concept of Implicit Religion: what, when, how, and why?", in *Annual Review of the Sociology of Religion*, (eds.) Enzo Pace, Luigi Berzano & Giuseppe Giordan, Vol. 2, *Religion and Politics* (ed. Patrick Michel & Enzo Pace), Leiden: Brill, 2011, 309-325
Hb. ISBN 978 90 04 20928 2, ISSN 1877 5233

"Pluralism and Implicit Religion" in *Testing Pluralism: Globalizing Belief, Localizing Gods*, (ed.) Giuseppe Giordan & William H. Swatos, Jr., Leiden: Brill, 2013, 161-174
(Vol. 23 in *Religion and the Social Order*, ISSN 1061 5210)
Hb. 978 90 04 25447 3, e-book 978 90 04 25475 6

(iii) Articles

"The Implicit Religion of Contemporary Society: Some Studies and Reflections," *Social Compass*, XXXVII, 4, London: Sage Publications, 1990:483-498; re-printed in (ed.) Bryan S Turner *Secularization* (Sage Key Debates in Sociology series) London: Sage, 2010.

'Implicit Religion: what might that be?' in
Implicit Religion: Journal of the Centre for the Study of Implicit Religion and Contemporary Spirituality,
Leeds: Maney, 1998; 1:9-22

'What has spirituality to do with the Church?', in *The Bible in TransMission: A Forum for Change in Church and Culture*,
Swindon: Bible Society, Summer, 1999: 6-7

'The Sacred, the Holy, and the Human, as tripartite symbols of ultimate reality and meaning', in *Ultimate Reality and Meaning: Interdisciplinary Studies in the Philosophy of Understanding*, XXIII, 3,
Toronto: University of Toronto Press, 2000: 277-284

'Living with Implicit Religion, 1967-2007: A Memoir'
(from the 30th Denton Conference),
Implicit Religion: Journal of the C.S.I.R.C.S.,
London: Equinox, 10, 2, 2007, 172-188.

'Implicit Religion: Journal of the C.S.I.R.C.S.', in *Religion*, 40, 2010: 271-8

'Implicit Religion": what might that be?', in
Implicit Religion, Journal of the C.S.I.R.C.S.
Sheffield: Equinox, 15.2, 2012:195-207

(iv) Entries

'Implicit Religion', in *A New Dictionary of Religions*, 2nd Edition, (Ed) John Hinnells, Harmondsworth & Oxford: Penguin and Blackwell, 1995; Hb. ISBN 0 631 18139 3,9 780631 181392

16 articles (on Christianity, Death and dying, Folk religion, Funerals, Groups, Implicit religion, Last Supper, Non-official religion, Popular religion, *"Religion"* (journal), Religious Education: Sacred, Secular religion, Supernatural, Surrogates for religion, and Ultimacy), in *Religion and the Social Sciences: An Encyclopedia*, (Ed.) William H Swatos, Jr. New York, Garland, 1998:82-3, 127-8, 190-1, 200, 235, 269, 334-5, 370, 405-6, 407-8, 443-4, 457, 502, 502-3, 532 (also, personal entry); Hb. ISBN 0 7619 8956 0

'Folk religion', in *The Oxford Companion to Christian Thought*, (Ed.) Adrian Hastings *et al.* Oxford: Oxford University Press, 2000:244; Hb. ISBN 0 19 860024 0

9 articles (on Baptism, Civic religion, Common religion, Confirmation, Confirmation preparation, Folk religion, Implicit religion, Rites of passage, Weddings) in *The New Dictionary of Pastoral Studies*, (Ed.) A Wesley Carr, London: SPCK, 2001
Hb. ISBN 0 281 05000 7, 9 780281 050000

'Implicit Religion', in *Encyclopedia of Contemporary American Religion*, (Ed.) Wade Clark Roof, New York: MacMillan Reference, 2000

Religion, Past & Present: Encyclopedia of theology & religion, VI, 2009: 433, (Ed.) H D Betz *et al.*, Leiden: Brill, 2007–2012, Hb. ISBN 978 90 04 14690 7, 978 90 04 14666 2

'Implicit Religion', in *Encyclopedia of New Religions, Sects and Alternative Spiritualities*, (Ed.) Chris Partridge, Oxford: Lion, 2002; Hb. ISBN 0 7459 5073 6

'Implicit Religion', in *Encyclopedia of New Religious Movements*, (Ed.) Peter Clarke, London: Routledge, c. 2004

C. Edward Ian Bailey (1935-2015)

A Biographical Sketch

Edward Ian Bailey was born on 11 October 1935, in Rawdon near Leeds, the third son of Noel and Beryl Bailey. He was educated as a small child at a school in Horsforth (the family having by then moved to Horsforth, a couple of miles from Rawdon). At nine he followed his brothers to a prep school near Ilkley and then from there went to Oundle School in Northamptonshire. After school, he did two years National Service, before going to Cambridge to read History for Part I and Theology for Part II of his B.A.

Then he went to India in 1959 with a scholarship from the World Council of Churches for a year, (which became two years), travelling in India and elsewhere. While a student at United Theological College Bangalore, his interest in the relationship between religion and society was fostered by contact with Christian Institute for the Study of Religion and Society and in particular with M. M. Thomas and P.D. Devanandan. Before being awarded his MA from Cambridge he studied for the priesthood at Westcott House, also in Cambridge. He was ordained deacon in 1962 and priest in 1963 before taking up a curacy at St John the Baptist, Newcastle upon Tyne and an assistant chaplaincy at Marlborough College. In 1969, he was awarded an MA by Bristol University and in 1977 a PhD also from Bristol. His doctoral research was completed under the Africanist F.B. Welbourn. This doctoral thesis was subsequently published with the title of *The Implicit Religion of Contemporary Society.*

While working as a parish priest for forty years, Edward encouraged others through teaching and conferences, to recognise the implicitly religious in the apparently secular. His three definitions of implicit religion were commitments, integrating foci, and intensive concerns with extensive effects. Just as recognising the implicitly religious so defined, as key to understanding the 'religion' of individuals and society, so Edward likewise suggested that applying the methods usually used in the analysis of religion, could also assist in understanding the 'secular.'

For Edward, the study of implicit religion brought together in one family the three different settings of the secular world, informal religion and organised religion. In the secular world, implicit religion is present in 'secular quests.' In the world of informal religion, implicit religion is connected to the sense of deep meaningful purpose (reflected in animal rights and politics, for example). In the world of organised religion, implicit religion is connected to non-religious motivations (reflected in seeking infant baptism for cultural or superstitious reasons, for example).

In 1968, Edward initiated the formal study of 'Implicit Religion,' which he termed 'secular faith.' He believed that this, 'opens up the possibility of discovering the sacred within what might otherwise be dismissed as profane, and finding an experience of the holy within an apparently irreligious realm. Above all, in contemporary society it allows for the discovery of some kind of religiosity within what conventionally might be seen as an unrelievedly secular sphere. The concept therefore gives credence to the opinion of the 'person in the street,' that while 'some who go to church really mean it,' others who go to church 'really have a different religion altogether'—but that 'everybody has a religion of some sort,' a faith by which they live, albeit as 'an unconscious core at the centre of their way of life and being.' For details, visit: http://hirr.hartsem.edu/ency/implicit.htm

Edward was a person who connected cultures, bridging past and future, church and academia, parish ministry and intellectual creativity, and theology and social science - a rare and impressive achievement. His feet were rooted in the very best historic traditions of the Church of England, in which the parish priest was granted the freehold of the rectory in which to reside and the living from which to be freed from undue material concerns. The responsible priest, thus inducted, was enabled to exercise pastoral care over the local community, and if so equipped, to engage in wide-ranging intellectual activities that both nourished the local community and served the wider benefits of church and society. For 36 years (1970-2006), Edward made Winterbourne Rectory (a suburb of Bristol) the centre of a rich and sincere pastoral ministry, and (increasingly) the location for academic advancement of international significance. All this was achieved (in the very best tradition of Anglican ministry) in the context of an engaged family life.

Edward's mind, while properly rooted in the intellectual heritage of the Anglican theological tradition, was actively searching for ways of connecting that heritage with the contemporary context for building bridges into the future. Edward's original doctoral research put in place the essential foundations for (and equipped him to undertake) his life-long commitment to the notion of 'implicit religion.' That quest, began in three related projects by a series of careful interviews, (the disciplined investigation of human experience, activity within an English public house, and the observed life of his parish), which generated the consultations in Winterbourne Rectory, the annual conference (since 1979) in Denton Hall, the Centre for the Study of Implicit Religion and Contemporary Spirituality, the research post in the Faculty of Divinity at Cambridge University, and the launch of the peer-reviewed journal *Implicit Religion*. It is through the journal in particular that Edward's legacy continues to inspire and nurture a new generation of scholars.

The achievements of earlier generations of Anglican priests in the arts and sciences have helped to shape many fields of studies, and in the past a few have become so influential that their names remain forever connected with their field of study. This phenomenon becomes rarer and rarer. Part of Edward's unique achievement in the late twentieth and early twenty-first century is that the name of Edward Bailey will remain always inextricably linked with the notion of implicit religion.

Behind Edward's distinctive profile and achievements lay a number of early formative influences in study and training, not to mention the family - wife Joanna (married in 1968) and their three children, Charlotte, Christopher, and Catherine.

For those who have enjoyed the privilege of travelling with Edward over the years, the annual Denton Hall conferences have been a key and core part of the experience of accessing and unlocking the significance and potential of implicit religion. Denton Hall (near Ilkly, west of Leeds), the headquarters of the family engineering business (N. G. Bailey) of which Edward was a non-executive director for many years, provided the ideal ambience in which to link the genteel ways of the Cambridge Senior Common Room with the connected expectations of contemporary engagement. The annual conferences began in 1978, and new entrants felt welcomed into a warm, open and generous community of scholars and friends willing to present their research, engage in critical but generous conversation, and to feast together around the oak tables discretely carrying the mouse trademark of the celebrated Yorkshire craftsman (Robert Thompson). While this academic community housed in Denton Hall was never compromised by personal matters of religious conviction, close to the Hall stood the parish church (1662) where the 8.00am Communion Service always seemed to attract a good number of the conference participants. Here, Edward was at home as priest, scholar and family man.

Since he initiated the formal study of 'Implicit Religion' in 1968, which he termed 'secular faith,' Edward was keen to propagate and promote the recognition and study of implicit religion through his attendance of the American Academy of Religion conferences and lecturing in universities in Europe. In 2009, Edward was invited to join the Steering Group of what subsequently became the British Association for the Study of Spirituality (BASS). Following the first international BASS conference in 2010, the committee structure of BASS was formalised to include a President and two Vice Presidents of the Association. Edward volunteered to become the first President, supported by Professor Wilf McSherry and the Venerable Arthur Hawes as Vice Presidents. Edward presided over the next two conferences in 2012 and 2014. Following the third BASS conference, he stepped down as President but remained on the Executive Committee. He is dearly missed.

A combined and edited summary of details provided by Joanna Bailey and tributes offered by Leslie J Francis, Professor of Religions and Education, University of Warwick, England and Canon Theologian, Bangor Cathedral, Wales, and Trustee of CSIRCS, and Arthur Hawes, President of the British Association for the Study of Spirituality, 2010-2014. - Editor

Index of Names and Key Terms

Contributors

Prof. Edward Baily, Founder Director of the Centre for the Study of Implicit Religion and Contemporary Spirituality, U.K.

Dr. Israel Selvanayagam, Professor of Religions Emeritus, Gurukul Lutheran Theological College and Research Institute, Chennai.

Dr. Songram Basumatary, Professor of Theology, Gurukul Lutheran Theological College and Research Institute, Chennai.

Dr. Mohd Fahim Akhtar, Associate Professor & Head of the Department of Islamic Studies, Maulana Azad National Urdu University, Hyderabad.

Dr. M. M. Abraham, Lecturer in Islamic Studies, Henry Martyn Institute, Hyderabad.

Dr. Limasangla Lemtur, Asst. Professor, Christian Social Ethics, Union Biblical Seminary, Pune.

Dr. T. Vanlaltlani, Professor in Religions, Aizawl Theological College, Aizawl.

Dr. Gabriele Dietrich, Professor of Religions and Social Analysis Emeritus, Tamilnadu Theological Seminary, Madurai.

Rev. Densingh Oliver, Lecturer in Religions, United Theological College, Bangalore.

Prof. Faizan Mustafa, Vice Chancellor, The National Academy of Legal Studies and Research (NALSAR), Hyderabad.

Dr. W. S. Annie, Asst. Professor of Theology and Women Studies, Gurukul Lutheran Theological College and Research Institute, Chennai.